FORTY NINERS
Looking Back

FORTY NINERS
Looking Back

By Joseph Hession

FOGHORN PRESS
SAN FRANCISCO

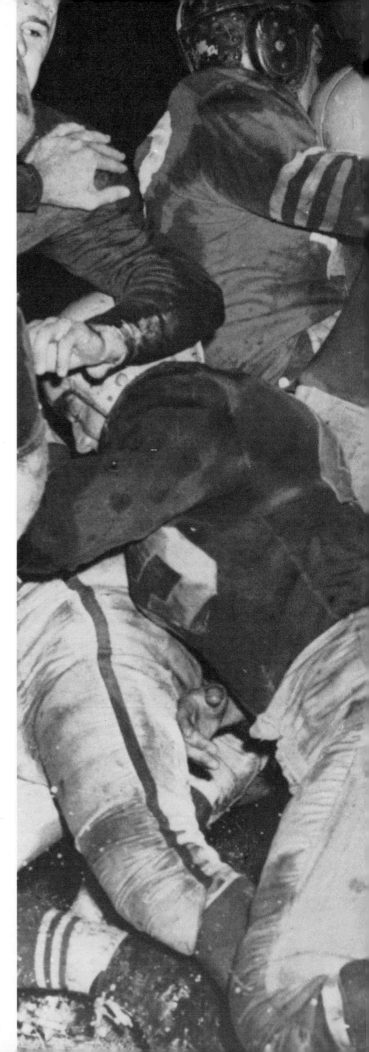

ISBN 0-935701-49-4

Printed in the United States of America

CONTENTS

FOREWORD

Though I've been a New Yorker for the past 25 years, and I'm a Southern Californian by birth, I'll take liberty with the song title and admit...I left a bit of my heart in San Francisco!

My four years in the Bay Area, from 1948 until 1952, of course, were concentrated on my activities as an undergraduate at the University of San Francisco, where, in my senior year, I also held the positions of Publicity Director and Assistant Director of Athletics. It was a wonderful time to be a part of the athletic program at USF.

But, *FORTY NINERS: Looking Back* is about the 49ers, and I certainly have fond memories of those early years of the franchise when they were charter members of the old All-America Football Conference, then, in 1950, brought into the National Football League.

It was the courageous and dedicated leadership of Tony and Vic Morabito in the front office and the direction of Coach Buck Shaw which established the foundation of a franchise that has become one of the most stable in the NFL.

Some of the names flash across my mind as if they were still running onto the field at old Kezar Stadium. Frankie Albert...Jim Cason...Leo Nomellini ...Joe Perry...and, a personal favorite and ex-USFer, Forrest "Scooter" Hall.

The 49ers have a proud tradition, and it is being carried on today by owner Eddie DeBartolo Jr., and Coach Bill Walsh and his staff and players. When fans talk about the best these days, the 49ers get lots of attention.

With a pair of Super Bowl trophies, why shouldn't they?

PETE ROZELLE
Commissioner
National Football League

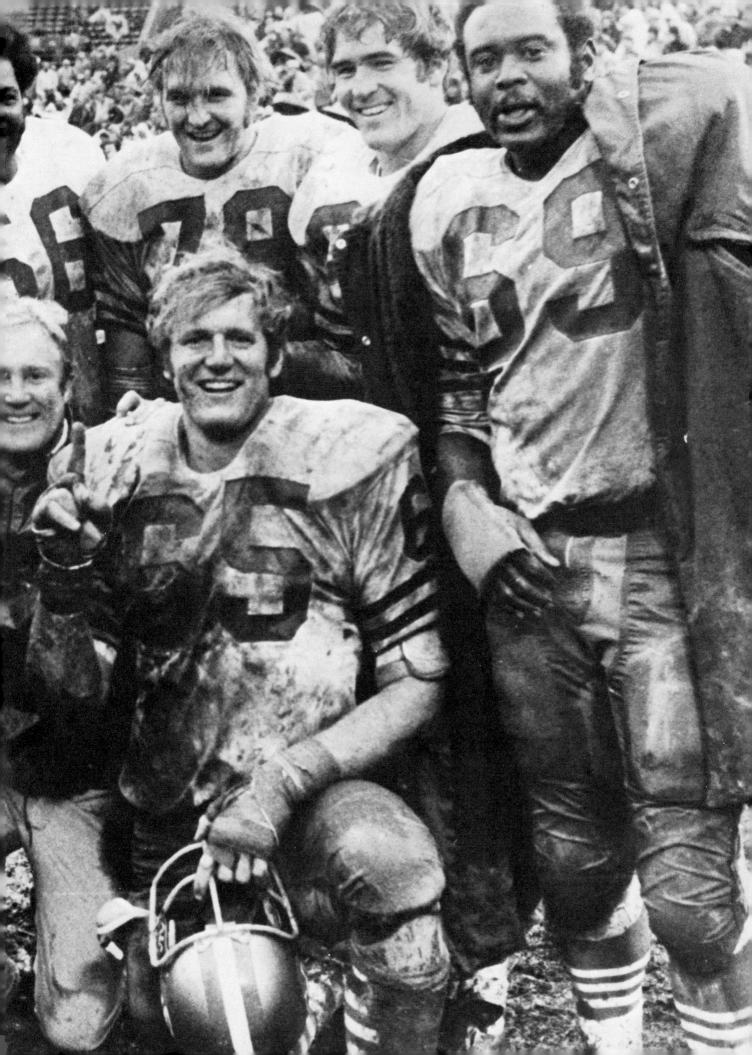

INTRODUCTION

It all started one fall afternoon in 1964. I remember it because a remarkable thing happened that day. Of course, I didn't know how unusual it was at the time. I was only nine years old.

What started as an innocent bus ride to Kezar Stadium, turned into a lifelong obsession. Along with some mischievous friends from Robert Louis Stevenson schoolyard in San Francisco's Sunset District, I hopped on the Muni's old 72-Sunset line. We had a couple of tickets to see the San Francisco 49ers. We'd clipped them off Christopher Milk cartons.

I'd never been to a football game and I wasn't sure where Kezar Stadium was located. When I asked the driver for help, he told me to get off when everyone else did.

As we approached the eastern edge of Golden Gate Park, everybody who was packed onto the bus disembarked. Following the bus driver's orders, we jumped off too. It was then that I spotted Kezar Stadium for the first time. It might as well have been King Arthur's castle. I was overwhelmed. The size of the stadium, and the enormity of the crowd as it moved along Lincoln Way toward the entrance gates, made the entire spectacle hard to comprehend.

We waded through the crowd and innocently tried to convince a ticket-taker our Christopher Milk ducats entitled us to admission on the 50-yard line. He patiently directed us to an area reserved for Christopher Milk patrons. It was fenced off from the rest of the crowd and intended for young fans under the age of 17. Inside, I realized the age requirement was loosely enforced. Men nearing retirement age sat next to me smoking Lucky Strikes and cussing at John Brodie.

I disliked them immediately. I hated cigarettes and Brodie was the only player with whom I was familiar. Before the day was over I would know about another 49er star.

It wasn't far into the game that I noticed Brodie connecting on passes to a wide receiver named Dave Parks. It wasn't the receptions that were so striking, it was the way Parks got to the football. He was like an acrobat, leaping and twisting to catch everything in his direction. Midway through the second quarter, he hauled in an 80-yard touchdown pass. I was hooked. That game opened a whole new world for me and the 49ers were at the center of it.

Parks wasn't the only person to make that game memorable. The Vikings' Jim Marshall picked up a fumble and ran 60 yards—the wrong way. As he outran everyone to the end zone, I wondered why the crowd was on its feet yelling and laughing. It seemed running toward the goal line was the logical thing to do. But, just like Marshall, I didn't know one end zone from the other at the time.

It was with men like John Brodie and Dave Parks in mind that this book was written. Faithful 49er fans have seen four decades of stars come and go at Kezar Stadium and Candlestick Park. Until recent years, individual heroics were all they had to cheer. Championships had a way of avoiding San Francisco.

Some of the greatest individual players in the history of the game have worn 49er uniforms, including five members of Pro Football's Hall of Fame. Dozens of others should be considered for induction. Y.A. Tittle, Joe Perry and Hugh McElhenny, part of San Francisco's "Million Dollar Backfield" in the 1950s, have all been enshrined at Canton, Ohio. A fourth member of that team, Leo Nomellini, has also been inducted in the Hall of Fame. San Francisco native O.J. Simpson is the fifth on display.

The book has been divided into five decades and is composed of two parts; an historical text which gives a running account of the team's fortunes and miseries, and individual profiles adding a personal flavor to the team's development.

an historical text which gives a running account of the team's fortunes and miseries, and individual profiles adding a personal flavor to the team's development.

Numerous people contributed to the book and without their help it would never have been written. Dave Morgan returned from a European vacation and spent weeks with his head buried in books and old newspapers checking facts. Pat Pacheco, Larry Parsons and Scott Williams lent their personal knowledge of the 49ers to the editing process. Lido Starelli offered his collection of 49er programs and memorabilia for our use. Lido is still searching for two programs to round out his collection of every 49er game program since the team's inception. The missing include a game with the Detroit Lions on Oct. 8, 1950, and a game with the Green Bay Packers in Minneapolis on Sept. 12, 1951. Kevin Bernie and Michelle Corbin provided counsel and helped smooth several rocky paths. Jerry Walker and Rodney Knox of the 49er staff opened their files and offered advice. Photos and illustrations were gathered with the help of Michael Zagaris, 49er team photographer, and Paula Perretty. The 49er players, both present and past, were enthusiastic and helpful in tracking down other former players. Gary Hession offered valuable assistance with production. Most importantly, designer Mark Olson sifted through hundreds of photos, then put them together in an artistic package. It was Mark's intricate knowledge of design and production that put the book in its final form.

Special gratitude goes to my parents, Joe and Dianne Hession, and my in-laws, Monte and Maita Morgan for their continuous support. A boisterous standing ovation goes to my wife, Vicki Morgan, for making me laugh when the project seemed futile.

—J. H.

PAGES ii–iii: San Francisco halfback Sam Cathcart (83) takes to the air to avoid a Cleveland Browns tackler. Bob Mike (47) gets in position to block. Sam teamed with his brother Royal Cathcart in the 49er backfield of 1950. PAGE iv: Baltimore receiver "Racehorse" Davis (51) stretches for a pass as the 49ers' Eddie Carr (85) defends. PAGES vi–vii: Green Bay Packer fullback Jack Cloud (82) tries to make his way through the 49ers' goal line defense in a night game at Minneapolis. He's stopped short of the end zone. PAGES viii–ix: San Francisco halfback Don Durdan (93) tries to turn the corner in the 49ers' first game at Kezar Stadium, a preseason contest in 1946. The 49ers outplayed the Chicago Rockets, 34-14. PAGES x–xi: The offensive line was nicknamed "The Protectors" in 1970 when it set an NFL record by allowing only eight quarterback sacks all season. The line celebrates here after beating the Oakland Raiders in the last game of the 1970 season and clinching the western division title. In the front row is Forrest Blue (75), line coach Ernie Zwahlen and Randy Beisler. In the back row is Len Rohde (76), Bob Hoskins (56), Cas Banaszek, Elmer Collett and Woody Peoples. PAGE xii: Dave Parks at Kezar. PAGE 2: San Francisco halfback Jim Cason (93) slips through the grasp of Baltimore's Win Williams on a punt return. Tackle John Woudenberg (41) attempts to block. Cason was one of the 49ers' most exciting punt returners. In 1949, he averaged 16.7 yards per return, a team single-season record which stood until 1982 when Dana McLemore averaged 22.3 yards per return.

1946–1949

CHAPTER ONE

THE FORMATIVE YEARS

The world was finally at peace in 1946. Harry Truman was president, Joe Louis was the heavyweight champion of the world and Stan Musial was the National League MVP.

In San Francisco, Mayor Roger Lapham ruled City Hall as professional football invaded Kezar Stadium.

The San Francisco 49ers were the dream of a young trucking executive named Tony Morabito who spent six years trying to make his dream a reality. Morabito was a native San Franciscan who attended the University of Santa Clara. After building a trucking empire that spanned the Pacific Northwest, he approached the National Football League in 1941 with a request for a franchise.

The league turned him down, reasoning that the Bay Area was inundated with college football teams. California, Stanford, St. Mary's, Santa Clara and the University of San Francisco were all playing major college schedules. A professional team could never outdraw the college talent in the area, according to NFL management. San Francisco had too much football.

Travel costs were another consideration of the NFL. A round-trip air flight from San Francisco to New York was $270, and all the professional teams were congregated on the Eastern seaboard or in the Midwest. There were no professional teams west of St. Louis. They were not prepared to incur that travel expense for their 32 players and assortment of coaches.

Although rebuffed by the NFL, Morabito did not give up hope of acquiring a franchise. He caught wind of a scheme to start a new football league. It was the brainchild of Arch Ward, sports editor of the *Chicago Tribune*. Eager to join the league, Morabito attended the first meeting of prospective franchise owners. He finally got his wish. The San Francisco 49ers were made charter members of the All-America Football Conference in June 1944 after posting a $25,000 admittance fee. Jim Crowley, one of Notre Dame's legendary Four Horsemen, was appointed the first commissioner. The league began operation in 1946.

Morabito enlisted two partners from his trucking business, Allen Sorrell and Ernest J. Turre, to become partners in the franchise. Victor Morabito, Tony's younger brother, later joined the enterprise as a partner.

Legend has it that Sorrell came up with the name 49ers, although no one knows for sure. It was originally spelled out Forty Niners and was an appropriate reminder of the pioneers who flooded Northern California during the Gold Rush of 1849. Those gold miners eventually helped build the city of San Francisco.

The team's original logo depicted the city's wild beginnings. It consisted of a prospector, clad in boots and a lumberjack shirt, firing a pair of pistols. One shot just misses the miner's head, the other misses his foot. The logo was taken from a design seen on the side of railway freight cars. In that picture, the prospector was in front of a saloon. The 49ers dropped the saloon from the logo.

Morabito recognized that his young team would need an experienced lead

John Colmer of the Brooklyn Dodgers is brought down by the 49ers' Gerry Conlee (22). Don Durdan (93) was in on the stop.

er, so he persuaded Buck Shaw to coach his new club before he even had any players.

Shaw came into prominence as a tackle at Notre Dame where he played under the guidance of George Gipp. At Santa Clara, the lean, silver-haired Shaw built a reputation as one of the finest coaches in the nation. His overall won-lost record with the Broncos was 46-10-2, including upset victories over Louisiana State in the 1937 and 1938 Sugar Bowls.

Shaw previously had been approached to coach several professional teams. He turned down the offers, preferring to stay in the Bay Area. During World War II, he served as a temporary coach at the University of California. For Morabito to land a coach of Shaw's caliber was a major coup. His image and national reputation brought instant respectability not only to the 49ers, but to the entire league.

Morabito then focused his attention on the rich supply of college talent in the Bay Area and turned it into an asset. He recruited players whose names were familiar to local football fans. Many of these players were returning from stints in the armed forces during World War II and had played for pow-

erful service teams like the El Toro Marines, St. Mary's Pre-Flight and Fleet City.

Frankie Albert was one of Morabito's first acquisitions. Albert had played his college ball at Stanford, then teamed with Len Eshmont at St. Mary's Pre-Flight. The left-handed Albert stood only 5' 9" and weighed 170 pounds, yet local writers called him the best T-Formation quarterback in the game.

Several other Stanford graduates, including Norm Standlee and Bruno Banducci, joined the 49ers in 1946. Banducci, who played with the Philadelphia Eagles prior to World War II, became an All-Pro guard for the 49ers in 1952, 1953 and 1954.

Standlee, known as Big Chief, starred in the backfield with Albert on Stanford's undefeated team of 1940. He signed with the Chicago Bears in 1941, where he had a spectacular rookie season, leading the Bears to the NFL title. He came to the 49ers after World War II and gave them the tough inside runner needed to complement Albert's aerial game.

Shaw returned to his Santa Clara roots and recruited some of his former players. He signed Alyn Beals, Visco Grgich, Dick Bassi, Eddie Forrest and several other Bronco stars. Beals turned into one of the great receivers of his time and holds the AAFC all-time scoring record.

Many other players with previous NFL experi-

Frankie Albert 1946–1952

He was called "the T-Formation Wizard" and for good reason. Frankie Albert threw 88 touchdown passes in four years of All-America Football Conference play, the league record.

Other than Otto Graham, a member of the Hall of Fame, no one came close to that. Remember, that was the era of three yards and a cloud of dust, a time when throwing the football was akin to witch-

craft. And maybe that's why Frankie Albert was called the wizard. He certainly could throw a football.

In 1948, he led the wildest offense in the nation, throwing 29 touchdown passes in 14 games. That was a 49er single-season record that stood until 1965 when John Brodie threw for 30, the current record.

At 5' 9" and 170 pounds, the southpaw from Stanford didn't look

like a football player. But on the field his wide array of talents took over. He could run, throw, kick and handle the ball like a magician. With Albert in control, the ball disappeared more times than a rabbit in a vaudeville show—now you see it, now you don't.

"I guess my ability to handle the ball made me effective," he said modestly. "I was pretty good on a bootleg. I could hide the ball and run it if I

had to."

But running the football wasn't what made Albert one of the highest paid players in the old league. It was tossing the pigskin. He credits Alyn Beals, a Santa Clara graduate, for helping him set the record for touchdown passes in a season. Beals caught 14 scoring passes in 1948, the AAFC record. The next year he caught 12 touchdown passes. Gene Washington and Dave Parks share

5

the "official" 49er single-season record set in the NFL with 12 touchdown catches.

"Beals was my main receiver," said Albert. "Boy, did he have some great moves. He was a good faker. I can remember several times setting up to pass and watching the defensive back fall down after Alyn put a fake on him. The back would trip over his own feet. I'd look at the defensive man lying on his butt while Alyn was wide open."

Albert was not just an offensive whiz, he mixed it up on defense as well. Against the Cleveland Browns and Otto Graham you could generally find Albert in the defensive secondary.

"I enjoyed playing defense," he said. "I didn't do it as often as I would have liked. I played back there in some of the important games like against the Browns."

Cleveland became the 49ers first great rival. In the AAFC, every game against them was important. Three times between 1946 and 1948, the 49ers finished second to the Browns. In the 1949 AAFC Championship Game, Cleveland beat San Francisco, 21-7.

"When we played Cleveland, it was like the Stanford–Cal game here," Albert said. "It was a real big rivalry. Whenever we beat them, it was a big thrill for me."

Albert had one of the best games of his career against the Browns. The year was 1949. San Francisco was on a roll. They had won four of their first five games and averaged 35 points per contest. When the 49ers battled

Cleveland at Kezar that day, Albert could do no wrong. He threw five touchdown passes as the 49ers whipped the Browns, 56-28.

In 1951, San Francisco acquired Y.A. Tittle from Baltimore. The two quarterbacks alternated for two years before Albert decided to retire in 1952.

"When he arrived there was quite a rivalry for the quarterback position," he said. "Of course, he was already an established star. I guess you could say there was a quarterback controversy. Whenever I see him now, I tell him he sent me to Canada."

Within a year after retiring from the 49ers, Albert went back to work for the Calgary Stampeders of the Canadian Football League.

"I was just getting into the car business," said Albert, "and it was a little slow at first. The Stampeders offered me more money then I ever made in the NFL, so I went up there for a year. We played two games a week, one on a Saturday and one on Monday. That was because the farmers would come to town on the weekends. They'd get drunk, go to the games and raise hell."

Albert returned to the states and was made an assistant coach of the 49ers in 1955 under Head Coach Red Strader. The team floundered under Strader, and Albert was thrown into the fire the next year when he was made the head coach.

"I liked certain aspects of coaching," he said impassively. "I enjoyed teaching the kids."

Albert lasted three years as the 49ers' head coach. His overall record

was 19-17-1. In 1957, he guided the team to an 8-4 season and a playoff spot against Detroit. But that game ended in another agonizing loss when the Lions rallied from a 27-7 deficit, to beat the 49ers, 31-27.

"I still can't believe that game," he said with disgust. "We were ahead and started playing conservative. That's what killed us. They scored once, then they scored twice, and the next thing you know they are ahead. It was embarrassing. It just goes to show you how quickly things can happen on a football field."

Although the 49ers came close to winning a championship several times with Albert at the helm, either as a quarterback or a coach, they never quite made it. That frustration is offset by the camaraderie and friendships Albert established as one of the original 49ers.

"There were some real characters on those teams," he said. "Bob St. Clair was one of them. He used to eat raw meat. We'd go to a nice restaurant and he liked beef so he'd order a steak or something. He'd tell the waiter to just have the chef heat the meat. He didn't want it cooked, just warmed up. A few minutes later the chef would look out from the kitchen to see who was ordering their meat like that.

"He's one of the few guys from the old teams that could be playing today. He was that good. And he had the size (6'9", 265). Besides Bob, Leo Nomellini was a good one on the line. In his

later years, he played only defense, but he was a pretty good offensive lineman too."

Behind those 49er lines were two of the most explosive running backs to ever strap on shoulder pads. Albert cultivated a reputation as an unpredictable gambler on the football field, but he admits that with Hugh McElhenny and Joe Perry in the backfield it was much easier to do the unexpected.

"I had good players to gamble with," he said. "You can't compare many backfields with Mac and Joe Perry. Mac was the best open-field runner from the T that ever played. Perry was a different runner. He was good straight ahead. Mac was always zigging and zagging around the field."

Albert played alongside some of the NFL's biggest stars. Several teammates and opponents are in the Hall of Fame. When he watches the current 49er team, he is reminded of the great quarterbacks of football's past.

"I wasn't bad as a scrambler or ball-handler, but after watching Montana play I don't think I could carry that guy's helmet," said Albert. "I've seen some great quarterbacks—Otto Graham, Bob Waterfield, Norm Van Brocklin—and I'd say Montana ranks with the top two or three to ever play the game. When things break down and people start to scatter, he's at his best. He can get out of trouble and do things no other quarterback can do. He makes plays out of nothing. That's a gift."

ence signed with the 49ers after finishing their military duties. Halfback Len Eshmont, a former New York Giant, Bob Titchenal, an end from the Washington Redskins, and Parker Hall, a halfback who played with the Cleveland Browns, were among those who offered their services to the 49ers in the club's inaugural season.

San Francisco quickly became one of the teams to beat in the AAFC. Unfortunately, they played in the same division as the Cleveland Browns, a perennial powerhouse in the new league. During their four years in the AAFC, the Browns would be a constant thorn in the 49ers' side.

The first professional game played by the 49ers was an exhibition match against the Los Angeles Dons on August 24, 1946, at San Diego's Balboa Park. Only 8,000 fans turned up to watch San Francisco defeat the Dons, 17-7. The first touchdown in the history of the franchise was scored on a 35-yard pass from backup quarterback Parker Hall to Hank Norberg.

A week later, the 49ers played their first home game, a preseason contest, at Kezar Stadium. Despite the sale of only 1,100 season tickets, nearly 40,000 curious fans crowded into Kezar to see the 49ers take on the Chicago Rockets and their spectacular halfback, Elroy "Crazy Legs" Hirsch. They weren't disappointed. Two local boys, quarterback Frankie Albert and receiver Alyn Beals, combined to lead the Niners to a 34-14 win. Albert's accurate passing earned raves in the local press.

The first showing of major league football in San Francisco was hailed as a huge success by local sports writers. Morabito had anticipated losing money in his initial season. Crowds of only 4,000 and 5,000 were expected at the gate. The large turnout at the first contest gave him higher expectations.

The 49ers' successful debut led *Chronicle* Sports Editor Bill Leiser to write, "Their team, we think, is as good as any professional team we ever saw, including the best of the Chicago Bear teams. It is much better than the present National League Champion Los Angeles Rams team." With the fans convinced that San Francisco had a quality football club, they flocked to Kezar on game days.

TOP: Buffalo Bills defensive back Steve Juzwik (88) knocks the ball away from 49er receiver Alyn Beals. Beals was the all-time leading scorer in AAFC history with 278 points. He caught 14 touchdown passes in 1948, a 49er record. BOTTOM: Head Coach Buck Shaw.

The 49ers' John Woudenberg (hidden) and Dick Horne (51) stop Monk Gafford (80), a Brooklyn Dodger running back.

The 49ers now had to tune up for their opening game against the New York Yankees, one of the class teams of the new league. A large crowd was expected at Kezar because of the 49ers' 2-0 preseason record. To avert long waits at Kezar ticket booths, general admission tickets went on sale the week of the game at Roos Brothers clothing stores and at the Crane Box Office.

Kickoff was at 2:30 p.m. The game was rated a tossup by local bookmakers. Experts agreed the game would be decided along the line of scrimmage.

New York's powerful line consisted of Jack Russell, Perry Schwartz, a four-time All-Pro in the NFL, and the intimidating brother combination of George and "Bruiser" Kinard. Schwartz had been an All-American at the University of California as an undergraduate. Ace Parker, Blondy Black and Spec Sanders rounded out the Yankees' offense.

San Francisco's smooth backfield of Albert, Norm Standlee, John Strzykalski and Len Eshmont was expected to carry the team. The line, consisting of

Dick Bassi, Bruno Banducci, John Woudenberg and John Kuzman, was not to be underestimated however. Said Yankee line coach Al Ruffo to the press before the game, "Nobody is going to push this 49er line around."

On game day, 35,700 fans turned out at Kezar despite the thick gray fog that hovered over the stadium most of the day. Things didn't go quite as expected for the 49ers. They were completely dominated by New York, 21-7. San Francisco's only score came in the first quarter on a nifty pass and lateral play. Frankie Albert tossed a 12-yard pass to John Strzykalski, who then lateraled to Len Eshmont. Eshmont took the lateral and romped 54 yards down the sidelines to score. The entire play covered 66 yards. Joe "the Toe" Vetrano added the extra point.

The novelty of professional football apparently wore off quickly because only 17,500 fans turned out at Kezar Stadium the following week to watch the 49ers battle the Miami Seahawks. Prior to the game, it was discovered that running back Norm Standlee had a knee injury that would keep him out of action. Buck Shaw intended to make up for the loss of his star runner by having Albert throw more passes. He did just that, completing passes at will to Alyn Beals, Parker Hall and Nick Susoeff. The 49ers had their first victory in the AAFC, 21-14. All three 49er TDs were scored by fullback Dick Renfro.

The third week of the season, the Niners won big, turning back the Brooklyn Dodgers, 32-13. Albert threw two scoring tosses to Alyn Beals and one to Len Eshmont. Eshmont also threw a 43-yard touchdown pass to Bob Titchenal and scored on an end run.

After the game, Dodgers' assistant coach Mal Stevens told reporters, "San Francisco has a team which its citizens should well be proud of. Either in exhibition or in league, we have played New York, Cleveland, Chicago and Los Angeles, and I can truly say San Francisco was the finest club we met. You have the most imaginative attack and the men to work it. Yes sir, the most imaginative style."

The 49ers continued to play surprisingly good football throughout the season. They beat Cleveland, 34-20, and ended the year with three straight wins over Brooklyn, Chicago and Los Angeles to give themselves a 9-5 record and second place in the Western Division. Most importantly, behind Frankie Albert and Coach Buck Shaw, they had developed the "imaginative style" that would become a 49er trademark for 40 years.

Alyn Beals 1946–1951

In 1948, Alyn Beals caught 14 touchdown passes. No 49er ever scored more in a single season.

The record is an obscure one. It was set while the 49ers were members of the All-America Football Conference. Beals' standard of excellence may be lost on a new generation of 49er fans, but to his peers, he was recognized as one of the best of his time. Three times they selected him to the AAFC All-Star team.

Beals toiled as the 49ers' right end from 1946 to 1951. He was al-ways a reliable receiver. In 1946, his first year in professional football, he tied for the league lead with 40 pass receptions. Ten of those catches were for touchdowns.

He had a knack for find-ing the end zone. In his four years of AAFC play, he scored 46 touch-downs and was the league's all-time scoring leader with 278 points.

Dante Lavelli is the only receiver to score nearly as many touch-downs and he has been in Pro Football's Hall of Fame since 1975. Yet Lavelli scored only 29 touchdowns in the AAFC.

Beals caught 177 passes in the old league to put him second on the all-time list. Lavelli caught just 142.

Beals played collegiate ball at Santa Clara under Buck Shaw. When Shaw was made coach of the original San Francisco 49ers, he immediately recruited his star pupil. Beals became the first in a long line of great 49er pass catchers.

"I got on the team while I was in Germany," Beals said. "The war had just ended. I was a cap-tain in the Army with a field artillery unit. I was making about $275 a month. Buck Shaw had coached me at Santa Clara, and he sent a contract to Germany asking me to play for the 49ers. The contract was for $5,000. Of course, I signed it immediately. That was good money back then. And I only had to work for six months. I think I was also supposed to get a signing bonus of $50 but I never saw that.

"Buck Shaw was a great innovator," he said. "He was offensive minded. He was one of the first coaches to start spreading the ends out. We used to have the ends spread only about a foot. He kept spreading them off the tackles a little at a time. It opened up the passing game a little more. Playing for Buck was a pleasure. It was just like being back at college."

Beals could not have caught all those passes unless he had a steady quarterback to get the ball to him. Quarterback Frankie Albert was just the man to do it. When Albert was at the helm, he saw to it that Beals got plenty of action.

"Frankie Albert was really something," Beals recalled. "He was a good team leader. What made him so effective as a quarterback was that he could do just about everything. He was a good scrambler. He could pass, run or kick the ball. He was probably the most famous athlete in the area at that time because he'd come from Stanford and got a lot of publicity there."

Like most good passing and receiving combinations Beals and Albert had a special relation-ship. They were able to predict what the other person would do in certain situations. When the blocking broke down and plays fell apart, Beals knew where to go.

"Whenever Frank was under pressure," Beals said, "I knew what he would try to do. He was left-handed and I knew he would roll out and throw in that direction. Whenever he started to scramble, I would change my pattern and go to his left. He must have known I would because I caught a lot of passes that way."

Beals and Albert put their talents together for six seasons with the 49ers, four years in the AAFC and another two in the NFL. Beals retired in 1951, while Albert played one more season.

In the early years of the franchise, the Cleveland Browns were football's powerhouse. Beals well remembers the awesome talent they had on their offensive unit. Four times the Browns edged out San Francisco for first place in the AAFC.

"The Cleveland Browns were our big nemesis back then," he said. "Just look in the Hall of Fame. A lot of Hall of Famers came from the old Cleveland Browns. There was Marion Motley and Otto Graham in the backfield. They had great receivers like Mac Speedie and Dante Lavelli. Bill Willis was a big lineman. Tom Colella was one of their defensive backs. He gave me a tough time."

Games between the Browns and 49ers drew enormous crowds while they were members of the AAFC. One game in 1948 attracted 82,000 fans. But that wasn't the game that Beals most remembers. A 56-28 trouncing of the Browns in 1949 is his personal favorite. Beals scored one of the touchdowns in that game.

Beals has fond memories of the original San Francisco 49ers during the team's formative years. He is proud of the part he played in the team's birth, like a man who has helped create something special.

"When we started out, we all had to stick together," he said. "We had a lot of things in common. The war was just over and most of us had just gotten out of the service. A large group of us lived out at Parkmerced —it was fairly new then —so we saw one another all the time. We are still good friends. A day doesn't go by when I don't hear from Joe Vetrano. I hear from all those guys.

"We had lots of fun back then. I think we were a lot closer than the guys today. We were a close-knit group. After the games we all went out and drank beer together. It wasn't uncommon to find about 25 of us going out to the same place. You don't see that today.

"When I think back, my biggest thrill wasn't any one game or play, it was just being part of the team. There was plenty of important games in my career, but it was the excitement of being with the 49ers back then. Not many people get a chance to be a part of something like that. We helped get the team started."

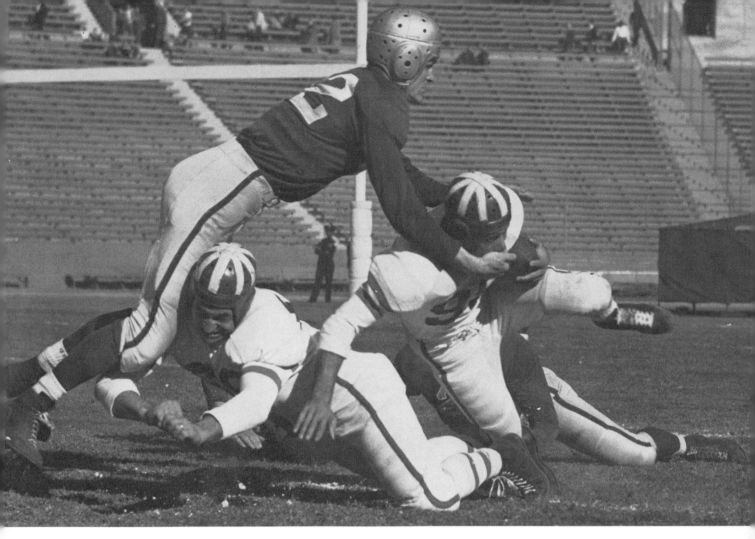

1947 During the off-season, owner Tony Morabito made headlines by trying to sign Glenn Davis and Doc Blanchard, West Point's "Touchdown Twins." The two collegiate stars were entitled to 90-day furloughs. Morabito invited them to play for the 49ers during their break. Army brass quickly put an end to Morabito's plan by prohibiting cadets from participating in activities for personal profit while on furlough.

Although unable to sign the "Touchdown Twins," the 1947 San Francisco club did sign the first Asian-American running back in professional football history. Wally Yonamine was a Japanese halfback from Farrington High School in Hawaii. He never played collegiate football, but Buck Shaw considered him an outstanding breakaway runner. An unexpected development prevented the 49ers from putting his speed to good use.

At Yonamine's first professional game at Kezar Stadium, 43,000 fans were on hand to watch the exhibition contest between the Los Angeles Dons and the 49ers. As the team made its way through the tunnel leading from the locker rooms to the field, Yonamine caught sight of the awesome crowd and froze in his tracks. A fear of large crowds plagued him all season. He played sparingly and never showed the running potential Shaw had hoped for.

Hermen Wedemeyer (94), a halfback with the Los Angeles Dons, has his jaw wrenched by 49er defensive back Paul Crowe. Wedemeyer was a running sensation with St. Mary's College in Moraga before turning pro. Crowe was also a St. Mary's graduate. FOLLOWING SPREAD: Len Eshmont (81) races down the sideline with an intercepted pass against the New York Yankees. Pete Wismann (22) lays a block for his teammate. Eshmont led the club in interceptions in 1947 with six. He also was a running back on offense, rushing for 1,181 yards in his four seasons with the 49ers.

The 49ers kicked off the 1947 season with fancy red-and-gold uniforms. The new outfits did little to fool the Los Angeles Dons in their first preseason match. Los Angeles defeated San Francisco, 14-7.

Despite the loss, several returning veterans looked good for the 49ers, particularly quarterback Frankie Albert. Albert sparked the 49ers to their only touchdown on the first possession of the game. Working from the 49ers' 48-yard line, he drove them the length of the field in 12 plays and scored on a three-yard run. The long gain in the drive was a 12-yard pass from Albert to Len Eshmont.

The following week, the 49ers opened regular season play at Kezar against the Brooklyn Dodgers and their star quarterback Glenn Dobbs. Unseasonable San Francisco sunshine greeted the 31,900 fans who watched the 49ers defeat the Dodgers, 23-7, for their first victory of the year.

Dobbs, considered by many to be the premier quarterback of his day, was stymied by a tough 49er defensive line. Ed Balatti, a 22-year-old defensive end from Oakland, led the charge on the line. Balatti teamed with Bruno Banducci and Eddie Forrest to pressure Dobbs into several errant throws. He ended the day completing only eight of 23 passes and had one intercepted.

The 49ers' first score came on a pass from Albert to Alyn Beals. Another Albert pass to Len Eshmont was lateraled to Strzykalski who then ran 17 yards for a touchdown. Reserve quarterback Jesse Freitas also threw a touchdown pass to Beals. Joe Vetrano added a field goal to round out the scoring.

The 49ers had posted a 5-1-1 record when the

Running back Sam Cathcart (86) is tackled by Tom Landry, a defensive back with the New York Yankees. Landry gained fame as the coach of the Dallas Cowboys. PAGE 17: Paul Salata (55), a 49er wide receiver, just misses a pass from quarterback Frankie Albert in a game against the New York Yankees at Yankee Stadium. Defensive back Harmon Rowe (90) stays close.

defending champion Cleveland Browns came to town for the most important game of the season. Paul Brown, head coach of the Browns, had put together one of the most potent offenses in football. The Cleveland scoring machine centered around quarterback Otto Graham, fullback Marion Motley and halfback Dan Greenwood. The previous year the Browns were a 20-point favorite in a game played at Cleveland against the 49ers. The 49ers had soundly defeated them, 34-20. Revenge was in the air.

Cleveland trotted into Kezar Stadium for the 2:30 p.m. kickoff a one-point favorite. A near sellout crowd of 54,500 waited impatiently for the game to begin. At that time, it was the largest attendance at a professional sports function in San Francisco history.

Otto Graham was too much for the 49ers. His pinpoint passes to Dante Lavelli and Mac Speedie led the Cleveland Browns to a 14-7 win. Between sideline tosses to his fleet ends, Graham sent bruising fullback Marion Motley through the middle on slants and trap plays.

San Francisco's only score came after taking the second half kickoff and marching 80 yards in 13 plays. The touchdown came on a one-yard plunge by fullback Norm Standlee. Standlee led the 49er rushing attack, gaining 72 yards on 11 carries for a 6.5-yard average.

Admiral Jonas Ingram, who replaced Crowley as commissioner of the AAFC, raved that the game demonstrated "professional football at its finest."

The 49ers' final game of the season was with the Buffalo Bills. Although the Kezar turf was slippery from rain, Frankie Albert had a fine day, gaining 49 yards on eight carries. He also threw a touchdown pass to Nick Susoeff. Halfback Ned Matthews scored twice for the Niners, once on a two-yard run from scrimmage, and later on an interception he returned 36 yards for the score. But it wasn't enough. The game ended in a 21-21 tie, leaving the 49ers with an 8-4-2 mark and second place behind Cleveland in the Western Division.

1948 In 1948, Buck Shaw was determined to produce the most powerful offense in the league. He unloaded numerous veterans and went after college talent. When final cuts were made, Shaw kept 17 rookies and 16 veterans. It's doubtful that any professional team ever started a season with so many rookies.

Len Eshmont 1946–1949

Len Eshmont was a legend on the East Coast before the San Francisco 49ers were even formed.

He was raised in the coal regions of central Pennsylvania and played high school football at Mt. Carmel Township in Easton, Pennsylvania, just a few miles from his home in Atlas.

At Mt. Carmel, Eshmont set several prep rushing records and was chosen All-State in 1936, his senior year of high school. His outstanding high school play caught the eye of Jim Crowley, one of Notre Dame's Four Horsemen. Crowley, then a recruiter for Fordham University, persuaded Eshmont to play collegiate ball in New York with the Fordham Rams. At that time, Fordham was one of the most powerful teams on the East Coast.

Eshmont entered Fordham in 1936 and quickly gained recognition as the "Fordham Flash." In his senior year, 1940, he was named to the All-America team.

Eshmont signed with the New York Giants in 1941 where he played for one year before joining the armed forces. In 1942, he was commissioned in the U.S. Navy and served as physical education instructor at Naval pre-flight schools around the country, including St. Mary's Pre-Flight.

For three years, Eshmont starred with the Navy's football teams and combined with Frankie Albert in 1943 to turn St. Mary's Pre-Flight into a local powerhouse. Eshmont was named to the All-Service football teams in 1942, 1943 and 1944, the only person to be named to the all-star team for three consecutive years.

After leaving the Navy, Eshmont decided to stay in the Bay Area and joined the original San Francisco 49er team of 1946 along with his teammate from

St. Mary's Pre-Flight, Frankie Albert. That year, he combined with Albert, Norm Standlee and John Strzykalski to give the 49ers one of the best running attacks in the AAFC.

Eshmont retired in 1949 as San Francisco prepared to enter the NFL. In his four years with the 49ers, he gained 1,181 yards on 232 carries, an average of five yards per carry.

In 1950, he began a successful coaching career by joining former 49er assistant coach Eddie Erdelatz at the U.S. Naval Academy as a backfield coach. In 1956, he left to coach at the University of Virginia. A year later, in May of 1957, he died of infectious hepatitis in Virginia. He was 39.

Each year the Len Eshmont Award is given to the 49er player who best exemplifies the inspiration and courageous play of Len Eshmont. The recipient is selected by a vote of his teammates. It is the team's highest individual honor.

"Me and Len were roommates for three years. They used to call us stumble and fumble. He was a typical Polack, just like me. That's probably why we got along so good. He'd been an All-American at Fordham then played for the New York Giants. When I was back east playing college ball, I remember hearing his name all the time. He was well known back there. When I heard he died I just couldn't believe it. Bruce Lee, the old *Chronicle* reporter, called to tell me. He was a great competitor. That's what

made him a good football player. He just loved competition."
—John Strzykalski

"Len Eshmont was always the old pro. Most of us had only played college ball or in the service. Len had played with New York (Giants) before the 49ers. That was important to a new team. He had experience. He was a hell of a good guy. He was a quiet leader. He led by example. He did have one funny habit. We called him 'thumbs' for it. Whenever he carried the ball, his thumbs stuck up in the air like he was hitchhiking."
—Alyn Beals

"Len Eshmont was a great guy. He was a dedicated football player. He showed a lot of courage, playing injured and stuff like that. He was one of those born leaders, just a natural leader. Some of the fellows on the 49ers now, I don't think they realize what they are getting when they get the Len Eshmont award. It's very special, something to be proud of. A guy like Bill Ring, now he is a lot like Len Eshmont. He has a lot of courage and plays hard."
—Joe Vetrano

"Len was pretty quiet. He was a team leader but he led by his example. He was one of those backs who always got the job done. He wasn't flashy or flamboyant. He just did what was necessary to win. I couldn't compare him to anybody playing now."
—Joe Perry

"Eshmont was a great player. I played with him at St. Mary's Pre-Flight before the 49ers. He led by demonstration and got a lot of respect from his teammates. He wasn't a holler guy. He had desire and was a hell of a competitor.

"He didn't have blinding speed but he knew how to use what he had. He was a smart player more than anything. He was one of those guys you went to in the clutch. I would remember his number in the clutch because he was effective. He was a good receiver. He never fumbled. He wasn't a great open field runner or anything, but when you needed two or three yards, that's who you went to."
—Frankie Albert

WINNERS OF THE LEN ESHMONT AWARD:
1957—Y.A. Tittle
1958—Joe Perry
1959—J.D. Smith
1960—Dave Baker
1961—Leo Nomellini
1962—Dan Colchico
1963—Bob St. Clair
1964—Charlie Krueger
1965—John Brodie
1966—John David Crow
1967—Dave Wilcox
1968—Matt Hazeltine
1969—Jimmy Johnson
1970—Roosevelt Taylor
1971—Ed Beard
1972—Tommy Hart
1973—Mel Phillips
1974—Len Rohde
1975—Jimmy Johnson
1976—Tommy Hart
1977—Mel Phillips
1978—Paul Hofer
1979—Paul Hofer
1980—Archie Reese
1981—Charle Young
1982—Dwight Clark
1983—Bill Ring
1984—Keena Turner

A pass intended for 49er receiver Hal Shoener (52) is broken up by Buffalo Bills defensive back Tom Colella (88) in a preseason game at Kezar Stadium in August, 1949.

Verl Lillywhite from the University of Southern California, Joe Perry from Alameda Naval Air Station and Hal Shoener from Iowa, were just a few of the prizes the 49ers added to their roster.

The nucleus of the team was made up of returning veterans Frankie Albert, John Strzykalski, Len Eshmont, Norm Standlee, Joe Vetrano and linemen Bruno Banducci and Alyn Beals. The rookies blended exceptionally well with the established players and the result was one of the most explosive offensive clubs in football history.

The 49ers averaged an incredible five touchdowns a game through the 14-game season and scored 495 points, a record topped only by the 1961 Houston Oilers with 513 points.

The fearsome running attack, led by Perry, Strzykalski, Standlee and Lillywhite gained 3,663 yards rushing, a professional football record. The 49ers averaged 6.5 yards per carry and over 261 rushing yards per game. The 1978 New England Patriots have the second highest rushing total of all-time with 3,165 yards over a 16-game season.

Frankie Albert sparked a 49er passing assault that accounted for another 2,104 yards. He threw 29 touchdown passes. Wide receiver Alyn Beals caught 14 of those scoring tosses, a 49er single-season record.

The 49ers began their scoring show against the Los Angeles Dons in their first preseason game. They whipped the Dons, 42-24, before 58,300 fans at the Rose Bowl. Albert connected on 17 of 21 passes for 222 yards, including three scoring tosses to Beals and one to Eshmont. Lillywhite also scored on a 41-yard run from scrimmage and Albert ran one in from the two-yard line. Joe Vetrano was good on all the conversion attempts.

The game marked the first professional appearance of St. Mary's College standout Herman Wedemeyer. Wedemeyer was drafted by the Dons and reported to the club straight from the College All-Star game. He practiced less than a week and played sparingly against the 49ers.

A week later, the Baltimore Colts came into Kezar for another exhibition game. The 49ers rolled up 42 points for the second successive week. Frankie Albert completed 10 of 13 passes for 190 yards in leading San Francisco to a 42-14 win.

The opening league game against the Buffalo Bills at Kezar Stadium proved the 49ers were a team to be reckoned with. They destroyed Buffalo, 35-14, before 33,950 fans. The 49ers' point total could have been higher but they lost three fumbles deep in Buffalo territory.

Joe Perry flashed his sprinter's speed, when he darted 58 yards for a touchdown. It was the first time he handled the ball in a league game. He gained 65 yards on just three carries for a 21.6-yard average. Strzykalski chipped in a 10.8-yard rushing average with 76 yards on seven carries. He also scored a touchdown on a 48-yard run from scrimmage.

Albert, who completed 13 of 18 passes, suffered a broken nose and rib damage when he was hit hard on a pass attempt. He regained composure and two plays later, scampered 17 yards to set up a 49er touchdown. Albert also threw a touchdown pass to Jim Cason, a rookie halfback out of Louisiana State, and a scoring pass to Hal Shoener.

The following week San Francisco beat the Brooklyn Dodgers, 36-20, putting its league record at 2-0. Interest in the 49ers skyrocketed. Football fans in the Bay Area knew if the team played well against its next opponent, the New York Yankees, they had a real contender on their hands.

In two years of AAFC play, San Francisco had

John Strzykalski 1946–1952

John Strzykalski was the strength of the 49er backfield during the club's first seven years.

At a time when rushing for 1,000 yards per season was considered superhuman, Strzykalski was picking up 900. In both 1947 and 1948, he gained over 900 yards to pace the 49er ground attack. He averaged over six yards a carry in those years and in 1948 was selected to the All-America Football Conference All-Star team.

Strzykalski, or Johnny Strike as he likes to be called, was a small halfback by today's standards. At 5' 9" and 190 pounds he wasn't overpowering, but neither was he shy about putting his head down and battling for extra yards.

Like so many of the original 49ers, Strike joined the squad in 1946 after leaving the armed forces. He had been a

star with the Fourth Air Corps football team when the 49ers noticed him and signed him to a $50 option contract. When he finished his stint with the Air Corps, he joined the 49ers rather than return to Marquette, where he had two more years of football eligibility.

"In those days we were like one big family," said Strzykalski. "Money didn't mean that much to us. We just wanted to play the game. To be a good football player back then, more than anything you needed guts and heart. And you had to love the game. We had guys playing with the worst injuries. If you had a broken nose you suited up."

Strike knows a few things about playing with injuries. During his seven-year career he suffered broken legs and plenty of broken noses.

In all, his nose was broken eight times playing the game he loves, a testimony to old-time football without facemasks. In fact, in the last game of his career, a day in which he was to be honored at Kezar Stadium for his service to the 49ers, he had to leave the field with a broken nose.

Strike recalls with affection the family-type environment of the original 49er team. In those days it wasn't uncommon for 12 to 15 players and their wives to live in the same apartment complex. The family environment even extended to owner Tony Morabito.

"For a while a bunch of us lived out at Parkmerced," he said." Rent was only $52. When we practiced out at the Polo Fields in Golden Gate Park we'd drop by Tony's house after and get a bite to eat or talk. He lived close by on 36th Avenue. He took good care of us."

Strike played for only one head coach with the 49ers. He remembers Buck Shaw with reverence, saying he was a perfect gentlemen.

"Buck Shaw never cussed," he said. "The worse thing he ever said was 'damn it to hell.' When he said that, you knew he was mad."

Under Shaw, the 49ers employed the T-Formation. The starting backfield consisted of Frankie Albert at quarterback, Norm Standlee at fullback and Len Eshmont and John Strzykalski at halfback. Strike's role in that backfield was as a breakaway threat.

"Norm usually got the short yards," he said. "Len and I caught a lot of passes. We picked up long yardage once in a while. In those days, you have to remember, you could get up and run after you were tackled. The tackler had to hold you until the ref blew the whistle. If he didn't blow it, I was up and running. I was pretty good at that."

Although Strike made his reputation as a running back, he also played defense, as did most of the team. He doubled as a defensive back.

"Back then we all played 60 minutes," he said. "We were young and healthy. After 60 minutes we still felt fresh."

The 49ers' rival in the AAFC was the Cleveland Browns. Their passing attack in those years is still considered one of the best ever produced. Quarterback Otto Graham had two Hall of Fame caliber receivers to throw at—Mac Speedie and Dante Lavelli. Speedie was an All-Pro twice in the NFL and three times in the AAFC. Lavelli was an All-Pro twice in both leagues. He was selected to the Hall of Fame in 1975. Speedie has yet to be selected.

"Cleveland was easily the toughest team back then, although the New York Yankees were good too," said Strzykalski. "Marion Motley was the best back I ever saw. He was powerful and he was fast. He could also catch the pass.

"I played man-to-man on Dante Lavelli and Mac Speedie. I'll probably put those guys in the Hall of Fame, they caught so many passes over me."

In 1950 San Francisco joined the NFL. Although it was considered a superior league, Strike saw no difference in the competition.

"The NFL was no tougher than the AAFC," he said. "They thought they were King Farouk over there. They had players with a little more experience but they weren't any more talented."

One of the most memorable players of that era was Les Bingaman. Bingaman was a defensive lineman with the Detroit Lions from 1948 to 1954. He was listed at 325 pounds but opponents say that was a conservative figure. According to Strike, Lou Groza of the Cleveland Browns was a tough man to block, but Bingaman was in a class by himself.

"One time, Frankie Albert called an off-tackle play," he said. "Bruno Banducci was supposed to pull out and hit Bingaman. Bruno weighed about 225 and was strong. He pulled and hit Bingaman as hard as he could and bounced back about five yards. I was right behind Bruno so I hit Bingaman and bounced about five yards, too. The play was a bust. We went back to the huddle and Bruno said, 'Hey Frank, don't call that play anymore.' You just couldn't move that guy. He was too big. He was a blacksmith in the off-season."

Although Strike was the 49ers' leading rusher during their years in the AAFC, he insists the offensive line should receive credit for that total. John Woudenberg, Bruno Banducci, Dick Bassi and Visco Grgich are just a handful of the linemen who opened holes for Strike in the AAFC. And it was in the AAFC that Strike really made his mark. He is fourth on the league's all-time rushing list with 2,454 yards. He averaged 5.7 yards per carry and scored 14 touchdowns during the league's four years of operation.

Before Strike could hang up his cleats, he gained another 960 yards in the NFL, giving him a total of 3,414 yards. His career average was 5.2 yards per carry.

During those later years he knew his days were numbered, he says, especially when a halfback named Hugh McElhenny showed up at the 49er training camp.

"McElhenny was just too good," he said, chuckling at the thought of being replaced by one of the greatest runners to ever handle a pigskin. "He stepped right in and took my place. I knew then it was time to go."

yet to beat New York. The Yankees came to town with two consecutive Eastern Division Championships to boast about. Spec Sanders, the most valuable player in the conference, was their starting tailback.

A paid attendance of 60,927—at that time the largest attendance in the franchise's history—crowded into Kezar Stadium. An additional 10,000 fans had to be turned away at the gates. Those in attendance were not disappointed.

Only 25 seconds into the game, the 49ers put the first score on the board, an omen of things to come. Joe Vetrano booted the opening kickoff to the two-yard line where it was juggled by Yankee Bob Kennedy. John Woudenberg and Bob Bryant promptly tackled Kennedy, the ball squirted into the end zone and Len Eshmont pounced on it for the first 49er touchdown.

After 60 minutes of play, the 49ers had demolished New York, 41-0. Albert completed eight of 13 passes for 135 yards and two touchdowns. He also scored on a one-yard run.

The 49er defense also played well, limiting New York to just 88 yards of total offense. Defensive linemen Paul Maloney, Nick Susoeff, Gail Bruce and Hal Shoener completely shutdown Yankee tailback Spec Sanders. And rookie defensive back Paul Crowe, a graduate of St. Mary's College, rounded out the 49er scoring by returning an intercepted pass 39 yards for a touchdown.

The 49ers continued to pile up lopsided scores against their opponents. They beat the Baltimore Colts, 56-14, and the Chicago Rockets, 44-21, enroute to a 10-0 record. After winning their tenth straight league game, they came up against the formidable Cleveland Browns.

Cleveland also had a 10-0 record and was terrorizing the league with the same lineup that won the 1947 conference championship. However, the 49ers were the only team in the AAFC that continually challenged the Browns. In past meetings, San Francisco had lost twice by identical 14-7 scores and had won once, whipping the Browns, 34-20. The two teams still had to play each other twice in the last four games of the season. A split would mean a playoff to decide the division champion.

A record crowd of 82,769 packed into Cleveland's Municipal Stadium. According to Joe Vetrano and others who were on the field that day, the 49ers were tense. The crowd size, and the importance of the game, played on the nerves of the visiting 49ers.

The tension led to three fumbles that killed San Francisco. Despite playing tough defense, they again lost, 14-7, the third time in three years Cleveland won by that score. It was the Browns' 19th straight win.

San Francisco was confident that a rematch at Kezar Stadium, just two weeks later, would turn things its way. The Browns were on the road those two weeks, and the San Francisco game would be their third during that time. They were tired and rumor had it that star quarterback Otto Graham might miss the game because of an injury. The 61,000 fans at Kezar Stadium were poised for an upset. A win by San Francisco would force a playoff between these two great teams to determine the Western Conference champion.

The 49ers started poorly. In the first nine minutes of play San Francisco mistakes allowed Cleveland to take a quick 10-0 lead. Otto Graham, though reputedly injured, was in the starting backfield. The 49ers fought back gallantly. They scored on a Joe Perry run and a pass from Albert to Beals to go into the locker room at halftime leading, 14-10.

Perry scored again in the second half to give the 49ers a 21-10 advantage, but that was it for San Francisco. Cleveland scored three touchdowns in the third quarter to put the game out of reach. The Browns' 31-28 victory gave them their third straight Western Division title. The 49ers ended the season with a 12-2 record. Despite their sparkling season, they finished in second place for the third straight year.

1949 Prior to the 1949 season, Tony and Victor Morabito bought out their partners, Allen Sorrell and E.J. Turre. Tony got three-fourths of the team stock and Victor got the remaining one-fourth. Then Tony gambled that the franchise would be a success and mortgaged his home to ensure operating capital for the upcoming season.

San Francisco opened the year at Kezar Stadium as 14-point favorites over the Baltimore Colts. Most of the starting lineup that led the 49ers to a 12-2 season in 1948 remained intact. Homer Hobbs, a guard from the University of Georgia, linebacker Pete Wismann out of St. Louis, and Paul Salata, an end who starred with the USC Trojans, were a few of the new names on the roster.

Several 49ers began the year hoping to build on personal records. Alyn Beals had caught at least one pass in 31 consecutive games. Tackle John Woudenberg had started 42 league games in a row—every 49er contest since the team's formation. Joe Vetrano had kicked 41 extra points in succession. And Joe Perry had scored a touchdown in nine straight games. However, Perry sprained his ankle prior to the opener and Coach Shaw vowed to use him only in an emergency.

The season's inaugural game was not broadcast on radio for lack of a sponsor. Loyal fans who became attached to the 49ers in the exciting 1948 season were furious. Radio station KSAN began broadcasting the games the following week with Bud Foster on the microphone.

Forecasts of light showers kept away many fans. Only 29,100 turned out at Kezar to see the opener. The rain never appeared and the game was played under clear skies.

In the first half, the 49ers' line disassembled the Colt attack, allowing just three yards of total offense. The 49ers took a commanding 17-0 lead into the locker room, but the Colts emerged in the second half a completely different team.

Colts quarterback Y.A. Tittle engineered a third-quarter comeback that netted 17 points for Baltimore. The 49ers fumbled the ball twice and Tittle capitalized on the mistakes by scoring two quick touchdowns. A field goal by Rex Grossman tied the game at 17-17 at the end of the third period. The 49ers were in trouble.

Frankie Albert then took matters into his own hands, marching San Francisco 73 yards in 11 plays. Standlee ran eight yards for the score. The 49ers put

Paul Salata (55) came to the 49ers as a wide receiver in 1949 after playing college ball at USC. Here, he stretches for a 50-yard pass from Frankie Albert at Cleveland's Municipal Stadium after slipping in the mud. The pass was just out of his reach. PAGE 25: Joe Perry races 49 yards to score a touchdown against the Cleveland Browns as the 49ers routed Cleveland, 56-28. When he retired in 1963, he had gained the most rushing yardage in NFL history. Jim Brown later broke the record.

Joe Vetrano 1946–1949

Joe "the Toe" Vetrano was with the 49ers in the beginning. He's seen the good teams and the bad. He's played with the all-time greats.

In 1946, the very first year the team came into existence, Vetrano was trying to win a starting backfield spot. The war was over and the 49ers were lucky enough to have the cream of the military crop in the Bay Area. Thousands of servicemen returned to San Francisco from overseas duty. From that talent pool came many of the players that made up the first 49er team, including Vetrano.

"A lot of the players we had on the original team came from the service teams that were around here," Vetrano said. "Some of those teams were almost as good as the pros. Fleet City, the Camp Pendleton Marines and St. Mary's Pre-Flight were all pretty good. Frankie Albert played for St. Mary's Pre-Flight. Johnny Strzykalski and Bruno Banducci came from the service teams too.

"Kezar was packed for some of those games. Even at the Coliseum in Los Angeles they drew big crowds."

Most teams in the newly formed All-America Football Conference lacked players with professional experience. Among the 49ers, Bruno Banducci had played with the Philadelphia Eagles and Len Eshmont had played for the New York Giants before their military days. This gave San Francisco valuable leadership in its initial season, says Vetrano.

Vetrano found himself competing with Len Eshmont and John Strzykalski for a starting backfield spot at the 49ers' first training camp. At 5' 9" and 170 pounds, Vetrano was much smaller than his rivals for the halfback position. He saw limited action behind the two 49er workhorses but he got plenty of playing time as a defensive back and a kicker. He is most noted for his kicking ability.

"In those days everyone played both ways to some extent," he said. "There wasn't a big roster like now. The coaches had to go with what they had. I ended up playing a little offense, a little defense and kicking.

"Being a kicker was a good deal though. You watch these kickers now and as soon as they kick off they run to the sidelines. You would never see that happen back then. We kicked off, then had to go down and help make the tackle."

Vetrano became one of professional football's first place-kicking specialists. He scored 247 points during his four years in the AAFC to rank him third on the all-time scoring list. That's just 12 points behind Lou Groza, Cleveland's noted kicker

who ranks second on the list. All but 12 of Vetrano's points were scored with the toe.

For two consecutive years, Vetrano led the league in extra points. In 1948, he booted 62, and in 1949, he sent 56 through the uprights. At one point, he kicked 107 consecutive extra points, a record at that time. He also led the league in field goal kicking percentage in 1948, making five of eight for a .625 percentage.

Like most of the original 49ers, Vetrano remembers the bitter rivalry San Francisco had with the Cleveland Browns during those AAFC days. San Francisco finished second to the Browns for three straight years. The fourth season, they lost to the Browns in the 1949 AAFC Championship Game. It was the league's last game.

"Cleveland and the New York Yankees were the toughest teams in the All-America Conference," Vetrano said. "The Los Angeles Dons were a rival, too, but Cleveland and the Yankees were excellent teams. To show you how good the Browns were, they went into the NFL and won that league too."

Cleveland had a dynamic backfield that was led by Hall of Famer Otto Graham. Fullback Marion Motley, another member of Pro Football's Hall of Fame, was one of the most punishing runners of his day. Vetrano considers Graham and Motley two of the best football players he faced. But a halfback from the New York Yankees ranks right along with them,

he says.

"Spec Sanders was a tough individual," Vetrano said. "He was very dangerous because he could run and throw. You didn't want him to have the ball."

Indeed, Sanders was named to the AAFC all-star squad in both 1946 and 1947. He led the league in rushing both those years and was first in the league in total offense in 1947. That year he gained 1,432 yards rushing and threw for another 1,442. He also scored 19 touchdowns to lead the league in scoring with 114 points. He's the only running back in the history of the AAFC to gain over 1,000 yards rushing in a season and the only player to score over 100 points in a season.

Professional football has changed quite a bit since Vetrano's days with the original 49ers. But he sees a striking resemblance between the way the 49ers were treated under original owner Tony Morabito and the way the current players are treated by Eddie DeBartolo.

"Tony Morabito was good to us back then," he said. "We were like a little family. It seems that's how the 49ers are today. DeBartolo seems to watch out for his players and take good care of them. Of course, Tony didn't have quite the money that DeBartolo does. He was a kind man though, a real nice guy. DeBartolo reminds me a lot of Morabito.

"I'm glad I had a chance to play with the early teams. I have nothing but good memories of those years."

seven more points on the board when Verl Lilly-white caught a 10-yard pass from Albert to ensure the 31-17 victory.

The 49ers continued their winning streak, running their record to 4-1, by clobbering the Chicago Hornets, 42-7, and the Los Angeles Dons, 42-14, before losing to the Buffalo Bills, 28-17.

The Cleveland Browns, who had not lost a game in over two years, were set to invade Kezar Stadium once again. Their overall record after three years in the AAFC was 42-3-2. The 49ers were 33-12-2 in AAFC play. Cleveland was now San Francisco's most intense rival.

Joe Perry started the day with a dazzling 11.6-yard rushing average. He gained 156 yards in 16 carries against the Browns and scored two touchdowns as the 49ers drubbed Cleveland, 56-28. It was Cleveland's worst beating in four years of AAFC play. The highest previous point total against the Browns was 34 points, and that was by the 1946 San Francisco club.

The 49ers ended the season with a 9-3 record after beating Buffalo, 51-7, and Los Angeles, 41-24. They lost a rematch with Cleveland, 30-28, but their record was good enough for second place in the AAFC and a chance to play the New York Yankees in a divisional playoff. The winner would meet Cleveland in the conference championship.

The week prior to the Yankee game an unexpected obstacle appeared in the playoff picture. The 49ers threatened to strike. The players demanded a $500 bonus to appear in the playoff game against the Yankees.

"We're not asking for a bonus, just extra salary for an extra game," Visco Grgich told the press on behalf of the players. If there was no bonus, there would be no game.

The team members demanded the bonus because they were not paid for the three preseason games they played, and they were not going to be compensated for the playoff game. In effect, they were playing the games for free.

Owner Tony Morabito refused the players' demand and threatened to forfeit the game if they did not show up for practice. An emergency meeting was called between Buck Shaw, line coach Ed Erdelatz and members of the team. Norm Standlee and Len Eshmont negotiated on the part of the players. They agreed to play the game out of loyalty to the fans, but they stood behind the principles put forth in their demands.

The playoff game was the third match of the year between the 49ers and the Yankees. Each team had won one. The Yankees were well rested. They spent a week preparing for the 49ers at the Sonoma Mission Inn in Sonoma County. It didn't help. The Yankees could not stop the passing and ball handling of Frankie Albert, who sparked San Francisco to a 17-7 win.

The 49ers' first championship game, played against the Cleveland Browns, proved to be anticlimactic. Two days before the game was played, the AAFC merged with the the National Football League. Three teams from the AAFC—Cleveland, San Francisco and Baltimore—were to join the new league in 1950.

Horace Stoneham, owner of the New York Giants baseball club (later the San Francisco Giants), was credited with negotiating peace between the two leagues. NFL Commissioner Bert Bell was appointed commissioner of the new circuit. Art Rooney, president of the NFL's Pittsburgh Steelers, summed up the attitude of management by saying the merger would finally end the "absurd" $20,000 salaries being paid to rookies.

The 49ers played their first championship game on a miserable, cold day at Cleveland before only 22,000 fans. Just a year earlier, these two teams drew over 82,000 to Cleveland's Municipal Stadium. The paltry showing was blamed on the merger, which made the championship game of a now-defunct league insignificant.

The Browns put the only points on the board in the first half after quarterback Otto Graham drove them 57 yards in the first quarter. Edgar Jones plunged over from the two-yard line for the score and a 7-0 lead.

In the third period, the Browns' powerful running back, Marion Motley, sprang loose on a 63-yard run to give the Browns a 14-0 advantage.

The 49ers stormed right back, marching 73 yards on 13 plays. Albert capped the drive with a 24-yard scoring pass to Paul Salata. It was the team's last score in the AAFC. Cleveland defeated San Francisco, 21-7.

PAGE 28: Leo Nomellini was the first player drafted by San Francisco in 1950. He started on both offense and defense for five years before settling into the defensive tackle position.

1950–1959

CHAPTER TWO

JOINING THE NATIONAL FOOTBALL LEAGUE

 new era began in 1950. The San Francisco 49ers were now part of the National Football League.

The preseason player draft proved to be a bonanza for the 49ers. With their first pick, they chose Leo Nomellini, a massive tackle from the University of Minnesota. Coach Buck Shaw was in desperate need of linemen since the retirement of John Woudenberg and Bob Bryant, the starting tackles on the 1949 team. Nomellini proved to be more than an adequate replacement. He went on to earn All-Pro honors six times and a place in the Hall of Fame.

Under pressure from other NFL club owners, Tony Morabito reluctantly raised ticket prices at Kezar Stadium. Midfield seats jumped from $3.60 to $3.75, reserved seats went from $2.40 to $3 and general admission tickets were raised from $1.80 to $2. Children were admitted for 50 cents. Even with the price hike the 49ers had the least expensive tickets in the league.

The team held its annual preseason scrimmage in August at Menlo College near Menlo Park. Over 3,000 curious fans showed up to watch the 49ers prepare for their first season in the NFL. Norm Standlee was named team captain for the third straight year.

Herman Wedemeyer was a new addition to the 49er roster after his previous team, the Los Angeles Dons of the AAFC, folded. Although he was a favorite of the fans, he didn't win a spot with the club and was waived prior to the season opener.

Halfback John Strzykalski proudly claimed that this 49er team was the best he'd ever seen and sports writers eagerly picked San Francisco as a contender for the league crown.

In their first exhibition game, the 49ers faced the Washington Redskins. They quickly discovered there was a new level of competition in the NFL.

The Redskins were led by "Slingin" Sammy Baugh. He last appeared in the Bay Area in 1936. That year, Baugh led Texas Christian to an upset win over the Sugar Bowl-bound Santa Clara Broncos. Ironically, the Broncos were coached by Buck Shaw.

Washington was not an NFL powerhouse. The team had finished the 1949 season with a 4-7-1 record. The 49ers had played for the AAFC crown a year earlier and they were confident of a win. Still, Washington was a slight favorite to win the game.

Season ticket sales had been brisk and a sellout crowd was expected at Kezar. In anticipation of a large turnout, San Francisco Mayor Elmer Robinson closed what was then Panhandle Drive, near the edge of Golden Gate Park, to allow public parking.

In his team's first game against the established league, owner Tony Morabito desperately wanted to impress his peers. Prior to the game he implored his troops to "pour it on."

The 49ers were soundly beaten, 31-14. *Chronicle* Sports Editor Bill Leiser wrote, "Frankly, they did not look capable of beating any team in the National Football League."

After the game, local favorite Joe Vetrano was released. Two days later, Gordy Soltau, a receiver and place kicker, was obtained from the Cleveland Browns. Coach Shaw reasoned that Soltau would be more valuable to the team because he was not simply a kicking specialist, as Vetrano had been.

San Francisco met the NFL champion Philadelphia Eagles a week later. They were trounced once again, 28-10. Eagle coach Earle "Greasy" Neale claimed the 49ers had a deceptive offense, but it was not well organized. "Frankie Albert is a wonderful faker, but he's not the passer some of the other

boys are," Neale told the press.

The coach was even less complimentary about the 49er defense. "You've got to have big men in there to handle what they throw at you in this league," he said.

During the exhibition season, the 49ers were able to win only one game. They were defeated by some of the worst teams in the NFL, including the Pittsburgh Steelers and the Chicago Cardinals. Their sole victory was against the Baltimore Colts before only 6,000 fans at Baltimore. Things looked bleak for the 49ers.

San Francisco opened league play against the New York Yankees, a former AAFC rival. Behind 21-17 in the fourth quarter, the 49ers were driving behind the passes of Frankie Albert and the running of Joe Perry. With less than two minutes to play, and the ball at the New York 40-yard line, the 49ers were caught with 12 men on the field. The resulting penalty killed the drive and ended their hope of a victory.

San Francisco continued to have a tough time in the NFL. The 49ers dropped their first five league games before sneaking by Detroit, 28-27. With Baltimore coming to town the next week, the 49ers hoped to put together a two-game winning streak.

In seven exhibition games and five regular season contests, the Colts had yet to win. San Francisco was established as a 20-point favorite by local bookmakers.

Only 15,000 fans showed up at Kezar Stadium. Despite a big day by Joe Perry, who romped for 142 yards on 16 carries, the 49ers needed a field goal by Gordy Soltau with 2:45 to go for a 17-14 win.

After the Baltimore game, San Francisco reverted to its losing ways, dropping four straight games. Entering the season's finale against Green Bay, the club's record was 2-9.

Before the contest, team captain Norm Standlee, who had announced his retirement, was honored for his five years of service to the 49ers as a fullback and linebacker. Mayor Robinson gave him a new 1950 Oldsmobile. It turned out to be a premature gesture. Owner Tony Morabito later convinced Standlee to return to the 49er backfield, and he played for two more seasons before retiring.

San Francisco ended the season on an upbeat note with a 30-14 drubbing of Green Bay. The 49ers were led once again by Joe Perry who scored two touchdowns and gained 146 yards on nine carries.

At the end of the season, the Baltimore Colts folded. Their players were drafted by other NFL

New York Yankee halfback Buddy Young (76) loses his helmet as he is brought down from behind by Lowell Wagner, a 49er defensive back from 1949 to 1955. Wagner had nine interceptions, tops on the club in 1951.

clubs. The 49ers came away with one of the team's prizes, quarterback Y.A. Tittle.

1951 The 1951 college draft considerably strengthened the 49ers. Among the rookies chosen were offensive ends Billy Wilson and Bill Jessup, halfback Joe Arenas and linebacker Hardy Brown, a devastating tackler.

The 49ers rolled through the 1951 preseason schedule with victories over Washington, Pittsburgh, Green Bay and the Chicago Cardinals. They opened the regular season against the Cleveland Browns. Cleveland was the reigning NFL champion, and a seven-point favorite over the 49ers. The Browns entered the game with four victories in exhibition play and a 33-0 win over the College All-Stars.

Frankie Albert edged out Y.A. Tittle for San Francisco's starting quarterback spot. Once again Joe Perry opened at fullback and Verl Lillywhite at left halfback. Rookie Pete Schabarum took over for the injured John Strzykalski at right half.

San Francisco rallied to score a 24-10 upset of Cleveland. Lillywhite gained 145 yards in 17 carries to lead the club. Talk of a league title once again surfaced in the Bay Area. The victory had its sour side though. Receivers Billy Wilson and Gordy Soltau were lost temporarily due to injuries.

Dissension also began to arise at Kezar Stadium. Y. A. Tittle and Frankie Albert started sharing time behind the center, and San Francisco had its first quarterback controversy. Fans at Kezar were split into different factions, demanding playing time for the quarterback of their choice. Albert had been a local favorite since his playing days at Stanford when he led the Indians to an undefeated season. But Tittle gradually was winning fans with his brilliant passing.

San Francisco defensive backs Sam Cathcart and Jim Powers use the goal post in an unsuccessful attempt to keep Los Angeles Rams running back Paul Barry out of the end zone. Dan Towler (32), Bob Waterfield (7) and Gil Bouley (66) look on.

Joe Perry (74) was inducted into Pro Football's Hall of Fame in 1969 along with Leo Nomellini. They were the first two 49ers to be enshrined at Canton, Ohio.

The 49ers had a 2-2 record when the Los Angeles Rams visited Kezar. The Rams were loaded with superstars in 1951. Bob Waterfield and Norm Van Brocklin shared the quarterbacking duties, while Elroy "Crazy Legs" Hirsch and Tom Fears took care of the pass-catching chores.

The game started slowly with the 49ers taking a 10-3 lead into the second quarter. Suddenly, they caught fire.

Y. A. Tittle hit Gordy Soltau on touchdown passes of 49 yards, 10 yards and 13 yards in the second quarter. The 49ers added another touchdown when Leo Nomellini blocked a punt and pounced on the ball in the end zone. At the half, the score was San Francisco 38, Los Angeles 10.

Los Angeles never rebounded as the 49ers posted a 44-17 win. Soltau scored 26 points—a 49er single-game record—by adding a 23-yard field goal and five extra points to his three touchdowns.

The 49ers played mediocre football the rest of the season, losing to the lowly Chicago Cardinals and playing the New York Yankees to a tie. Going into the final game of the year against Detroit, they had a 6-4-1 record.

Prior to the Detroit game, owner Tony Morabito called the 49ers "the Robin Hoods of football." They took from the rich by beating the good teams, and gave to the poor by losing to the bad teams.

Yet, in the season finale, San Francisco still could salvage a tie for the divisional title. If the 49ers beat Detroit, and Green Bay beat the Rams, the 49ers would end the season deadlocked with the Lions.

With the 49ers behind 17-14, and a little over four minutes to play, Joe Arenas fielded a Detroit punt and raced 53 yards to the Detroit 17-yard line. Tittle and Albert had shared time at quarterback throughout the game, but now it was Tittle's turn. After Joe Perry picked up three yards, Tittle threw a 10-yard pass to Gordy Soltau. From the three-yard line, Tittle bootlegged around right end and ran the ball into the end zone to give San Francisco a 21-17 victory.

Unfortunately, the Rams beat Green Bay leaving the 49ers in second place, behind division champion Los Angeles.

Hugh McElhenny 1952–1960

Hugh McElhenny knew he was breaking a cardinal rule when he fielded a punt on the four-yard line, juked a couple of Chicago Bears, and took off on a 96-yard scamper for a touchdown.

A veteran would have allowed the punt to go into the end zone. But McElhenny wasn't a veteran, he was a rookie playing in his fourth league game in 1952. McElhenny's rookie mistake was ignored, but his running ability wasn't overlooked.

"After the game in the locker room," said McElhenny, "Frankie Albert gave me the game ball and said, 'You're now the King.' Then he turned to Joe Perry and said, 'Joe, you're just the Jet.' "

That's when the legend was born. "The King" was finally coronated. And McElhenny was definitely royalty. In the open field he had no peer, dancing past bruising tacklers with the grace and beauty of Baryshnikov. He was an artist unleashed on a canvas of green grass, sprinting and slashing like no one before him.

McElhenny began to make his presence known barely 24 hours after reporting to the 49er training camp. He played in the College All-Star game on a Friday night, reported to camp on Saturday and was in uniform on Sunday for an exhibition game against the Chicago Cardinals. He hadn't even had time to learn the names of his teammates when he found himself in the 49er backfield.

"Frankie had called a time out and asked Buck Shaw to put me in the game," McElhenny said. "Buck told him I didn't know the plays yet. At that time, Frankie pretty much had his way with Buck, so Buck went along with him. In the huddle, Frankie drew a play on the ground and told everybody what to do. He threw me a pitchout and I ran 42 yards for a touchdown."

It's hard to find a Hugh McElhenny story that doesn't in some way involve Frankie Albert. If not for Albert's acute judgment of talent and character, McElhenny might have played elsewhere. It was at the Hula Bowl in 1952 that Albert first laid his eyes on "the King." The game matched the best college players in the country against top professional talent. Albert happened to be on hand to represent the pros. McElhenny played in two games, made the All-Hula Bowl team and attracted Albert's eye. Frankie immediately got on the phone and told Buck Shaw he had to pick McElhenny in the upcoming draft. The 49ers made him the ninth college player picked in 1952.

When Albert introduced McElhenny to his new teammates for the first time he said, "I'd like you to meet a man who took a cut in pay to become a professional."

McElhenny considers it a curious joke because it was Albert who advised him what kind of contract to ask for when he was bargaining with team owner Vic Morabito. The contract negotiation took place at the Sheraton Hotel on Wilshire Boulevard in Los Angeles.

"Vic Morabito sat down and said to me, 'Well Hugh, what do you want?' I said I wanted $30,000, I was a first-round pick. He told me they were thinking about something in the range of $5,000. I told him I could have signed with the Los Angeles Dons for $10,000 when I got out of high school. At that point he excused himself, got up and never came back. I even had to pick up the check." McElhenny eventually signed for $7,000.

It was a bargain for the 49ers. McElhenny's exceptional running skill earned him *Sport* magazine's Player-of-the-Year award in his rookie season. But his reputation as a game breaker made him a marked man around the league. Everywhere he went defenses devised plans to stop him. Some devised ways to cripple him. They didn't want to just tackle him, they wanted him out of the lineup.

The Chicago Bears had one of those fierce defenses. In 1954, the 49ers and McElhenny were on their way to an exceptional season when he separated his shoulder against the Bears. Joe Perry, John Henry Johnson and Y.A. Tittle, the three other members of that Million Dollar Backfield, couldn't take up the slack. With McElhenny out of action, they lost three straight games and finished 7-4-1.

That year still evokes good memories for McElhenny because it was the first year the Million Dollar Backfield was together. McElhenny rates it the best backfield that ever played.

"That was one hell of a backfield," he said. "Even with all that talent, we could never quite win it. We had an injury here, an injury there. In 1954 we had nine starters injured.

"Perry was an exceptional guy to be with in the backfield," he said. "He was such an outstanding team player. Running backs are only as good as the guys in front of them. I don't know how many times he laid a block that sprang me. I'm just proud to say I was in the same backfield as him.

"Now I keep waiting for John Henry Johnson to go into the Hall of Fame. I don't know why he isn't. That would really be something. We probably would have the only backfield in history to all be in the Hall of Fame.

"Y.A. Tittle used to joke about trying to keep us all happy by giving us the ball. He certainly had his hands full because we all had egos."

One of the disappointments of McElhenny's nine years with San Francisco was the team's inability to win a championship despite having such outstanding individual players as Tittle, Johnson and Perry. Nevertheless, the 49ers were competitive throughout the 1950s. The highlight of that decade was 1957 when San Francisco forced a playoff with Detroit. One of the games that got the team there is etched in McElhenny's memory.

With two games left in the season, the 49ers needed a win against the Baltimore Colts to stay alive in the race for the Western Division title. San Francisco was behind, 13-10, but driving, when Tittle was hurt.

Rookie John Brodie was motioned off the bench and onto the field.

"When Brodie came into the huddle, he looked around and said, 'What do I call?' I told him to throw me the ball. I was going to do a little down and out and he could throw it to the sidelines."

Brodie threw the pass under a heavy rush, McElhenny caught it, and the 49ers won.

McElhenny regards the ability to run with a football as something of a mystery. He had been a prep hurdling champion at George Washington High School in Los Angeles, and that training helped him develop as a running threat. But there is something undefinable that the great backs possess, he says. The intuitive cutbacks and changes of direction that were McElhenny's trademark, are something that can't be programmed.

"Speed is one ingredient," he said. "I had pretty good speed but I couldn't beat Joe Perry in the 50. I could beat him in the 100 though. To be a good running back, well it's just God's gift. It's not something you can teach. I did things by instinct. Running, balance, all of it was instinct. You also have to know where other people are on the field."

He generally doesn't like to compare the modern players with those of his era because he disagrees with the argument that today's players are better athletes.

"We'd probably be just as good as these guys playing today," he said. "They are bigger and faster, but we'd probably have been bigger and faster if we had the same training methods, the vitamins, and all that."

McElhenny remains a 49er faithful to this day. He credits the success of the present team to the system used by Bill Walsh more than the individual players.

"You have to look at Bill Walsh's system," he said. "How do the 49ers evaluate their players? How do they find players that fit into the system that well? If one guy gets hurt, it won't affect the team. They have other talented players that will fit into the system and do just as well.

"The loss of the quarterback might make a difference, but (Matt) Cavanaugh does a good job when he's in there. They have great athletes on that team but the important thing is Walsh knows how to use them. He knows how to get the maximum effort out of his players.

"The organization is great to us. Eddie DeBartolo and Bill Walsh always try to keep in touch and make us part of the organization. They invite us on road trips every year. That's real gratifying to know they want you to still be part of the team. Many teams just forget about us old guys.

"I don't want to be overly sentimental, but I'll always be a 49er."

John Strzykalski (91) was the 49ers' leading ground gainer during their four years in the AAFC. When the league folded in 1949, he was fourth on the all-time rushing list with 2,454 yards. He averaged 5.8 yards per carry in the AAFC.

1952 In 1952, the 49ers had the ninth pick in the draft. It was a year of enormous collegiate talent. Among the players chosen before San Francisco had a chance to pick were Ollie Matson, Les Richter, Bill Wade, Frank Gifford and Babe Parilli. When it was San Francisco's turn to choose, Buck Shaw was astonished to find Hugh McElhenny from the University of Washington still available. He quickly picked McElhenny and never regretted it.

The first time he touched the ball as a 49er, McElhenny ran 42 yards for a touchdown. His shifty runs and elusive moves inspired quarterback Frankie Albert to call him "the King," a name he later would take to Pro Football's Hall of Fame.

San Francisco's third year in the NFL began innocently enough with preseason games against local semi-pro teams. The 49ers demolished the San Francisco Broncos, 79-0, and the San Jose Packers, 76-0. They also dominated the NFL teams, beating the Rams and Cleveland on the way to a 7-0 preseason mark.

They opened the season against the Detroit Lions, a team they knocked out of the playoff picture on the last day of the season a year earlier. Detroit had won all six of its preseason games.

Hugh McElhenny was making his debut as a 49er starter along with rookie tackle Bob Toneff,

defensive end Pat O'Donaghue and J.R. Boone at halfback. Frankie Albert opened the season again as the starting quarterback.

It was Albert who guided the team to its opening game victory. His 47-yard touchdown pass to Boone in the third quarter gave the 49ers a 17-3 lead they never relinquished.

The 49ers continued their winning streak by beating the Dallas Texans, and then Detroit again, before meeting the Chicago Bears in the Windy City.

A standing-room-only crowd of 48,400 gathered at Wrigley Field to see the game. The 49ers had not beaten the Bears since joining the NFL. This time things were different. The 49ers humiliated the Bears, 40-16.

McElhenny was awarded the game ball for his part in the triumph. He broke the game wide open in the second quarter with a 94-yard punt return that put the 49ers in front, 21-9. He also carried from scrimmage 12 times for 103 yards. For his efforts, the

35

Rex Berry, a 14th-round choice in the 1951 draft, stops the New York Giants' Frank Gifford (16) after a short gain.

Chicago fans gave him a standing ovation when he left the field. The 49ers were now the only undefeated team in football, two games ahead of the pack.

The 49ers beat the Dallas Texans the next week, 48-21, to post a 5-0 record, then disaster struck. They lost five of their next six games. Injuries played a big part in the club's decline. Team captain Norm Standlee contracted polio, and Tittle and Perry were in and out of the lineup with less serious ailments. San Francisco finished the year at 7-5, but it was the end of something special.

Three members of the 49ers' original starting backfield retired after the season. Besides Standlee, John Strzykalski, 30, and Frankie Albert, 32, ended their careers.

For Strzykalski, the end wasn't a pleasant one. Just prior to halftime of his final game against the Green Bay Packers—a day when he was to be honored for his achievements—he broke his nose for the eighth time as a professional. He carried the ball only six times for 22 yards that day. His lifetime totals compiled entirely with the 49ers were 3,414 yards on 662 carries.

Albert's final game against the Packers was more satisfying. He completed 16 of 26 passes for 213 yards and a touchdown. His lifetime totals were 631 completions in 1,564 attempts for 10,795 yards and 115 touchdowns.

Gordy Soltau ended the 1952 season as the league's top scorer and Hugh McElhenny was named *Sport* magazine's Player-of-the-Year. He ran for 684 yards on 98 carries, nearly a seven-yard average.

1953 The most memorable part of the 1953 opening game was the bench-clearing brawl that occured near midfield. Tempers began to flare early when 49er linebacker Hardy Brown flattened Philadelphia Eagle halfback Toy Ledbetter with one of his famous shoulder tackles. The jarring tackle left Ledbetter unconscious and crushed his cheekbone.

Minor confrontations continued throughout the game until it finally erupted into a helmet swinging free-for-all. Among the combatants were Hugh McElhenny, who used his helmet to club the Eagles'

Pete Pihos, and Joe Perry, who charged off the sidelines to tangle with Bob Walston. Once the battle was under way, about 150 fans swarmed out of the stands at Kezar Stadium to help their hometown heros. It took the referees nearly 10 minutes to restore order. Even the pleadings of Buck Shaw and Eagle coach Jim Trimble were ignored by the players.

Joe McTique and the 49er band tried to soothe the unruly crowd by playing the national anthem. When that failed, they used their instruments to help break up the fight.

San Francisco won the battle on the field and the scoreboard that day, beating Philadelphia, 31-21. Joe Perry paced the winning club with 145 yards rushing in 16 carries.

The following week the Rams brought their high-flying passing attack to Kezar. Quarterback Norm Van Brocklin led the team to a 20-0 lead in the second quarter. San Francisco battled back and, with three minutes to play, had a 28-27 lead. The Rams quickly regained the lead, 30-28, on a Ben Agajanian field goal.

San Francisco took the ensuing kickoff to the 20-yard line. With less than a minute to play, the Rams' secondary prepared for a long bomb from Tittle. Instead, "the Bald Eagle" tossed a screen pass to Hugh McElhenny, who galloped 71 yards to the nine-yard line. With five seconds on the clock, Gordy Soltau kicked a field goal for a 31-30 win.

A rematch with the Rams at the Los Angeles Coliseum attracted 85,900 fans. The 49ers brought a 4-2 record to town after losing twice to the Detroit Lions. The Rams were 5-1.

Y.A. Tittle was returning to action with a newly designed face mask after his cheekbone was shattered in three places against the Lions. The 49ers trailed the Rams, 27-24, with four minutes to play. Tittle then marched the club 80 yards in 11 plays. Twice on third down and 10 yards to go, he hit receivers for first downs. The winning score came on a Tittle-to-Soltau pass with 1:12 to play. The 49ers won another cliffhanger, 31-27, behind Tittle's 18 completions and 301 yards passing.

The 49ers went into the last game of the season with an 8-3 record. They needed a win over the Colts and a loss by the Detroit Lions to tie Detroit for the league title. The 49ers walloped the Colts, 45-14. But the New York Giants couldn't beat Detroit, and the 49ers again finished in second place, this time with a 9-3 record.

For the second season in a row, Gordy Soltau

led the league in scoring. His 114 points beat runner-up Lou Groza of the Cleveland Browns, who had 108. Receiver Billy Wilson tied Philadelphia's Pete Pihos with 10 touchdown receptions on the season. The team's 372 points topped every other offense in the league. Their 2,230 rushing yards was also the league high.

1954 The 49ers opened the 1954 season as 28-point favorites over the Washington Redskins. For two consecutive seasons, San Francisco had the strongest running attack in the league with Perry and McElhenny. Now, John Henry Johnson, obtained in a trade with Pittsburgh, was added to the backfield.

Hugh McElhenny was nicknamed "the King" by Frankie Albert after he returned a punt 96 yards against the Chicago Bears in his rookie season.

Halfback Jim Cason loses his helmet in a night game against the New York Yankees at Yankee Stadium.

San Francisco's potent offense got rolling immediately. It scored two touchdowns in the first five minutes against Washington and cruised to a 41-7 win. Perry scored two rushing touchdowns.

San Francisco tied the Rams the following week and defeated its next two opponents before meeting Detroit at Kezar Stadium. The 49ers had not been beaten in 15 straight games, including the preseason and the tail end of the 1953 season. Detroit was riding its own streak of 16 straight wins.

The Lions were two-point favorites, largely because Tittle had suffered a broken hand. Midway through the week, it had been announced that 49er rookie Maury Duncan would be starting at quarterback. A capacity crowd of 59,600 was on hand at Kezar Stadium.

Tittle thrilled the crowd by opening the game at quarterback despite the injury. On the second play from scrimmage, Hugh McElhenny set the tone for the day by scampering 60 yards for a touchdown. San Francisco continued to pour it on and jumped out to a 24-7 halftime lead. Detroit fought back and cut the margin to 37-31 in the fourth quarter, but it

was not enough. The 49ers held on to win behind the excellent running of McElhenny, who gained 126 yards on seven carries for an 18-yard average.

The 49ers string of undefeated games came to a halt the next week when the Chicago Bears entered Kezar Stadium and beat the 49ers, 31-27. After that, injuries began to hamper the team. Tittle missed several games with his injured hand. McElhenny separated his shoulder in the sixth game, after piling up 515 yards rushing, and was lost for the season. Gordy Soltau, Don Burke, Jim Cason, Bruno Banducci and Joe Manley all missed games due to injuries. The 49ers finished the season in third place with a 7-4-1 record after beating Baltimore, 10-7, in the season's final game.

Joe Perry gained over 1,000 yards rushing for the second straight year becoming the first man in NFL history to have successive seasons gaining over 1,000 yards.

It was also Buck Shaw's last season as the 49er coach. Tony Morabito was still searching for a championship. He thought a change of coaches might do the trick, so he fired Shaw and hired Norm "Red" Strader. Morabito believed the easy-going Shaw was too lenient with his players and that a different style might rejuvenate the team.

Shaw ended his 49er coaching career with a

Leo Nomellini 1950–1963

Leo Nomellini was a predator. His territory was the line of scrimmage, his prey, opposing ball carriers.

His nickname was "the Lion," an appropriate monicker for a man who pursued and devoured offensive backs. For 14 seasons, Nomellini anchored the 49er defensive line. His presence, like that of a lion, was quickly detected and avoided.

At 6' 3" and 265 pounds, his size, strength and agility were more than most opponents could handle. Nomellini used techniques he learned as an off-season wrestler to manhandle opposing linemen who often double- and triple-teamed him.

On the line of scrimmage he was a picture of intimidation. His crew cut and jutting jaw fit snuggly inside a 49er hel-

met. A frightening scowl revealed missing teeth through which he exhaled grunts and groans. The bestial sounds were designed to strike fear in opposing linemen.

Although Nomellini is noted for his defensive prowess, he was also a stellar offensive tackle. For five years, from 1951 to 1955, he was a starter on both offense and defense for the 49ers.

"I tell you, it was difficult sometimes to stand out there and watch the other 21 players run on and off the field," Nomellini said."I never had much time to rest. In fact, the only rest I got was when the other people were changing over from offense to defense. If I had a choice I would have played just defense. I guess I didn't know any better."

Nomellini should also be known as "the Iron-man." When he retired in

1963 at age 39, he had played in 174 consecutive league games. In 60 of those games, he never left the field, playing both offense and defense. In addition, he played in 77 preseason games and 10 Pro Bowls. Incredibly, he never missed a game.

San Francisco made Nomellini its first draft choice in 1950. Luck played a part in his coming to San Francisco.

The Los Angeles Rams originally picked Nomellini in the 1950 NFL draft. After the draft, however, the NFL and All-America Football Conference merged. The draft was held again, and the Rams skipped over Nomellini to choose a fullback named Ralph Pasquariello. The 49ers chose the big lineman from the University of Minnesota.

Nomellini was born in Lucca, Italy. His family immigrated to America when he was an infant and settled in Chicago's West Side. He played no high school sports because he worked after school to help support the family.

During World War II, Nomellini enlisted in the Marine Corps and saw combat in the South Pacific. It was during his Marine Corps days that he began playing football.

Minnesota offered Nomellini a football scholarship based on his performance with the Cherry Point Marine football team. In his first year at college, he won a starting guard position. Ironically, the first college game Nomellini saw was the first one he played in. Later, he was switched to tackle, and for two years he was an All-American. He was also a Big Ten wrestling champion.

Nomellini was a unanimous All-Pro choice six times and played in 10 Pro Bowls. He nostalgically recalls those early 49er days.

"I had some great teammates with the 49ers. There were so many outstanding players—Joe Perry, Y.A. Tittle. I went through 22 roommates on that team. Every one was a joy.

"We considered ourselves pioneers back then. The league was just starting to grow and professional football was gaining popularity. I was just happy to be part of the sport. It's grown quite a bit since those days."

In the early days of football, life on the road was often exhausting. It wasn't uncommon for the 49ers to be on the road for more than three weeks at a time as they swept through the Midwest or the East Coast. Round-trip flights were on propeller-driven planes rather than chartered jets. The trips to a game were often as tough as the contests themselves, Nomellini says.

"We went on road trips back east that lasted 17 to 21 days," he said. "We'd play in Chicago, Detroit, Green Bay and stay back there the whole time. It was tough being away from the family and friends for so long. We'd practice every day, have team meetings and maybe go to a show at night; nothing out of the ordinary. The trips themselves took forever. We flew on props. It would take about 20 hours to fly back from New York."

Nomellini has been honored in many ways for his outstanding play. In addition to his selection to 10 straight Pro Bowls, he was inducted into the Hall of Fame in 1969. His greatest honor, however, is the Len Eshmont Award he received in 1961. The award is given to the 49er who best exemplifies Len Eshmont's spirit and inspiration.

"That award stands out because it was voted by my teammates," he said. "It's special when the people you play with single you out for something like that."

Nomellini played in more than 250 professional football games. He says there is one he will never forget. It stands out for the wrong reason.

"We had some great rivalries back then," said Nomellini. "The Rams were always tough. Of course, we wanted to beat them and be considered the best team in California. Cleveland came over to the NFL with the 49ers so there was a natural rivalry there. Later, the Packers under Vince Lombardi were awfully tough. But I guess the game I most remember was the 1957 playoff game against the Detroit Lions. That game really hurt. We should have done better. Some way or other they just caught us. There was no let down or anything. We were just ahead and we blew it."

The 1957 playoff game against the Detroit Lions was one of the tragic days in 49er history. San Francisco held a 27-7 lead in the third quarter. It seemed certain the 49ers would win the division title. Fans left Kezar Stadium early to celebrate along Haight Street and in Golden Gate Park. But the Lions rallied and won the game, 31-27.

Nomellini remembers Kezar Stadium as a wonderful place to play, a stadium that many teams were happy to see.

"Kezar was a beautiful park," he said. "All the NFL players liked Kezar. The weather was always good for football. It was always cool, which was unlike New York or Chicago where it could be very humid or very cold. Kezar was definitely my favorite place to play.

"The fans were pretty good out there. They could make it hard on some people, the quarterbacks especially, but overall they were pretty knowledgeable. They knew their football."

Hall of Fame cornerback Emlen Tunnell (45), of the New York Giants, intercepts a pass intended for San Francisco's Billy Wilson (84) at the Polo Grounds. Wilson was drafted out of San Jose State on the 22nd round of the 1950 draft.

72-40-4 record. His sparkling .638 winning percentage is still the best among 49er head coaches. He also won more games than any other coach in team history. After leaving the 49ers, "the Silver Fox" coached at the Air Force Academy. In 1958, he moved on to become the head coach of the Philadelphia Eagles. With the Eagles in 1960, he won the NFL championship that had eluded him with the 49ers and promptly retired.

Strader was a local product who had played and coached at St. Mary's College. Later, he became the head coach of the New York Yankees in the AAFC. His methods differed dramatically from Shaw's. He was a strict disciplinarian who prohibited smoking and drinking, while Shaw often looked the other way. Strader recruited Frankie Albert and Red Hickey as assistant coaches.

1955 Prior to training camp for the 1955 season, Bruno Banducci, an All-Pro guard and the 49er team captain, held out for a salary raise. Instead of receiving a raise, Banducci was given his outright release. The team's other starting guard, Nick Feher, was traded prior to the season, leaving a void in the offensive line.

The preseason was a success. The team finished 5-1, but once the league games got under way the 49ers fell apart.

They opened the regular season with five rookie starters. Dick Moegle, Matt Hazeltine, Carroll Hardy, George Maderos and Lou Palatella all worked their way into the lineup. In their first game against the Rams, they were nine-point favorites.

The oddsmakers had the right point spread but picked the wrong team. Los Angeles walked all over the 49ers, 23-14. Five Y.A. Tittle passes were intercepted. The only 49er highlight was a 42-yard scoring pass from Tittle to McElhenny.

The 49ers struggled along trying to play .500 ball and found themselves in Washington midway through the season. They had a 3-4 record, including wins over Chicago and Detroit. At Washington, the situation grew worse. San Francisco was shutout for the first time in five years.

With little Eddie LeBaron at quarterback, the Redskins downed the 49ers, 7-0. It was a frustrating day for San Francisco. The team had three touch-

Left to right, Hugh McElhenny, Frankie Albert, the injured Gail Bruce and Bruno Banducci watch helplessly as the Chicago Bears' George Blanda kicks a last minute field goal to beat the 49ers, 20-17. PAGE 47: Chicago Bears receiver Bill McColl was unable to hang on to this pass as Rex Berry (23) tries to bat it away. McColl is the father of Milt McColl, a member of the 49ers since 1981.

downs called back due to penalties. Another potential scoring strike of eight yards, from Tittle to Soltau, hit a goal post. The Redskins' sole score came after they recovered a fumble on the 49ers' 33-yard line.

The season turned from gray to black after the Washington game. McElhenny injured a foot and was used sparingly the rest of the season. He gained only 326 yards rushing all year. Joe Perry also missed several games with injured knees. San Francisco closed out the season by losing five of its last six games.

Despite finishing with a 4-8 record, San Francisco set a new single-season home attendance record of 281,780.

1956

Prior to the 1956 season, Red Strader was relieved of his coaching duties, although he had a two-year contract. He was replaced with

Frankie Albert. Under Albert's guidance, the 49ers won their first three exhibition games. The optimism soon faded when they lost the next three in a row.

Bruno Banducci tried a comeback. But after playing the exhibition season, he decided his legs had had enough and retired. The Million Dollar Backfield was reduced by half when Perry and McElhenny were injured and started the season opener on the bench.

McElhenny wasn't out of action for long. He came off the bench in the opener to score twice in a 38-21 loss to the New York Giants. Earl Morrall, San Francisco's first-round draft pick in 1956, made his first league appearance as a 49er. He relieved Y.A. Tittle late in the game and completed two passes for 52 yards.

Albert got his first league coaching victory the following week with a 33-30 win over Los Angeles before 57,000 at Kezar Stadium. It was the only win for the 49ers in the first half of the season. After losing six of their first seven games, the 49ers rallied to win three and tie one game, finishing with a 5-6-1 record.

The Baltimore Colts came to town for the season finale with a backfield every bit as potent as San Francisco's. Johnny Unitas was at quarterback with Alan Ameche and Lenny Moore behind him at the running back slots. The star of the day did not start

R.C. Owens 1957–1961

It seemed unlikely that a rookie receiver playing in his sixth NFL game would leap into the stratosphere, grab a 50-yard pass above Detroit's All-Pro secondary and score a winning touchdown with 10 seconds on the clock.

But that's exactly what R.C. Owens did in 1957 when he and Y.A. Tittle made the Alley-Oop pass as much a part of San Francisco as Coit Tower and the Golden Gate Bridge.

Owens' touchdown reception against the Lions that day was not the first time the Alley-Oop was put to use, but it was certainly the most dramatic.

San Francisco trailed Detroit, 31-28, with 1:20 to play. The 49ers had the ball on their own 38-yard line. Three straight pass completions by Tittle moved the ball to the Lions' 42. There was 11 seconds to go. Everyone

at Kezar Stadium knew what was coming. The Lions completely surrounded Owens all the way downfield. Tittle let fly a rocket that sailed about 50 yards in the air. In the end zone, All-Pro Jack Christiansen covered Owens along with Jim David. Owens leapt, grabbed the pigskin over the defenders and scored. San Francisco won, 35-31.

"That Detroit game was probably the most satisfying win for me," Owens said. "Detroit had just scored to go ahead and Abe Woodson made a good kick return. Y.A. went to work after that. Overall, it was a great game played by two great teams."

The Alley-Oop pass was a standard part of the 49ers' offensive plan in 1957. Tittle claims it was developed by accident. Owens says it was an accidental design.

While preparing for the second league game of 1957, the 49er defense was devising ways to stop the Los Angeles Rams. Coach Red Hickey had Y.A. Tittle throw long, high passes into the secondary to prepare it for Bill Wade and Norm Van Brocklin, the Rams' quarterbacks. They gradually realized that R.C. Owens was leaping over the defensive backs and catching the passes.

"It was noticed that I could outjump the defenders," said Owens. "Red Hickey, Frankie Albert and Y.A. Tittle all decided this might be something we could use in a game. Then we wondered what to call it. Somehow we decided on Alley-Oop. In the first game against the Rams, it was used twice for completions, one of those was a touchdown."

Actually, that was not the Alley-Oop's first appearance. It had been used once before in a preseason contest aganst the Chicago Cardinals in Seattle.

"When we used it against Chicago, we had no name for it at the time," he said. "It was still the Alley-Oop but nobody recognized it."

Owens' jumping ability, which he cultivated as a basketball star at College of Idaho, was one of the factors that made the Alley-Oop successful. Tittle's confidence in the unorthodox pass was another.

"Y.A. Tittle believed in it," said Owens. "When a quarterback believes in something he'll use it. The team believed in it so everyone came together when it was called. The line blocked well because they knew it would work.

"I guess you could say the Alley-Oop was the same as a Hail Mary pass, except we didn't pray."

The 1957 San Francisco team was loaded with offensive weapons. No other team in the league could match the backfield of Tittle, Perry and McElhenny. Billy Wilson, Clyde Conner and Owens gave Tittle a trio of excellent pass receivers. But the 49ers rarely demolished their opponent. Virtually every game that year was a cliffhanger.

"It was the best 49er team I played on," said Owens, who spent five years, from 1957 to 1961, in a 49er uniform. "Mac and 'Joe the Jet' were something. The Jet was good on those quick openers. Mac was a zig and zag type runner. He had great peripheral vision.

"Abe Woodson was another weapon. He was a

spectacular kick returner who always got us in good position. He was a Big Ten hurdles champ. You'd always see him hurdling over people. We were always in it with Abe because he would get us good field position."

Since Owens contributed to one of the most exciting seasons in the team's history, one would expect him to choose a heart-stopping Alley-Oop reception as his most thrilling moment that year. Not quite. It was a last-minute reception against the Chicago Bears, but the Alley-Oop was not involved.

With the Bears leading, 17-14, and 20 seconds to play, Chicago went into its prevent defense in an effort to stop the long pass by Tittle.

"The Bears were all set to stop our last-second drive," he said. "I was going downfield and someone knocked me down and out of bounds. I crawled back into the end zone on my knees. Tittle kept pumping the ball looking for someone. Finally, he threw to me. I was still on my knees. It was a touchdown. The refs didn't see me out of bounds or it wouldn't have been allowed. Halas was irate. He was kicking the dirt and kicking at the referees. It was a thrill just to beat George Halas."

Although Tittle and Owens hooked up successfully for several years, it was in 1961, when John Brodie was running the offense, that Owens had his best statistical season. That year, he caught 55 passes for 1,032 yards. He became the first 49er receiver to

gain over 1,000 yards through the air.

As a wide receiver, Owens became intimately familiar with some of the hardest hitting defenses in football.

"The Chicago Bears and Detroit Lions were always tough," he said. "Both teams had tough traditions, tough players and tough defenses. They gave you headaches. When they hit you, they really tattooed you. Bill George from Chicago, for example, was a headhunter. Doug Atkins was another who liked to hit."

Kezar Stadium had a growing reputation in the 1960s as a haven for rowdy fans. At one time city officials considered building a moat around the stadium to keep fans off the field after the game. Owens memories of the fabled stadium on the edge of Golden Gate Park are more peaceful.

"Kezar was a nice stadium," he said. "There's a lot of nostalgia there. One thing I remember about Kezar was the seagulls. There was always seagulls at one end of the stadium and as soon as the play went to that end, they all took off and flew to the other end.

"Another memorable thing about Kezar Stadium was the wrong-way run by Jim Marshall. Bruce Bosley ran after him and shook his hand.

"Fans got a little upset out there once in a while. They threw a few things. One time a guy got upset at a Bears game and ran on the field and kicked Papa Bear—George Halas. Overall the place is full of good memories. I enjoyed it."

LEFT, TOP: Joe Perry had a facemask designed to protect his jaw after it was broken earlier in the 1953 season. Here, he blasts through the Green Bay Packer line on the way to a touchdown. LEFT, BOTTOM: Hugh McElhenny (39) was named *Sport* magazine's Player-of-the-Year and UPI Rookie-of-the-Year in 1952. Here, he gives the Bears' Stan Wallace a straight-arm as he picks up six yards. RIGHT, TOP TO BOTTOM: John Henry Johnson lunges forward to score before 90,000 fans at the Los Angeles Coliseum in 1954. Johnson was acquired in a trade with the Pittsburgh Steelers prior to the 1954 season.

ABOVE: The opening game of the 1953 season at Kezar Stadium between San Francisco and the Philadelphia Eagles turned into a free-for-all. A shoving match between 49er Clay Matthews (83) and Eagle Ken Farragut quickly escalated as the hometown fans raced onto the field to help the 49ers. Police were needed to break up the brawl. LEFT: San Francisco's Rex Berry tries to unscrew the head of Washington Redskins receiver Ed Barker (87). Berry had seven interceptions for the 1953 49ers, the club high.

in either backfield, however. It was tiny Joe Arenas, a Choctaw Indian from Omaha, Nebraska. The 49er halfback returned a punt 67 yards for a touchdown and ran back a kickoff 96 yards to set up another touchdown as San Francisco defeated the Colts, 30-17.

1957 The year 1957 was both magical and tragic for San Francisco football fans. Heart-stopping finishes became the 49ers' trademark as the team continued its winning ways and innovative tradition.

The 49ers were a box office smash around the league. Average attendance at their games was 60,000. In a game with the Rams, 102,368 fans packed into the Los Angeles Coliseum. It was the largest crowd in professional football history.

Joe Perry 1948–1963

Joe Perry was designed to be a fullback. He carried the ball with the power and grace of a panther, defying tacklers to strike. The first time he touched the ball in a league game, he bolted through a hole in the Buffalo Bills' defense and dashed 58 yards to score.

Y.A. Tittle, the quarterback for most of Perry's years in the 49er backfield, took extra haste when handing the ball to "Joe the Jet." He was so quick off the snap, he often shot past Tittle before the quarterback could turn to make the handoff.

His playing weight was 195 pounds and that was distributed over a six-foot frame. Opponents claimed he was bigger. He could run to daylight, or create his own running room by bowling over potential tacklers. He made a habit of carrying opposing players for extra yards.

Perry gained 8,378 yards in the National Football League and another 1,345 in the All-

America Football Conference. He averaged over five yards per carry. After 16 years of professional football, "Joe the Jet" retired in 1963 with more rushing yards than any player in NFL history. That record stood until someone named Jim Brown came along to break it.

In the mid-1950s, Perry teamed with Y.A. Tittle, Hugh McElhenny and John Henry Johnson to form the most famous backfield in football. With three great running backs hungry to carry the ball, Tittle's chore was to keep them all happy.

"Tittle would try to divide the ball between us back there as much as possible," Perry said with a laugh. "He kept me satisfied anyway."

Indeed, Perry's 1,929 lifetime carries has been surpassed by only seven other running backs in NFL history.

Perry was discovered playing football when he was a running sensation for the Alameda Naval Air Station Hell Cats.

John Woudenberg, an offensive tackle for the 49ers at the time, is credited with the find that became a 49er gold mine.

After playing two years with the 49ers in the All-America Football Conference, Perry and the club moved to the NFL. Although the established league was reputed to have fiercer competition, Perry saw little difference between the two leagues.

"The first year in the NFL we weren't too successful," he said. "We were 3-9. The next two years we almost won the thing. There wasn't a real big difference. There was one game, though, when we played the Bears that I noticed it. They won, 13-7. But they beat the hell out of us physically. We were beat up pretty good. I guess that was the only game where I noticed a difference in the leagues.

"They could play good defense in the old league, too. I remember one game in the AAFC against the New York

Yankees. They had a middle linebacker who followed me everywhere.

"There is quite a difference between my era and football now. The game is more scientific now. There are more specialists. In my day we had 33 players and 22 of them went both ways. As far as I am concerned football is football, just get out there and play."

Perry has nothing but praise for the quarterbacks he worked with in the 49er backfields. Frankie Albert and Y.A. Tittle had different styles but they excelled in their own way, he said. They were quarterbacks that reflected their separate eras.

"Frankie Albert was like a riverboat gambler," Perry said. "He had a sharp mind and did the unexpected. He was unpredictable. But if you gave him something he would run the same play 20 times until you stopped it. He used to throw a quick pass to Strzykalski. One game he threw the same pass over and over for about five yards. We marched right down the field and scored.

"Y.A. Tittle was a brainy quarterback. He was a thinker and he had a strong arm. He would stay in that pocket and wait for the man to get open. He'd wait until he got done what he had to do."

Perry is diplomatic about praising his peers on the gridiron. All the running backs he saw had something that made them professionals. But he is not shy about praising his fellow running back, Hugh McElhenny.

"Mac was the best open field runner of our era. He was a will o' the wisp out there. Sayers was a great open field runner, too, but he was different than Mac. It's hard to pinpoint what it was."

Not all of Perry's memories of life in the NFL are rosy. He was one of the first black men in professional football, joining the 49ers just a year after Jackie Robinson broke the color line in professional baseball. He encountered racism both on the field and off. His teammates were very supportive, he says, as was the club management.

"I was the first black to play football here," he said. "It was rough as hell. There were a lot of unpleasant things that happened. Lots of things were said on the field. You could imagine what they were. It was probably worse playing football instead of baseball, like Jackie Robinson did, because football is such a physical game.

"The 49ers were great though. If one person was in a fight, the whole team was in a fight. We were like a big family. That was part of the Morabito influence. Italians always do things family-style. We always had meals family-style. In training camp, the food was on the table and you just served yourself."

Like most former 49ers who played in the 1950s, the year 1957 is one that stands out. Many players recall the playoff loss to Detroit that year. Others remember the 49ers' powerful offense and the Alley-Oop Pass. Perry remembers the game against the Chicago

Bears at Kezar Stadium.

"That game stands out for me because it is the game when Tony Morabito died," Perry said. "I had been hurt for several weeks. At halftime, Chicago was ahead, 17-3. We got word that Tony had died. The mood turned pretty somber. You could hear people crying, that's how much people loved the guy. I played the second half and we all made a great comeback. We ended up winning, 21-17."

Perry played 14 years with the 49ers and another two for the Baltimore Colts. He was the first man in NFL history to rush for over 1,000 yards in two consecutive years. In 1953, he rushed for 1,018 yards, a feat that inspired owner Tony Morabito to reward Perry with a $5,090 bonus, $5 for every yard. In 1954, he ran for 1,049 and was named the NFL's Player-of-the-Year. He is also the 49ers' all-time leading rusher. Although proud of his accomplishments, there is one award that tops them all.

"The biggest thrill for me has to be making the Hall of Fame," he said. "There is no way anything could surpass that."

Since retiring, Perry has not missed the game. He doesn't miss the long flights in propeller-driven planes or the games on frozen fields in Green Bay and Cleveland. He has remained a devoted 49er fan, however, and the new version of the 49ers is a sight to behold, he says.

"I think they'll be there for years to come. They have depth and talent at every position. That's what it's all about."

ABOVE: Clyde Conner was the 49ers' leading receiver in 1958 when he caught 49 passes. Here, he reaches back for a Y.A. Tittle pass that is picked off by Yale Lary (28) of the Detroit Lions.

They drafted consensus All-America quarterback John Brodie out of Stanford and were blessed with three of the finest signal callers in the game. Brodie competed with Earl Morrall and Y.A. Tittle for the starting job. However, before the start of the regular season, Morrall was traded to Pittsburgh for linebacker Marv Matuszak.

In the league opener, the 49ers were soundly defeated by the Chicago Cardinals, 20-10. Former University of San Francisco star Ollie Matson returned to Kezar Stadium and ran through the 49er defense. After the game, local writers said there was no reason to believe the 49ers would be contenders. In 12 weeks they would eat their words.

In the second week of the season, the Los Angeles Rams met the 49ers at Kezar Stadium. The Rams had mauled San Francisco in a preseason game, 58-27. They were favored to win the league championship.

The Rams held a 20-16 lead late in the fourth quarter. But just as the 59,700 fans at Kezar were preparing to head for home, Tittle got the team untracked. With short passes to his receivers, and several fine runs by McElhenny, he drove the team 50 yards to the Rams' 11-yard line. With four minutes to play, Tittle dropped back and threw a high arching pass to the corner of the end zone. R.C. Owens, a rookie from College of Idaho, leaped into the sky. He outjumped Los Angeles defensive back Jesse Castete and came down with the football. The Alley-Oop pass was born. San Francisco had itself a 23-20 win.

Spectacular finishes eventually became commonplace. The following week in Chicago, the Bears were in the driver's seat with a 17-14 lead and four minutes to play. Tittle dropped back and looked for Owens again but the receiver had been knocked to the turf by a Chicago defender. Undaunted, Tittle threw a low pass to the squatting Owens and he caught it on his knees to give San Francisco a 21-17 win.

Two weeks later they played Chicago at Kezar. Behind at the half, 17-7, the team received word in the locker room that owner Tony Morabito had suffered a heart attack while in the stands. He died a short time later. The inspired 49ers battled back and defeated Chicago, 21-17.

Dick Moegle (47) was the 49ers' top pass defender in the mid-1950s. He was the team's first draft choice in 1955 and led the club in interceptions for three straight years from 1956 to 1958. Here, he deflects a pass intended for Green Bay's Max McGee. PAGE 57: Abe Woodson (40) breaks up a pass from Baltimore's Johnny Unitas to receiver Raymond Berry. Woodson thrilled 49er fans with his spectacular kick returns. He ranks second on the NFL's all-time kickoff return list with 5,538 yards.

The next week they were behind Detroit, 31-28, with less than a minute to play. Tittle valiantly worked the ball downfield. With 11 seconds to play, he launched a rocket into the end zone. R.C. Owens came down with the pigskin. The Alley-Oop had done it again. The 49ers won it, 35-31.

With two weeks left in the season, San Franciso was 6-4. They needed wins in the last two games to tie for the league title.

Baltimore was the first hurdle. The Colts were a pass-oriented team with Johnny Unitas at the helm. The day before the game, a crowd formed at the Kezar Stadium ticket booths to buy tickets. When the booths finally opened, a near riot ensued and thousands of fans had to be turned away.

The game was a defensive battle most of the way. With less than two minutes remaining in the game, Baltimore held a precarious 13-10 lead. But the 49ers had the ball and Tittle was moving the

club. A pass to Hugh McElhenny picked up 28 yards and put the ball on the Colts' 15-yard line.

On the next play, Tittle was belted by Baltimore's defensive line as he tried to get off a pass. Afterward, he lay motionless on the field. His teammates carried him to the sideline while rookie John Brodie quickly warmed up. With precious seconds remaining on the stadium clock, Brodie took the field. Then, with 46 seconds to play, Brodie found McElhenny wide open. He drilled a pass to "the King" and San Francisco won, 17-13.

The Green Bay Packers were next. A win would leave the 49ers tied for the league crown with Detroit.

Before the game Tittle was still hobbling on pulled leg muscles suffered in the collision against the Colts. Brodie got the starting assignment. Rain soaked Kezar Stadium throughout the day but 59,530 paying customers remained in their seats.

Green Bay took a 20-10 lead into the locker room at halftime. Coach Frankie Albert decided to go with the old master, Y.A. Tittle, in the second half. On the 49ers first offensive possession in the third quarter, the fans roared their approval at the sight of Tittle leading the team onto the field. He didn't let them down.

The 30-year-old Tittle completed 10 of his 14 passes for 94 yards and Joe Perry gained 130 yards

Y.A. Tittle 1951–1960

When Y.A. Tittle joined the 49ers in 1951, he found himself in a new role. Frankie Albert was still in command of San Francisco's offense and he wasn't about to give up the controls. For the first time in his life, Tittle was a backup quarterback. It was a role he did not enjoy.

Tittle became a 49er after the Baltimore Colts folded in their first NFL season. Baltimore was originally a member of the All-America Football Conference and joined the NFL with Cleveland and San Francisco in 1950.

Near the end of the 1951 season, Coach Buck Shaw began to take notice of Tittle's strong throwing arm and started alternating his two quarterbacks. Albert would play the first and third quarters of a game, while Tittle played the

second and fourth. The 49ers' first quarterback controversy began to brew. By 1952, Tittle and Albert were alternating full time.

"Frank was more of a roll-out type quarterback," said Tittle. "He used a lot of play action. There was more running than passing when he was in there. His whole style of play was built off the run. I was more of a drop-back quarterback, so defenses had to shift according to our styles.

"Frankie Albert was a big influence on me. Of course, we were intense rivals for the quarterback position, but I learned a lot just watching him play. His leadership qualities were unparalleled.

"He gave me another dimension. I never had been around someone who was such a loose quarterback and had so much freedom. I was

more of a coach's quarterback. I did what I thought the coach wanted done. Frank was unpredictable. I learned from him that being unpredictable can be a good quality, that nutty things sometimes will work.

"The bootleg is another thing I got from him. After I left the 49ers, it helped me win a championship at New York."

Tittle got the freedom he wanted under Coach Buck Shaw. Shaw allowed Tittle to call his own plays or improvise when necessary. Such independence instilled Tittle with confidence. For that reason, he considers Shaw one of the best coaches he played under.

"Buck Shaw was probably the easiest coach to play for," he said. "As a quarterback, he let you be yourself. He had re-

spect for your ability. He would never second guess you. If I called a long pass on third down and two, he wouldn't say, 'What did you call that for?' He let me play the way I wanted."

The 49er backfield of the 1950s was among the best of all time. Tittle played alongside Joe Perry, Hugh McElhenny and John Henry Johnson. All but Johnson are in the Hall of Fame.

"I was lucky to play with the greatest running backs in history," Tittle said. "Joe Perry and Hugh McElhenny were probably the best running combination ever together on one team. McElhenny was the greatest broken field runner I ever saw play. There's no doubt about that. Perry was great because he was so quick to hit the hole. He was fast and powerful."

The first time they played together Perry's quickness startled Tittle. On several handoff attempts, Perry was past the quarterback and into the hole before Tittle could hand him the football.

"I told him he was jumping offsides," Tittle said jokingly. "He just wanted to beat the handoff and make me look bad."

The 1957 season was one of triumph and agony for Tittle. Last-second victories became a 49er trademark. The Alley-Oop pass became their most potent weapon.

"The Alley-Oop was developed by accident," Tittle recalled. "R.C. (Owens) wanted to try it out. We practiced it a few times, but I never thought we would use it in a game. In 1957, we won five games in the last couple minutes using the Alley-Oop. What made it work was timing and R.C.'s jumping ability. The defenses knew it was coming. They would put extra defensive backs on R.C. It didn't help though. They just got in the way of each other."

The Alley-Oop couldn't help the 49ers on Dec. 22, 1957. It was the 49ers' first playoff appearance in the NFL. They jumped out to a commanding 24-7 halftime lead over the Detroit Lions. On their first series of plays in the second half, Hugh McElhenny raced 71 yards with a pitchout, only to be dragged down at the nine-yard line. The 49ers had to settle for a field goal, but a berth in the championship game looked secure. Suddenly, the team fell apart. De-troit came back to win, 31-27. Tittle sighs painfully as he recalled the game in his Texas drawl.

"We watched the clock too much," he said. "Once we had that 20-point lead, I thought we could wait it out. We tried to kill the clock by running the football. It was the pass that got us the lead and we should have stayed with the pass. We should have been more aggressive and continued to throw the ball."

Throwing the football is a passion for Tittle. He believes it is the game's ultimate weapon. In his prime, he could toss the pigskin 60 yards with the same ease as Ray Wersching kicking an extra point. His strong throwing arm kept defensive coaches scribbling X's and O's that would stop him.

"I'd like to play now," Tittle said. "The new rules make it easier for the passing game to succeed. It's much more wide open. You can't put your hands on receivers like you could before. I'd love to play against the zone defense. A strong arm can succeed against the zone. Marino has shown that. The field is still 53 yards wide so it's only a matter of time before someone gets open. You just have to be patient.

"Don't get me wrong. I'd prefer to play during my era. I'm not saying we were better or anything, I just liked our rules better. I liked the individual matchups, players going man-to-man. You knew who your opponent was going to be. You knew what defensive back was going to be watching which receiver. With the zones you don't know who is watching who. In our day, you had a four- or five-man rush. Now they use stunts and turns and all kinds of funny games on the line. You don't know what's going on."

Not all the teams of Tittle's era played conventional defense. The Chicago Bears were one team that was always a thorn in Tittle's side.

"I hated to play the Bears," he said. "They were the one team that didn't do anything normal. They made you look bad even when you played good. For some reason, you felt like you played a sloppy game. Chicago always did crazy things on defense. They used safety and corner blitzes. They did things to screw up the blocking. Now the Bears are doing all this stuff again under Ditka.

"Cleveland was another tough team when I played. Paul Brown was the coach. But they were a very disciplined team. Unlike the Bears, they were an orthodox team. Brown had them well trained."

Tittle was traded to the New York Giants prior to the 1961 season and it was there that he had his greatest success. He led the Giants to three straight appearances in the NFL Championship Game, which he considers his greatest thrill as a player. He never forgot his ties to the Bay Area, however, and relished his return trips to Kezar Stadium.

"Kezar Stadium was one of the unique stadiums in football," he said. "The fans were so close to you. It seemed like they were right on top of you. In my day it was a great place to play. It was really something just driving there because of the surroundings in Golden Gate Park. You had all these people walking through the park to the stadium. Driving to the games I just felt it was a beautiful place to play."

Ask Tittle about the most fearsome defensive players of his day and he'll tell you about his 49er roommate. He was Hardy Brown and he was a legend around the NFL. He was small for a linebacker, weighing in at 190 pounds, but rumor has it he knocked out more teeth than a country club full of oral surgeons.

"We called him Hardy the Hatchet," said Tittle. "He may be the hardest hitter that ever played the game. Butkus would maul you when he made a tackle, and Nitschke, too. They were strong and would bring you to the ground with arm strength. Hardy just exploded. He popped you. In 1951, we played the Washington Redskins and he knocked out the entire backfield. He knocked the running backs out cold."

Tittle was honored for his outstanding ability when he was selected to the Hall of Fame in 1971. It was a thrill unsurpassed by anything he ever achieved.

"Well that's got to be my most cherished memory," he said. "I'm in great company. You can't get much better than the Hall of Fame."

on 27 carries. There was no need for magical Alley-Oop passes this day. Perry scored two second-half touchdowns on runs of nine yards and two yards. That was all the scoring the 49ers needed to take a 27-20 win. They had gained a first-place tie with Detroit. A playoff was needed to determine who would face Cleveland in the NFL Championship Game.

The playoff was held at Kezar. Frenzied fans scrambled to get tickets. People began lining up at Kezar ticket booths on Friday night in hopes of purchasing a ticket on Saturday. The game was blacked out on local television. Busloads of fans unable to obtain tickets went to Reno to see the game on television.

The 49ers found themselves 3½-point favorites at game time. The favorable odds were due in part to the broken leg suffered by Detroit quarterback Bobby Layne. He was replaced by Tobin Rote.

In the first quarter, Tittle connnected on a 34-yard Alley-Oop pass to R.C. Owens to put the 49ers in front 7-0. A 47-yard pass to McElhenny made the score 14-0. Before the half, Tittle threw another touchdown pass, this one a 12-yarder to Billy Wilson. Gordy Soltau added a 25-yard field goal and the 49ers looked unbeatable. The halftime score read 24-7.

McElhenny opened the second half by taking a pitchout and racing 71 yards to the nine. The 49ers couldn't push it in and had to settle for a field goal. Their 27-7 lead looked insurmountable.

Suddenly, the Lions came to life. Three interceptions and two lost fumbles contributed to the Detroit cause. When it was all over the 49ers had lost a heartbreaker, 31-27.

1958
The 49ers hobbled through a mediocre 1958 exhibition season with a 3-3 record. Quarterback John Brodie showed flashes of brilliance, however, and Albert named him the starting quarterback. Brodie had taken the starting position from the 1957 Player-of-the-Year, Y.A. Tittle.

Several other newcomers worked their way into the starting lineup. Among them were John Thomas, who began the year at left tackle, and John Wittenborn, who opened at right guard.

The opening game was against the Pittsburgh Steelers. Former 49er Earl Morrall was the quarterback.

Brodie played brilliantly in his first game as a

starter. Down 20-7 in the closing minutes of the third quarter, he marched the club 73 yards in eight plays cutting the margin to 20-13. On the next possession, he took the 49ers 30 yards to tie the game at 20-20. Finally, with 2:30 remaining, he set up the winning field goal by throwing three passes to Owens for gains of 12, 15 and eight yards. Overall, Brodie completed 19 of 28 passes for 244 yards.

The game proved to be one of the highlights of a lackluster year. Brodie and Tittle alternated at quarterback much of the season. Tittle completed 120 of 208 passes for 1,467 yards over the course of the season. Brodie hit on 103 of 172 for 1,224 yards.

The 49ers suffered some drastic defeats in 1958, including the worst loss in the history of the franchise when Los Angeles embarrassed them, 56-7, before 96,000 at the Coliseum.

San Franciso salvaged some respect by defeating the Baltimore Colts, champions of the Western Division, 21-12, on Albert's last day as coach. He resigned after the season with a 6-6 record. He had a three-year coaching record of 19-17-1.

After the victory, a riot broke out at Kezar as young fans attempted to tear down the goal posts. When police tried to disperse the mob, the largely young crowd threw cans, seat cushions and dirt at police.

1959
Howard "Red" Hickey took charge in 1959. Under their new coach the 49ers jumped off to their best start since joining the NFL by winning six of their first seven games. They beat Los Angeles twice, 34-0 and 24-16. They also defeated Detroit twice, 33-7 and 34-13. Their only loss was a 21-20 squeaker at the hands of Green Bay.

But things went bad in a hurry. The 49ers dropped four of their next five games. They still had a shot at first place on the last weekend of the season, but a victory by Baltimore, coupled with San Francisco's 36-14 loss to the Packers, knocked them out of contention. The 49ers ended the year with a 7-5 record and tied for third place.

PAGE 60: Defensive back Elbert Kimbrough (45) receives a straightarm that looks more like a right cross from Green Bay halfback Elijah Pitts. Kimbrough played in the 49er secondary from 1962 to 1966.

1960–1969

CHAPTER THREE
THE LEAN YEARS

Coach Red Hickey began to reshape the team in 1960 by adding two draft picks that had an immediate impact. Monty Stickles, a tight end from Notre Dame, was used as a spot starter and caught 22 passes in his first season. Mike Magac, a guard from Missouri, helped strengthen the offensive line.

San Francisco opened the 1960 season with a 21-19 loss to New York. Kicker Tommy Davis missed four field goal attempts in the game, including a 37 yarder with 30 seconds to play.

Tittle won the starting quarterback position over John Brodie and completed 21 of 34 passes in the opener. As the season wore on, Tittle saw less action, and it became clear John Brodie was the quarterback of the future.

The 49ers unveiled a new offense on Nov. 27, 1960, when they surprised the Baltimore Colts with the Shotgun Formation. The 49ers had been struggling all season and had a 4-4 record. The Colts were two-time NFL champions and 21-point favorites. San Francisco did not look capable of an upset.

The week prior to the game, Coach Red Hickey decided to try the Shotgun Formation because it would allow his quarterbacks to run, pass, pitch out, handoff, or kick. The new weapon helped the 49ers defeat the Colts, 30-22.

Using the formation, the 49ers won four of their last five games in 1960 and finished in second place with a 7-5 record.

In the off-season, Hickey drafted UCLA's Billy Kilmer, a skillful passer and runner. Kilmer was the ideal man for the Shotgun Formation. To make room for his new quarterback, Hickey traded veteran Y.A. Tittle to the New York Giants. Tittle, a drop-back passer, was uncomfortable with the Shotgun.

Tittle wasn't the only veteran to go after the 1960 season. Two other members of the Million Dollar Backfield departed as well. McElhenny was picked up by Minnesota in the expansion draft, and Joe Perry was traded to the Colts for a third-round draft pick. In addition, Ed Henke was traded to the St. Louis Cardinals.

1961 In the 1961 season opener, Brodie got the starting call and immediately made the 45,000 fans at Kezar forget about Y.A. Tittle. He threw four touchdown passes as the 49ers defeated the Washington Redskins, 35-3.

After a 30-10 loss to the Green Bay Packers, the 49ers were set to play the Detroit Lions. The Lions were 10-point favorites. Their defense, rated the best in football, was led by All-Pro linebacker Joe Schmidt.

To counter the Lions' defense, Hickey used the Shotgun, but with an additional twist. He rotated his three quarterbacks—Brodie, Kilmer and Bob Waters—on every down and sent in plays from the bench. San Francisco walloped the Lions, 49-0, the most overwhelming win in the team's history.

San Francisco's rotating quarterbacks were devastating against the

Lions. Kilmer ran for 103 yards out of the Shotgun and scored two touchdowns. Waters ran for another 38 yards and Brodie, who did most of the passing, completed five of 12 for 108 yards.

The victory set several team standards. It was the highest number of points scored by the 49ers in NFL play. It established the largest margin of victory in team history. And it handed the Lions their first shutout in 10 years.

The Los Angeles Rams were the 49ers' next opponent. Before 59,000 paying customers at Kezar Stadium, San Francisco accumulated 521 yards of total offense and scored a 34-0 win. It was the second consecutive shutout for the 49ers and only the second time Los Angeles had been held scoreless in 140 games.

Dave Wilcox (64) pulls Frank Nunley (57) away from the referees as Nunley argues a pass interference call. PAGE: 65 R.C. Owens goes high in the air to grab an Alley-Oop Pass. Owens became the first 49er receiver to gain over 1,000 yards through the air in 1961.

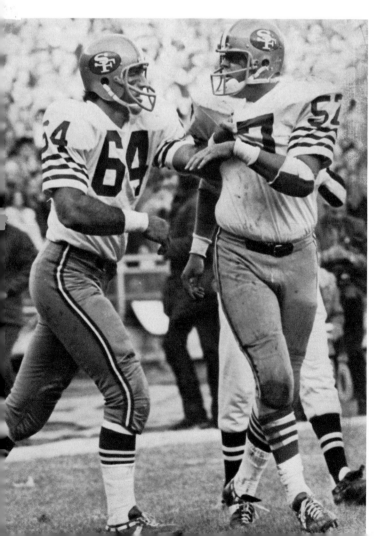

Once again, Hickey rotated his quarterbacks and they responded with an even better performance than the one against the Lions. They combined for 201 rushing yards and another 261 yards passing to account for all but 58 yards of San Francisco's total offensive output.

Kilmer gained 131 yards in 19 carries and scored two touchdowns. Brodie threw for 151 yards, completing 12 of 17 passes. Waters completed seven of eight passes for 53 yards and one touchdown.

After five games, the 49ers led the league in points scored, passing yardage and running yardage. They looked invincible.

Two weeks after routing Los Angeles, the 49ers were matched with the Chicago Bears. Clark Shaughnessy, the man who perfected the T-Formation, had been scouting the 49ers for Chicago. He detected a slight flaw in the Shotgun. To snap the ball, the center had to look between his legs to see the backs. Shaughnessy thought it would be easy for the Bears' middle linebacker, Bill George, to shoot past the center before he had a chance to look up and block.

The adjustment worked. San Francisco netted only six first downs and 132 yards of total offense all day. Hickey used the formation sparingly the rest of the year and ended up with a 7-6-1 record. His experiment with the Shotgun ended as abruptly as it began.

1962 In the 1962 college draft, the 49ers made Lance Alworth their first-round choice. Alworth was a spectacular runner and pass catcher out of the University of Arkansas. The 49ers were unable to sign him after a bidding war with the San Diego Chargers of the American Football League. Instead, second-year man Jimmy Johnson started the season in the flanker position. Johnson later became an All-Pro defensive back. Alworth went on to become one of the greatest deep threats in history, averaging 19 yards per reception. He was selected to the Hall of Fame in 1978. Long-time fans still marvel at the thought of Alworth and Dave Parks, a first-round selection in 1964, catching passes together for the 49ers.

When the 1962 season started, most of the Bay Area's attention was riveted on the San Francisco Giants, who were in the midst of a tight pennant race. Later that year, they would appear in their only World Series.

Bruce Bosley 1956–1968

Ask Bruce Bosley who his toughest opponent was and he'll recite a virtual who's who of the Hall of Fame.

Imagine bumping heads with Dick Butkus, Ray Nitschke, Joe Schmidt, Sam Huff and Bill George. Or trap blocking Roger Brown, Rosey Grier, Bob Lilly, Alex Karras and Merlin Olsen. Bosley's played against them all. To rate one of those stars over the rest is impossible, he says. They all stood out in their own way.

Bosley came to the 49ers as a second-round pick in the 1956 college draft. At 6' 3" and 245 pounds, the 49ers originally planned to use the West Virgina graduate as a defensive end.

"I remember my first game with the 49ers," Bosley said. "I just got in from the College All-Star Game. It was a pre-season game against Cleveland and I'd been in camp for three days.

Leo Nomellini, the old pro, was going to be playing next to me. He said, 'Don't worry rook, I'll take care of you.' We ended up beating Cleveland. I played the whole game and did pretty good. Nomellini gave me the game ball afterward. It was the only one I ever got."

In 1957, Bosley was switched to the offensive line where he made his home for the next 12 years. Four times he was selected to play in the Pro Bowl, once as a guard and three times as a center. It was from his offensive line position that he encountered the game's greats.

"Butkus wasn't really mean like everyone said he was," Bosley recalled. "He wouldn't deliberately try to twist your leg off. He was just rough. He liked to hit. In fact, he loved to hit. But I'd hit him back as hard as he hit me. I wanted him to respect me."

Eugene "Big Daddy" Lipscomb was a massive defensive tackle who terrorized ball carriers in the 1950s and early 1960s while playing with Los Angeles, Baltimore and Pittsburgh. He stood 6' 6" and weighed 300 pounds. He was more than most linemen could handle. Bosley tried to neutralize him by holding him when the referees weren't looking. Finally, Lipscomb had had enough.

"He turned around and started yelling and screaming at me," Bosley said. "Saliva was coming out of his mouth. He said to me, 'Bosley, if you hold me one more time, I'll kill you.' "

Not wanting to lose his starting center to penalty or injury, John Brodie grabbed Bosley and pulled him back to the huddle. On the way, Bosley could not refrain from adding one more retort.

"I didn't want anyone to think I was afraid so I

yelled back and told him we were going to run right over him. I guess Brodie thought I was serious because in the huddle he asked me if I wanted to run a 31 trap on him. I said, 'Hell no, that guy's going to kill me.' But Brodie called it anyway.

"As I walked up to the line, Lipscomb was snorting and digging his feet in. He's all set to tee off. At the last minute, Brodie calls an audible so the play would be going the other way. I look up and Lipscomb is grinning at me. He says, 'Boz, I was just kidding you.'

"Later we got to be good friends. I'd see him in the off-season and tell him I voted for him for All-Pro. That was just a little psychology to butter him up so he'd take it easy when we played."

One of Bosley's teammates at West Virginia was Sam Huff, a Hall of Fame linebacker who was the leader of the New York Giants fabled defense in the 1950s and 1960s. When they faced each other, they never allowed their friendship to surface.

"Sam always tried to distract me," he said. "Dick Modzelewski was a defensive lineman for the Giants. Huff would yell out for everyone to hear, 'Boz, Modzelewski is going to tear you up.' Then he'd smile at me.

"Huff had a reputation for piling on. Once a referee was getting everyone off a pileup. I heard someone in the pile say, 'We can't, Huff isn't here yet.' I guess he figured the play wasn't over until Huff jumped on the pile.

"Bill George was another nasty linebacker—

tough as nails. He used to call me a snake eater because I was from West Virginia. I had to laugh at that."

During Bosley's tenure with San Francisco, he had the priviledge of blocking for some of the game's most talented backs. Joe Perry, Hugh McElhenny, Ken Willard and John David Crow all owe thanks to Bosley for the holes he opened for them.

"McElhenny was the best to block for," Bosley said. "He wasn't the fastest, but he was very elusive. It was easy to throw a block for Hugh because he set the block up himself with his moves and great running ability. He made us look good. A lot of backs tend to outrun their blockers. McElhenny's greatness was his ability to use blockers, to set the block up for his linemen."

The 49er teams of 1965 and 1966 were exciting, according to Bosley. Although the team record was only 7-6-1 in 1965, they had a potent offense that averaged 30 points a game. They scored over 40 points four times.

"Brodie was really on the stick then," said Bosley. "He was hitting long passes, short passes, everything. And Ken Willard was grinding out yardage. It really pumped you up when Brodie completed those 50-yard passes."

On the receiving end of many of Brodie's tosses was Dave Parks. Parks was the first college player chosen in the 1964 draft. He led the league in receptions in 1965 with 80. Bosley has fond memories of the Texas

Tech star.

"That Parks was a great competitor," he said. "I hated to see him go. A lot of receivers are prima donnas. They don't like to get in there and block. Dave wasn't like that at all. He was a tough nut. He liked to get in there and mix it up."

The starting running backs in the mid-1960s were characters in their own right. Ken Willard was a hard-running fullback who was well known as a prankster. John David Crow, a former Heisman Trophy winner, was a respected team leader.

"Ken had a poker face," recalled Bosley. "But don't let that fool you, he was always up to something."

The mere mention of the name John David Crow stirs Bosley's memory. The 49ers obtained him in a trade with the St. Louis Cardinals in 1965.

"I always heard about John when he played for St. Louis," Bosley said. "I was real excited when he came to the 49ers. First of all, he was a great guy. He was also a heck of a competitor. He always wanted to run with the ball. It jacks you up when you have a guy come into the huddle and say, 'Give me the ball.' That's what he did."

Bosley made four trips to the Pro Bowl but he'd gladly trade those games for the chance to have played in a championship game, the one goal that eluded him.

"A championship is what every professional plays for," he said. "It's something I never attained. I wish I had gotten just one shot."

The 49ers never really got going in 1962. Green Bay, led by Vince Lombardi, continued to dominate the NFL and the 49ers were no exception. The Packers beat up on the 49ers in both their meetings, and San Francisco finished with an uneventful 6-8 record. It was the club's first losing season under Red Hickey.

1963 Hickey's troubles continued into the 1963 season. Injuries to key players hampered the 49ers. The club's first- and second-team quarterbacks were injured in separate car accidents. Brodie walked away with a broken arm that kept him out of several games. Kilmer broke a leg and was out for the season.

The team got off to its worst start since joining the NFL, dropping five exhibition games and its first three league contests. Hickey decided he'd had enough. He called it quits, ending his career with a 27-27-1 record as the 49er head coach.

Assistant coach Jack Christiansen took over the controls after the third league game, but he fared no better. He directed the team to just two victories in 1963. The 49ers ended their worst season in professional football with a 2-12 record.

1964 Prior to the 1964 season, tragedy struck the 49er front office when team owner Victor Morabito died of a heart attack. The wives of Victor and Tony Morabito retained control of the team but hired Lou Spadia as team president. Spadia had been with the team since its inception, and had worked in virtually every job imaginable from ticket salesman to equipment manager.

In the 1964 college draft, the 49ers selected Texas Tech receiver Dave Parks on the first round. Parks teamed up with Bernie Casey and Monty Stickles to give the 49ers one of the best pass-catching trios in football.

In mid season, knee injuries to the 49ers' two top running backs, J.D. Smith and Don Lisbon, prompted the team to recall Gary Lewis, one of the draftees they had released in training camp. Lewis was a pounding fullback who played his high school football at San Francisco's Polytechnic, located directly across the street from Kezar Stadium. Lewis lasted six seasons with the 49ers and gained over 1,400 yards

Jim Marshall, a defensive end with the Minne-

Running back J.D. Smith (24) rushed for 4,370 yards with the 49ers between 1956 and 1964, an average of 4.3 yards per carry. Here, he hurdles over the Chicago Bears' line for a touchdown. He also played defensive back. PAGE 68: The 49ers made Dave Parks the first player chosen in the 1964 draft. He caught 208 passes in just four seasons with the team and was the league's leading receiver in 1965 when he caught 80 balls. Parks was an excellent runner after making the catch, averaging 16 years per reception. PAGE 71 Bernie Casey (30) caught 277 passes for the 49ers from 1961 to 1966. He led the club in receptions three times. Casey teamed with Dave Parks and Monty Stickles in the mid-1960s to give the 49ers one of the best pass-catching trios in football. He was sent to the Atlanta Falcons in 1967 in a trade that gave the 49ers the draft rights to Steve Spurrier.

sota Vikings, made the 1964 season memorable in the seventh week when he scooped up a Billy Kilmer fumble and rambled 60 yards—the wrong way. Thinking he'd scored a touchdown for the Vikes, he threw the ball into the air and ensured the 49ers a two-point safety. The safety didn't help the 49ers though, they lost to Minnesota, 27-22.

A quarterback controversy that would rage on and off for five years got under way in the Minnesota game when Brodie had four passes intercepted. The fans booed him steadily in the second half until rookie quarterback George Mira entered the contest. Mira was unable to get the offense moving either and before the game was over, he also was showered with boos. Although Brodie continued to start regularly during the next five years, there was always a contingent of fans at Kezar anxious to see Mira play. The quarterback debate lasted among fans until Mira was traded to Philadelphia in 1969.

Outstanding rookie performances by Parks, Mira and linebacker Dave Wilcox helped take some of the bitterness out of the 4-10 season.

1965 In 1965, the 49ers molded their most explosive offense since the record-setting 1948 season. Ken Willard, a 220-pound fullback from North Carolina, was the team's number-one choice. He stepped into the starting slot and held it for eight seasons. Halfback John David Crow, a former Heisman Trophy winner, was acquired from the St. Louis Cardinals for Abe Woodson. Crow solidified the 49ers' weak running game. They now had a pair of running backs to complement an already potent passing attack. Up front, Bruce Bosley, Howard Mudd and John Thomas anchored one of the best offensive lines in the league.

Charlie Krueger 1959–1973

Charlie Krueger vividly recalls his start in pro football. He'd been with the 49ers only a couple of weeks when he found himself on the defensive line in a game against the Chicago Bears.

"Willie Galimore carried the ball about six times against us in that game and three of those were touchdown runs," he said. "I thought to myself, 'Jesus what am I up against here.' This is quite an introduction."

Krueger was selected by the 49ers on the first round of the 1958 college draft. He'd been a standout at Texas A&M, where he played under Paul "Bear" Bryant. He began his career with the 49ers as a defensive end. When Leo Nomellini retired, Krueger was moved into "the Lion's" defensive tackle position. He became a fixture there until his own retirement in 1973.

"I tell you, we saw some great runners," he said with a hint of a Texas drawl. "Jimmy Taylor was in his own league as far as toughness. He was a physical animal. He pre-ferred running right over you instead of around you. He was not a polished runner like Jim Brown, but he was fierce. Taylor would demolish defensive backs. He loved that contact. He was a great blocker, too."

The Chicago Bears have had their share of outstanding runners. In addition to Galimore, Krueger spent some time chasing after Gale Sayers. He ranks Sayers as one of the greatest backs of all time. Krueger was on the field on Dec. 12, 1965, when Sayers put on a one-man show, scoring six touchdowns against the 49ers.

"It was cold and wet that day, just miserable," he said. "We were playing in the mud at Chicago. I looked at the scoreboard near the end of the game and saw the 61 points the Bears scored and thought, 'This is a hell of a way to treat visitors.' "

Krueger, a two-time Pro Bowl participant, was a nightmare for offensive linemen. He was often double- or triple-teamed. But there was one lineman who didn't need any help, according to Krueger. He played for the Green Bay Packers and was in a class by himself.

"The Green Bay line was always one of the best," he said. "Some others came close but were never quite as good. On the Packers' line, Forrest Gregg was the one who stood out. He was 6' 4" and about 245 pounds, not a real big lineman. He was smart, agile and he had a lot of guts and stamina. That's what made him good."

Dick Nolan built the 49ers into a solid defensive team in the 1970s. Krueger anchored the defensive line with Tommy Hart, Roland Lakes, Cedrick Hardman and Bill Belk. Although Krueger was one of the senior members of the team, he says he wasn't the leader of that unit. That distinction belonged to a hard-hitting linebacker.

"You want to talk about a stud," Krueger said. "Dave Wilcox, now he was a stud. He had a lot of physical ability. He was strong, fast, he set a good example. He was the leader.

"Tommy Hart was another one. He had a lot of ability too, but he didn't get the recognition he deserved back then."

The 49er defense had 46 quarterback sacks in 1972 to lead the NFC. In 1971, they were second with 38 sacks. As good as that defensive unit was, Krueger insists the teams of 1960 and 1961 were better.

Official records for quarterback sacks were not kept then, but the defense gave up only 205 points in 1960, lowest in the NFL. The same year, quarterbacks completed just 47 percent of their passes against the 49ers.

"That defensive backfield was just outstanding," he said of the teams of the early 1960s. "There was Dave Baker and Eddie Dove and Abe Woodson and Jerry Mertens back there. They did a damn good job."

Defensive linemen are paid to harass quarterbacks, and Krueger did his share of annoying. But with certain quarterbacks, that harassment often turned into long-term chases. The elusive Fran Tarkenton was one quarterback that gave fits to the 6' 4", 250-pound Krueger. Tarkenton's scrambling ability exhausted defensive lineman. Krueger remembers one game in 1965 that Minnesota won, 42-41.

"Tarkenton just got going in that one and ran us to death," he said. "His line really knew how to block for him. Once he started moving around

back there, you'd run from one end of the field to the other chasing him. His linemen would wait and just pick you off as you ran across the field. It's hard on you chasing those guys around. Staubach was a scrambler, too, but nothing like Tarkenton."

Krueger has more pleasant memories of two Hall of Fame quarterbacks. "Johnny Unitas was my hero," he said. "Sammy Baugh, too, but I never played against him. Johnny was a fine guy on and off the field. On the field, he'd talk to you like you were friends. I'd think, 'Geez, he's a nice guy. He remembers who I am.'"

According to his teammates, Krueger never got the recognition in the NFL he deserved. He was selected for two Pro Bowls, but his teammates say he consistently was one of the top defensive linemen in the league.

Bruce Bosley, a former Pro Bowl center with the 49ers, was Krueger's teammate for 10 years. In practice, they lined up on the opposite side of the line of scrimmage and battled each other daily.

"Charlie was a real hard knocker," Bosley said. "They always had two or three guys blocking on him in a game. That enabled the other linemen to do their job. He got a lot of respect. With the 49ers, he was a quiet leader. He was like E.F. Hutton. When he said something, people listened."

Every Sunday was a challenge for Krueger. Despite playing for 15 seasons, he never had trouble getting

motivated.

"Every game was a big game for me," he said. "I didn't want to get my butt whipped out there. I didn't want to embarrass myself. I think a lot of jocks work in that way. Every game was important to me from that respect."

Krueger was honored by his teammates in 1964 when they voted him the Len Eshmont award. He was also honored when he became one of only six 49ers to have his uniform number retired. Yet one simple moment stands out as Krueger's biggest football thrill.

"The first game ball I ever got is something I won't forget," he said. "We were playing Cleveland at Cleveland. There was snow flurries blowing across the field and about five-foot snow banks. I was playing against Lou Groza, who must have been about 34 at the time, and I was about 21. I made a few tackles and stopped Jim Brown for a couple of losses. The team captains, Bob St. Clair and Y.A. Tittle, gave me the game ball."

With his playing days over, Krueger is content to watch football on television or make an occasional trip to Candlestick Park. He does not miss the Sunday hoopla.

"Missing football is like missing a car wreck," he said. "I'm older now. I don't miss it. I'm proud I played for the 49ers though. I'm sure happy for them and proud of them now. Eddie DeBartolo and Bill Walsh sure turned things around. It's that combination that made them successful."

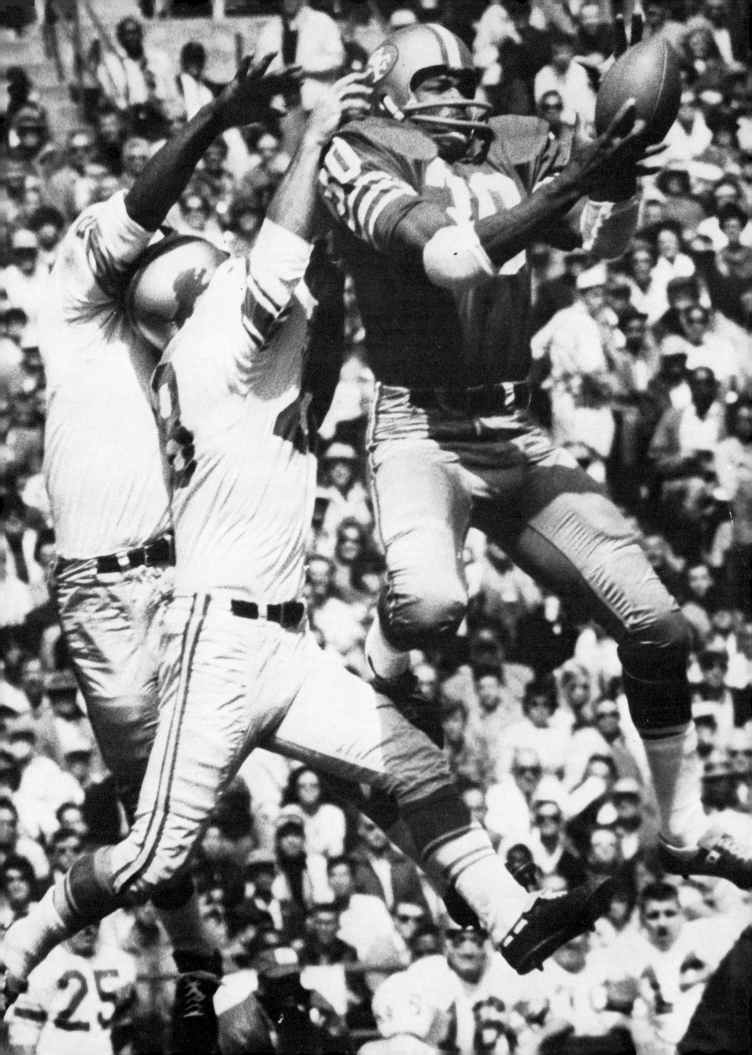

Doug Cunningham was a reliable running back for seven seasons. His best year was 1969 when he gained 541 yards. He added 51 receptions that year to tie for the team lead with Gene Washington. Cunningham started alongside Ken Willard when the team played for the 1970 NFC Championship.

The 49ers exhibited the effectiveness of their new offensive combination when they mauled the Chicago Bears, 52-24, in the season opener. It was the most points ever scored by the 49ers in the NFL. Brodie was on target, completing 14 of 20 passes for 259 yards and four touchdowns. Gary Lewis gained 91 yards on seven carries and scored one touchdown. Crow added 39 yards on six carries. Parks caught five passes from Brodie for 90 yards. And defensive tackle Charlie Krueger scored the first touchdown of his career when he picked up a fumble and plowed six yards into the end zone.

In the Chicago game, the 49ers got their first peek at a running back named Gale Sayers. The defense held Sayers to just 44 yards in 12 carries. It wouldn't be so lucky the next time. Sayers ran circles around the 49ers in the second game of the season, scoring six touchdowns.

San Francisco's offense almost burned out the

scoreboard lights in 1965. The 49ers scored 421 points, an average of more than 30 points a game. They beat Minnesota, 45-24, and the Rams twice, by scores of 45-21 and 30-27. Dave Parks' 80 receptions led the league, and Brodie's 30 touchdown passes set a club record. Brodie also was voted the Len Eshmont award by his teammates for his outstanding play.

But San Francisco's defense was giving up points faster than the offense could score. The team lost to Minnesota, 42-41, Dallas, 39-31, and Chicago, 61-20, on the way to a 7-6-1 season. Obviously, defensive help was needed.

1966 Part of the problem was solved when Stan Hindman, a number-one pick in 1966, was signed. Hindman, from the University of Mississippi, was regarded as the best interior lineman in the nation. The 49ers planned to use him as a defensive end. Alvin Randolph and Mel Phillips were also selected in the player draft. They reinforced a weak defensive backfield.

The bidding war between the AFL and NFL got nasty prior to the 1966 season. Brodie came close to signing a contract with the Houston Oilers of the AFL. After deciding to continue his career with the 49ers, he missed the first two weeks of training camp

Jerry Mertens 1958–1965

Jerry Mertens was a 20th-round draft choice out of tiny Drake University in 1958. He was a long shot to make the team. Six months after reporting to the 49ers' rookie camp, he was playing in the Pro Bowl.

Mertens was drafted as a receiver and was paid a $10 signing bonus. When he showed up at training camp he ran into Billy Wilson, Gordy Soltau and R.C. Owens, the 49ers' established receivers. He had to win a spot from one of the veterans to make the team and get a $4,500 salary.

Mertens figured he had a better shot at that $4,500 if he was playing another position. He tried the defensive backfield. Because he was an excellent athlete, he was

able to make the adjustment from offense to defense. In his rookie season, he became a starter. By year's end he was playing in the Pro Bowl.

For eight seasons, from 1958 to 1965, he quietly roamed the secondary, earning the respect of his teammates and opponents with his steady play. Abe Woodson, the team's other cornerback, gained the headlines with his spectacular kick returns, while Mertens remained unheralded. A fractured neck in the last game of the 1965 season ended his playing days.

"Playing for the 49ers was like a dream come true," he said. "When I joined the 49ers they had just come off the 1957 season when they were in the playoffs against

Detroit. I grew up back east and was a fan of the Bears, but it was exciting coming out here. This was when they had the Million Dollar Backfield of Perry, McElhenny and Tittle. When I got here from Wisconsin I was in awe of these guys. Here I was with some of the greatest players in the game."

From his cornerback position, Mertens confronted the legends of football. Paul Hornung, Jim Brown, Lenny Moore and Ollie Matson all came his way at one time or another. But there is one fullback who was in a class by himself. Mertens will never forget him.

"Jim Taylor of the Packers was the toughest back I ever faced," Mertens said. "He was a

73

punishing runner." It was a collision with Taylor that ended Mertens' career.

"I remember Taylor was sweeping around end," Mertens said. "There were a couple of blockers out in front, the usual Packer sweep. I was coming up to make the play. I hit him behind the line of scrimmage for about a four- or five-yard loss. I went down and he went down. For some reason my neck didn't feel right. I thought maybe I'd torn something. After about 70 X-rays, the doctors found a fractured Atlas vertebra. Luckily, I wasn't paralyzed or anything. Those things happen in football though."

The passing game reached new heights in the late 1950s, and Mertens, from his cornerback position, was right in the middle of it. Johnny Unitas, Sonny Jurgensen and Bart Starr revolutionized football with their aerial shows, changing the responsibilities of the defensive secondary. The long pass became a standard part of every offensive arsenal, and defensive backs were matched against bigger and faster receivers.

Mertens was tested repeatedly by Johnny Unitas when Baltimore was in town. And the Colts' stable of fine receivers were a constant challenge to the entire San Francisco secondary. Mertens' usual chore was to cover elusive Raymond Berry, a dangerous assignment. Baltimore quarterback Johnny Unitas was probably the

best in the game at that time, Mertens says. The combination of Unitas and Berry, both now in the Hall of Fame, was often overwhelming.

During Mertens' tenure with San Francisco, he was party to numerous memorable games. The old rivalry with the Cleveland Browns began to fade and the intrastate rivalry with the Los Angeles Rams grew intense. Enormous crowds packed the Los Angeles Coliseum and Kezar Stadium every time the two teams battled.

"The crowds we got against the Rams were incredible," Mertens said. "In L.A. we'd draw nearly 100,000 people. Kezar was pretty well packed, too. That place was a different story, though. Going onto the field at Kezar reminded me of going into the Roman Coliseum. (Coach) Frankie Albert used to remind us to keep our helmets on when we went through the tunnel. If we didn't play well, we could expect a few beer cans to come our way. Of course, as tough as the fans could be at Kezar, it was always more comfortable playing here than on the road."

One of the interesting developments Mertens witnessed with the 49ers was the birth of the Shotgun Formation in 1960. It really wasn't new at all but a variation of the old short-punt formation, he says. It was the Shotgun that led to one of Mertens' most satisfying wins.

"We didn't beat the Rams much when I was playing so when we did, it was something special," he said. "They just

seemed to be tough every year. Early in the 1961 season, *Sports Illustrated* had written a story on the Rams and their offense. About a week after the story came out, we played them at Kezar. They were favored. We went out and shut them out. It was one of the few times we beat them convincingly."

The 49ers beat the Rams that day, 35-0. A week prior to that, they beat Detroit, 49-0. A lot has been said about the use of the Shotgun Formation in those victories, but it wasn't the Shotgun that stopped two powerful offenses in consecutive weeks. Indeed, the 49er defense of the early 1960s was better than it was generally given credit for. And most of that credit should go to the defensive backfield of Mertens, Eddie Dove, Dave Baker and Abe Woodson. All of them made at least one Pro Bowl appearance between 1959 and 1962.

A year after the bone-cracking collision that ended Mertens' playing days, the AFL and NFL merged. The merger was a ticket to riches for many players. The average NFL salary nearly doubled. Mertens missed out on the big money. In his last season with the 49ers, the former All-Pro was paid $22,000. But the money meant little to Mertens.

"I was just thrilled to play with the 49ers," he said. "Playing pro football was a tremendous opportunity. It was a dream come true. I'm just happy to say I made it."

while negotiating a contract. It took several weeks for him to regain his form.

As Brodie worked his way into shape, the 49ers dropped two of their first three games and tied the other. Then they got hot, beating the World Champion Green Bay Packers while registering four wins in five games. Going into the final game of the 1966 season, the 49ers were 6-5-2 and in position to make the Playoff Bowl which was held each year for the league's runner-ups. A berth in the bowl could mean an additional $3,000 for each player.

Apparently the monetary incentive was not enough for the 49ers. The Baltimore Colts routed them, 30-14. The game closed out another wild season at Kezar Stadium. But most of the excitement was generated by the fans.

During the Baltimore game, the 40,000 people in attendance at Kezar grew irritable after several questionable calls went against the 49ers. Late in the fourth quarter, after a penalty was marched off against San Francisco, one woman sprinted onto the field, picked up an official's penalty flag and threw it at him.

The crowd grew even more restless when the game was over. As head linesman Gerard Bergman made his way to the tunnel leading to the Kezar dressing room, a drunken fan heaved a whisky

bottle that caught Bergman in the head. Bergman had to be helped off the field. Meanwhile, fans stormed out of the stands to rip down the goal posts.

After the contest, George Mira voiced his desire to be traded. An irritated Coach Christiansen said there would be big changes before the 1967 season got under way. He was right.

1967 Among Christiansen's changes was the trade of Bernie Casey, guard Jim Wilson and defensive end Jim Norton to the Atlanta Falcons for their first-round draft pick in 1967. With Atlanta's pick, San Francisco selected Heisman Trophy winning quarterback Steve Spurrier.

Besides Spurrier, the 49ers chose a host of future stars in the college draft including Cas Banaszek, Frank Nunley and Doug Cunningham.

Just two days prior to the start of the regular season, the 49ers acquired flanker Sonny Randle from the St. Louis Cardinals for a future draft pick. Randle, a four-time All-Pro, was needed to take the

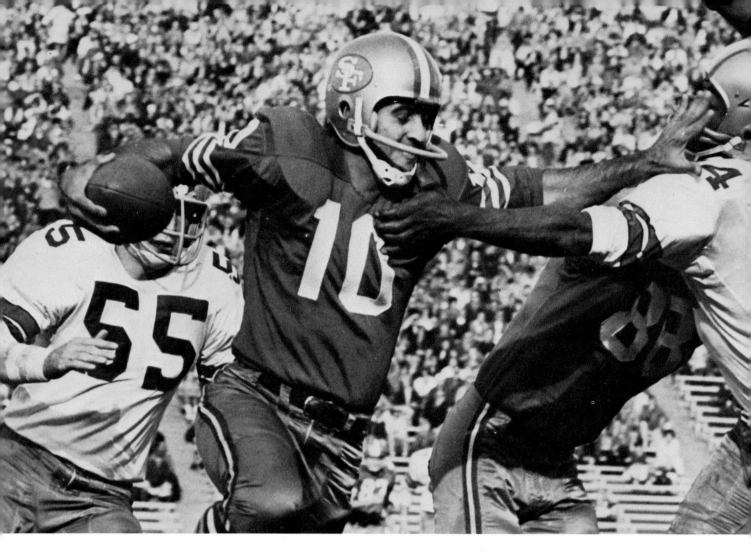

San Francisco quarterback George Mira (10) was an excellent scrambler. Here, he takes off on a 20-yard run and gives Cornell Green (34) of Dallas a stiff-arm along the way. Mira played five seasons with the 49ers behind starter John Brodie.

pressure off Dave Parks. After three spectacular seasons, Parks was a prime target for head-hunting defensive backs.

Randle was put to work immediately. In the league opener, against Minnesota, Parks and flanker Kay McFarland were injured. Despite less than an hour of practice with his new club, Randle was pressed into service. He responded admirably by catching three passes, including a 41-yarder.

The 49ers beat Minnesota and got off to an excellent start winning five of their first six games. At midseason they went into a slump and lost six consecutive games. Backup quarterback George Mira got the starting call for the last four games of the season and rumors began to circulate that Brodie was about to be traded to the Detroit Lions.

The rumors began to look more credible when Mira led the team to convincing wins over Atlanta and Dallas in the last two games of the season to give San Francisco a 7-7 record. Once again, Mira said he would not return to the 49ers unless he was guaranteed a starting role.

Mira played one more season with the 49ers before he was traded to the Philadelphia Eagles in 1969, but several other familiar faces did not return for the 1968 season.

1968 Jack Christiansen was relieved of the head coaching chores and replaced with Dick Nolan. Nolan brought with him a reputation as an excellent defensive coordinator. The 49er offense was always able to score points. Now it was up to Nolan to prevent the other team from getting into the end zone.

Several veterans were traded during the offseason, including Dan Colchico, Monty Stickles, Walter Rock and Dave Kopay. In addition, Dave Parks left the club after a contract squabble to play with the New Orleans Saints. Draft picks Forrest Blue, Skip Vanderbundt and Tommy Hart joined the team as Nolan prepared to shape a winner.

Brodie firmly established himself as the starting quarterback in the opening game of the 1968 season by connecting on 23 of 42 passes for 200 yards. Fumbles and miscues hampered the team, however, and Baltimore soundly beat the 49ers, 27-10.

Bolstered by Nolan's confidence in him, Brodie had a banner year in 1968, throwing for 3,020 yards

Dave Parks 1964–1967

It didn't take long for Dave Parks to become John Brodie's favorite receiver.

Just six games into Parks' rookie season, he established a 49er record when he caught an 83-yard touchdown pass against the Los Angeles Rams. It was the longest reception in team history. A week later, he caught an 80-yard touchdown pass against the Minnesota Vikings, the second longest in team history. And two weeks after that, he caught a 79-yard touchdown pass.

Dave Parks, the first player chosen in the 1964 college draft, had clearly established himself as the premier deep threat in the NFL. His records for the longest receptions in team history stood for 13 years.

"After that first season, the defenses tightened up on me," he said. "I didn't have any more 80-yard receptions. They covered me pretty good."

Opposing defenses may have stopped the long bomb but they didn't stop Dave Parks. In 1965, he caught 80 passes for 1,344 yards and 12 touchdowns. He led the league in all three categories.

That was the year the 49ers lit up the scoreboard everywhere they went. They led the league in scoring in 1965 with 421 points, an average of 31 points a game. Unfortunately, the defense was giving up points faster than the offense could score them. They lost games with final scores of 42-41, 61-20, and 39-31.

"My feeling was, if we had the ball last, we would score and win," he said. "Brodie could always get the ball into the end zone.

"The number of balls I caught was never really a big factor. I didn't think about the statistics. Neither did John Brodie. I remember a game against Pittsburgh where I could have caught 20 balls. No one could cover me effectively. John only threw me three passes. We just did what we had to do to win."

The offensive line of Walter Rock, Len Rohde, Bruce Bosley, Howard Mudd and John Thomas played a big part in the 49er scoring show of 1965. Each of them played in at least one Pro Bowl.

"We had the best line in football at the time and the best quarterback," he said. "All they had to do was give Brodie a little time and that was it. As a receiver it was simple. John just had to throw it to me.

"I don't know how they choose people for the Hall of Fame, but John Brodie was the best quarterback I was ever around," he said. "I don't think anyone even came close. I know I wanted him in there at quarterback. There may have been others that were just as good, like Bart Starr, but I was more than satisfied with the man I had."

Like so many good passing combinations, Brodie and Parks were able to detect what defenses were doing and react to it. They were able to spontaneously adjust to each other on the field. Despite facing double coverage for most of his career, Parks had an uncanny ability to find the open area in a secondary. And Brodie had the talent to find him. Good communication played a vital part in their relationship.

"Me and John always thought along the same lines," he said. "If we saw something with the defense that we could take advantage of, we were able to adjust accordingly. If I saw something that I thought would work, I told him about it and if he wanted to use it, he did. He had a great knack for adjusting and getting me the ball."

During his 10 years of professional football, Parks caught 360 passes for 5,619 yards and 44 touchdowns. His ability to catch the ball is well chronicled but his blocking ability stands out as well. It is a rare receiver that combines both of those talents.

"I always liked to block," said Parks. "The way I figure it, the back had to pick up a linebacker and throw a block while I was catching a ball, so it's just as important for me to block for the running back when he has the ball. The point is, we were a real close team back then. That's

how we got it done. We didn't have the individual player that could break open the game. We had to count on each other."

Although San Francisco had some potent offensive teams with Dave Parks at wide receiver, the team's best finish while he was on the roster was 7-6-1 in 1965. The mediocre records are a reflection on the 49ers' porous defense at the time.

"People scored a lot of points against us, but they never went over to Jimmy Johnson's side," he said. "He was the best damn cornerback in the game but nobody ever heard of him until the end of his career. The reason nobody heard of him was that nobody challenged him."

Parks played out his option during the 1967 season and left for New Orleans. With the Saints he wasn't as successful statistically, but he says he was just as effective.

"At New Orleans we didn't have Brodie at quarterback or the great line they had at San Francisco," he said. "I was open just as much but they didn't have the time to get me the ball.

"I get together down here (Dallas) with some friends that played with the Dallas Cowboys and they get to talking about big games they played in. When they do that, I really don't have anything to talk about. In New Orleans, we were just another team on everybody's schedule. I didn't like it but that's the way it was."

Although Parks ended his career at New Orleans, it was his days at San Francisco that were

the highlight of his 10-year career. Three times he played in the Pro Bowl from 1965 through 1967. He recalls with laughter some of the memories of his days in San Francisco.

"I remember going to Kezar on game days," he said. "That was when the hippies were coming around. Sunday was the big day for them out there by Kezar. We'd go down Haight Street on the way to the game looking at all the hippies. That's kind of a funny thing to remember, but that's what I remember most about the place."

Like almost all of Ken Willard's teammates, Parks has a favorite story about the talented fullback. This one occurred at the 49ers' training camp.

"Someone, I won't say who, ran a garden hose up the side of the building to Willard's room. It was on the second floor. He stuck the hose at the head of the bed so when it was turned on it would spray on Willard's head. When the water was turned on, Willard came running out and knocked on my door. He thought I did it. He was mad because he just bought some new shoes and they were floating around in his room. To this day he still thinks I did it.

"I think about those years with the 49ers a lot. That was the best bunch of guys I played with. That's what I hated most about leaving the team. There was a lot of comradeship. New Orleans was fun too, but San Francisco, well, they were a class bunch of guys."

and 22 touchdowns. He led the team to a 7-6-1 record, including upset wins over the New York Giants and the Green Bay Packers. Receiver Clifton McNeil was Brodie's primary target, catching 71 passes. McNeil was obtained in the off-season from the Cleveland Browns and in his first year with the 49ers was selected All-Pro.

John David Crow ended a magnificent career when he retired after the season. He gained 4,963 yards in his 11 years of pro ball for a 4.3-yard rushing average.

1969 The passing game went from good to great in 1969 when receivers Gene Washington from Stanford, and Ted Kwalick from Penn State, both were selected on the first round of the college draft.

Although the 49ers looked good on paper, the league standings revealed something different. They went winless through their first five games. Injuries to several key starters caused the team to nose dive.

Defensive ends Kevin Hardy and Stan Hindman were lost for most of the season and John Brodie injured a knee that hampered him for several games. The linebacker position was decimated when Matt Hazeltine retired, and Ed Beard was hurt midway through the season.

The team wound up a disappointing season with a hobbling John Brodie coming off the bench to spark the 49ers to a 14-13 win over Philadelphia. The Eagles were quarterbacked by Brodie's old nemesis, George Mira. The win gave San Francisco a 4-8-2 record in 1969.

The 1970s brought the merger of the American and National Football Leagues. It also brought about a new winning tradition for the 49ers. Finally, a championship was on the horizon.

The 49ers' left defensive tackle spot was anchored by Charlie Krueger for 15 seasons. He was drafted on the first round in 1958 after starring at Texas A&M under coach Bear Bryant. The 49ers honored Krueger by retiring number 70 at the end of his career. Only five other 49ers have had their numbers retired—Leo Nomellini, Joe Perry, Hugh McElhenny, Jimmy Johnson and John Brodie. PAGE 80: Running back Gary Lewis (22), a graduate from San Francisco's Poly High School, shakes off the Cowboys' Cornell Green (34). Lewis gained 573 yards in 1968, his most productive as a 49er. PAGE 84: Coach Dick Nolan gets a ride from the field on the shoulders of Skip Vanderbundt (52) and an unidentified teammate, after the 49ers clinched the NFC Western Division Crown in 1971 with a win over Detroit. Jim Sniadecki (58) unwraps the tape from his hand.

Abe Woodson 1958–1964

The longest kickoff return in 49er history was a 105-yard run by Abe Woodson. The second longest return in team history was also by Woodson, and so was the fourth longest and the fifth longest.

In fact, Woodson has five of the longest kickoff returns in 49er history. All of them were touchdowns. In nine years of NFL service, he brought back 193 kickoffs for 5,538 yards, ranking him second on the all-time yardage list. His average of 29 yards per return is topped only by Gale Sayers with a 30.5-yard average.

"You have to remember we did a lot of losing back then," he said. "The other teams scored a lot so I got a lot of kicks to return. The odds were with me to break one once in a while."

In a more serious vein, the former Big Ten hurdles champ credits Red Hickey, the 49ers' head coach from 1959 to 1963, for the emphasis he placed on kick returns. It was Hickey's belief that good returns led to good

field position and good field position enabled a team to score points. To get good returns, Hickey used his best linemen in punt and kickoff situations.

"Red Hickey used to put the All-Pros out there like Bob St. Clair," Woodson said. "He wanted his best blockers out there. Good blocking had a lot to do with our success returning kicks."

Woodson is proud of his 105-yard return against Los Angeles that set the 49er record, but he is more satisfied with a 99-yard touchdown run against the New York Giants.

The Giants took the 49ers apart that day in 1963, winning 48-14, but they were wary of Woodson's running skill. After each touchdown, they sent squib kicks bouncing down the field, making it hard for Woodson to return them. After the Giants' fourth touchdown of the day, Woodson fielded one of the squibbling kicks, followed a couple of good blocks and took off on his 99-yard touchdown run.

That return was satisfying because he scored despite the Giants persistent effort to keep the ball away from him.

The 49er defensive secondary in the early 1960s consisted of Jerry Mertens, Eddie Dove, Dave Baker and Woodson. It was considered one of the best of its time. Jack Christiansen, an All-Pro safety with the Detroit Lions, and a member of the Hall of Fame, was the coach of that unit. It was Christiansen who helped the backfield develop its aggressive style.

"We were one of the first teams to use the bump-and-run," said Woodson. "The man-to-man competition was something I enjoyed. It was with the bump-and-run that we were able to defense people like Raymond Berry. He was good because of his moves and precise patterns. The bump-and-run took that away. That 1961 team was probably our best defensive team."

Woodson was selected All-Pro four times between 1959 and 1963, but even All-Pros had certain receivers that gave them trouble.

"I always seemed to have problems with Max McGee," said Woodson. "The Packers had good timing and Bart Starr was very accurate on those kinds of passes. No matter what I did against McGee, it was wrong."

Returning kicks and preventing pass completions was just part of Woodson's job. From his cornerback position, he had a unique perspective from which to judge the great runners of his time. And as a gifted runner himself, he knew what to look for.

"Well, Jim Brown was probably the best," he said. "He was powerful, he had that great stiff-arm and he was also a very shifty runner. He was damn fast for a man his size. I remember chasing him 70 yards and just barely catching him on about the one-yard line.

"Gale Sayers was the most elusive runner I faced. He was probably the most difficult to tackle, especially in the open field.

"Jim Taylor was a harder runner than anybody. When he carried the ball, he went after defensive backs. Most people ran away from a tackler. Not Taylor. Even if he had a clear path to the goal line, he'd look for a defensive back to run over on the way."

Woodson's memories of the 49ers are laced with comical moments. He recalls one game against Green Bay in Milwaukee in late November of 1958. Vince Lombardi was in his first year as the Packers' coach. The 49ers won the game, 33-12, in

ice-cold conditions.

"In Milwaukee, the stands were real close to the bench," he said. "In those days when you were thirsty there was just a water bucket and dipper. Well, somehow one of the fans got on the field and poured scotch into our water bucket. It was a real cold day so you really didn't need a lot of water, but people kept getting water. Players would run off the field and take a big swig. The coaches started wondering why the players were having such a good time over at the water bucket.

"One game I'll always remember was against the Los Angeles Rams in 1961. What is funny is what happened after the game. I remember it because we were using the Shotgun and we beat them, 34-0. After the game there was a call to the locker room to see who won. Whoever answered gave out the score. The person on the other end said, 'Young man, this is the commissioner. I want to know the score of that game.' He didn't believe that we could beat the Rams."

One of the characters of the 1959-1960 49er teams was a tackle who played at USC and Trinity College named Henry Schmidt. He was affectionately known to his teammates as "wedge buster." On kickoffs, Schmidt's assignment was to run downfield and hurl himself at the wedge set up by the kick-return team.

"We used to get a per diem allowance for our meals," recalled Woodson. "To save money, Henry would come down to the hotel kitchen,

order a bowl of hot water and pour ketchup in it to make himself some soup. Then he'd pocket the money. One time he even pitched a tent out at training camp and lived in a tent right on the field."

Whenever the Chicago Bears were in town, strange things happened. Rumor had it that Bears coach George Halas regularly sent spies to the 49er practices to diagram the team's plays. The 49er coaches solved that problem by placing large pieces of canvas along the fence so nobody could see the team practice, said Woodson.

"One Bears' game at Kezar, a strange thing happened," he said. "Willie Galimore was carrying the ball and he fumbled. We recovered, but Halas started arguing with the referees and they changed their call. It was right before the half and as we were leaving to go to the locker room, some guy came running out of the stands and kicked Halas right in the butt. It was one of the funniest things I've ever seen."

Woodson sees quite a difference from the players of his era and the present day stars. Although the current crop is more talented, that does not make the game more interesting.

"Today's guys are bigger and stronger and faster," he said. "Especially on the artificial turf people are faster. The defenses are more complex. There's more substitution. But I think all the substitution takes away from the man-to-man competition. To me it makes the game less of a challenge."

1970—1979

CHAPTER FOUR

FROM CHAMPIONSHIP TO THE CELLAR

In 1970, the club's 25th year of operation, the 49ers finally put it all together. Coach Dick Nolan, the NFC's Coach-of-the-Year, assembled a solid defensive team led by All-Pro's Dave Wilcox at linebacker and Jimmy Johnson at defensive back. The defensive line of Cedrick Hardman, Tommy Hart, Charlie Krueger and Roland Lakes intimidated opposing quarterbacks. And defensive back Bruce Taylor was selected Rookie-of-the-Year, due in part to his 12-yard punt return average, which ranked him first in the NFC.

The 49ers' offense played well also. In the first game against Washington, Brodie completed 17 of 20 passes, including one for a touchdown. San Francisco came out on top, 26-17.

The offense continued to chalk up points, beating Chicago, 37-16, and Green Bay, 26-10, enroute to a 7-1-1 record at midseason. Ironically, the one tie came against the New Orleans Saints when two 49er castoffs, Bill Kilmer and Dave Parks, teamed up for a touchdown in the closing seconds of the game.

The team suffered consecutive losses to Detroit and Los Angeles before it got back to its winning style. In the final game of the season, the 49ers needed a win or a tie against the rival Oakland Raiders to secure the NFC Western Division title.

Going into the game, Brodie had been sacked only eight times behind a fine offensive line consisting of Len Rohde, Woody Peoples, Forrest Blue, Randy Beisler and Cas Banaszek. Oakland defensive end Ben Davidson predicted to the media he would personally tear apart the line and get to Brodie at least twice.

The Oakland Coliseum was packed with 55,000 Raider fans who sat through a steady drizzle. San Francisco got off to a quick 10-7 lead after a Bruce Gossett field goal and a 26-yard touchdown pass from Brodie to Ted Kwalick. An intercepted pass, returned 34 yards for a touchdown by Jimmy Johnson, and a three-yard touchdown pass to Gene Washington, put the 49ers well in front at the intermission, 24-7.

Many veteran San Francisco fans had a frightening recollection at halftime. The 24-7 score was the same margin the 49ers held at the half of the 1957 playoff game against Detroit. Of course, the 49ers went on to lose that one, 31-27.

The 49ers came out and played another half of solid football. Ben Davidson and the rest of the Raider defense were unable to get to Brodie, ensuring the 49er offensive line of an NFL record for allowing the least sacks in a season. Behind the line, Brodie threw three touchdown passes and San Francisco beat Oakland, 38-7. The 49ers' next opponent was the dangerous Minnesota Vikings.

The week of the Minnesota game, Brodie was honored as the NFC Player-of-the-Year, but his mind was on the Vikings. Minnesota was rated a seven-point favorite.

The temperature in Minnesota at game time was 10 degrees and the field

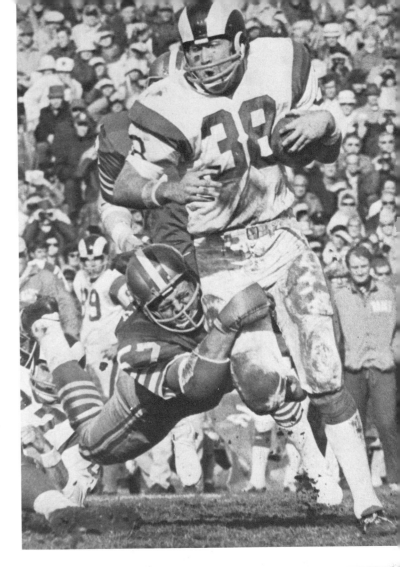

was in danger of freezing over. San Francisco was given little chance to beat the Vikes on their icy turf.

The frozen terrain worked to the 49ers' advantage. The Vikings' fearsome pass rush, consisting of Alan Page, Carl Eller, Gary Larsen and Jim Marshall, was unable to get any footing. The "Purple People Eaters," as they were called, had terrified opposing quarterbacks all year and went into the game with 49 sacks for the season. Against the 49ers they managed only one and that was due to a confused blocking assignment.

With the defensive line unable to operate effectively, Brodie took to the air and completed 16 of 32 passes for 201 yards. Several other passes were dropped due to the cold. Fullback Ken Willard complemented the passing game by gaining 85 yards on the ground to lead all rushers.

The 49ers scored on a 24-yard pass from Brodie to Dick Witcher and a one-yard plunge by Brodie. Gossett rounded out the point total with a 40-yard field goal in the 17-14 win.

The 49ers were established as 3½-point favorites to defeat the Dallas Cowboys in the NFC Championship Game at Kezar Stadium. At City Hall, San Francisco Mayor Joe Alioto boldly predicted the 49ers would demolish Dallas on the way to the Super Bowl. The winner of the championship game would not only go to the Super Bowl but would pocket $8,500. The loser's share was $5,500.

Long lines of faithful fans waited at the Cow Palace to purchase the $12 game tickets. They were anxious to see the 49ers in their first championship game. The contest also would mark the 49ers' last appearance at Kezar Stadium before moving to Candlestick Park.

The Cowboy offense was led by moody running back Duane Thomas. The Dallas defense had not given up a touchdown in 21 quarters prior to the game.

San Francisco got on the scoreboard first. Gene Washington hauled in a 42-yard Brodie pass and was downed at the 10-yard line. The 49ers had to

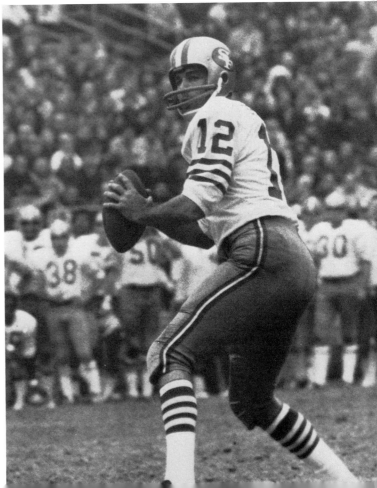

LEFT: Receiver Gene Washington (18) goes high in the air to make a spectacular catch against the Rams. Defending Washington is Kermit Alexander (39). Alexander was a 49er defensive back from 1963 to 1969. He led the team in interceptions in six of those seven years. RIGHT, TOP: Frank Nunley (57) grimaces as he grabs the legs of Rams running back Larry Smith (38). Nunley, nicknamed "fudge hammer" was a 49er linebacker from 1967 to 1976. RIGHT, BOTTOM: John Brodie.

Ben Davidson (83) and Tom Keating (74) of the Oakland Raiders charged through the 49er offensive line to grab John Brodie (12). The play was disallowed because of a penalty. The 49ers beat Oakland, 38-7, in 1970 to clinch their first division title.

settle for a Bruce Gossett field goal. The first half remained a defensive game and both teams went into the locker room tied at 3-3.

Two interceptions by Dallas in the third quarter gave the Cowboys excellent field position. They capitalized on the mistakes, scoring touchdowns both times and building a 17-3 lead. Late in the third quarter the 49ers began to battle back. Brodie drove the team 77 yards and capped the drive with a 10-yard scoring strike to Dick Witcher.

With a 17-10 lead, the Dallas running game ate up the clock in the fourth period. With 12 seconds left in the game, San Francisco finally got the ball back but was 72 yards from the goal line. Brodie quickly completed a 30-yard pass to Bob Windsor. He was dragged down as time ran out.

1971 After their appearance in the championship game, the 49ers no longer were a team to be taken lightly. They were made over-

whelming favorites to win the division title in 1971. They were also favorites to appear in the Super Bowl.

In the league opener against Atlanta, San Francisco didn't look like a Super Bowl team. The Falcons beat the 49ers, 20-17. They intercepted four Brodie passes and recovered three fumbles. With 30 seconds on the clock, and the 49ers within range to tie the game with a field goal, Brodie tried one more time to pass the ball into the end zone. As he dropped back to pass, he was sacked and fumbled away the ball.

The fumble sparked a bench-clearing brawl. After picking up the loose ball, Falcon Tom Hayes rambled about 10 yards ending the game. He then threw the ball toward the 49er bench where it hit Cas Banaszek. Bedlam broke loose.

The team settled down after that initial loss and won six of their next seven games. Late season losses to New Orleans, Los Angeles and Kansas City seemed to end the 49ers' championship hopes. But several losses by the Rams put them right back in it. Going into the final game of the season, they had an 8-5 record and could still win the Western Division title with a win over the Detroit Lions.

Several key players had injuries in that game including Mel Phillips, Bill Belk and Jim Sniadecki.

John Brodie 1957–1973

When John Brodie retired in 1973, he had passed the football 31,548 yards, or about the equivalent of one long pass from Kezar Stadium to Half Moon Bay.

And that's how Brodie made his living really, by throwing the long ball. For 17 years he wore the red-and-gold uniform of the San Francisco 49ers. He was the one constant in a sea of changing football faces. Among them were some of the best receivers to set foot on NFL turf. Brodie remembers them all. Billy Wilson, Gordy Soltau, Dave Parks, Bernie Casey, Ted Kwalick, Monty Stickles and Gene Washington were just a few of the men that contributed to those 31,548 yards.

"I can't pick out one as my favorite receiver," he said. "I had a good relationship with all the receivers I played with. Most of them fit in with what I liked to do, throw the ball."

During his tenure, Brodie guided the 49ers to two NFL Championship Games and one playoff appearance. He played in two Pro Bowls and was the NFL Player-of-the-Year in 1970. But none of that seems to impress Brodie. He stresses the fun he had playing the game and the friendships he made as a member of the 49ers.

"Football was a great experience," he said. "I was fortunate to be a part of it. I met some great people playing here. I was lucky to be able to play in my home-town and stay here for 17 years as a professional.

I was able to play in the same place that I grew up and went to college. All I can say is I enjoyed the hell out of it."

Brodie was picked by the 49ers in the first round of the 1957 college draft. He had been an All-American at Stanford. The 49ers already had Y.A. Tittle at quarter-back so Brodie saw little action that first year. But in one game, late in the 1957 season, he was forced to take over in a tense situation. It was a game the 49ers needed to win in their drive for the playoffs. It was Brodie's first test as a professional.

Baltimore had a 13-10 lead over San Francisco. With less than a minute to play and the ball on the Colts' 15-yard line, Tittle was injured trying to pass. Brodie was quickly summoned and sent into the game. He looked around and asked if anybody had a play they wanted to run. Hugh McElhenny, the old pro, told Brodie to throw him a pass out toward the sideline. The play worked, the 49ers scored, and eventually they made the playoffs.

"I never even saw the pass," Brodie said. "I got buried by Art Donovan as soon as I threw. I heard the crowd respond, that was about it."

It was ironic that 16 years later in the twilight of his career, Brodie would be called off the bench again to save the 49ers' playoff hopes. This time Brodie was the old pro.

He had been sidelined most of the 1972 season with an ankle injury, but backup quarterback Steve Spurrier had filled in admirably. In the last game of the season, San Francisco needed a win over Minnesota to propel itself into the NFL play-offs. Spurrier had been struggling against the Vikings for three quarters. In the fourth period, with Minnesota leading, 17-6, Brodie got his chance. In just eight minutes, Brodie led the team to two touchdowns and another playoff appearance.

Under Brodie's guid-ance the 49ers were a perennial playoff team for three years from 1970 through 1972. But the year that stood out for him was 1965. That year he threw 30 touchdown passes, a 49er record, and completed 62 per-cent of his 391 tosses. Dave Parks caught 80 passes to lead the league

and had 12 touchdown catches. The 49ers aver-aged over 30 points a game.

"I think that year turned everything around for me offen-sively," he said. "That was the start of our best offensive years. We had excellent running backs with Ken Willard, John David Crow and Doug Cunningham. Our line was very good too. I don't like to compare athletes, but we had some outstanding play-ers on that team."

Y.A. Tittle returned to San Francisco as an assistant coach in 1965. Under his tutelage, Brodie began to blossom.

"I learned a hell of a lot from him as a coach," Brodie said. "When we played together, it was a little different. The most important thing I learned then was that there was only room for one quarterback."

The 49ers really have had only four starting quarterbacks in the history of the franchise. Frankie Albert was the quarterback from 1946 to 1951, Y.A. Tittle from 1952 to 1959, John Brodie from 1960 to 1973, and then a string of journey-men ran the show until Joe Montana popped onto the scene in 1980.

Brodie commanded the 49er offense longer than anyone. He com-pleted 2,469 of 4,491 ca-reer passes to put him fourth on the all-time list for pass completions. His 214 career touchdown passes ranks him eighth among the all-time leaders.

So what is it that made Brodie a consistently ef-fective quarterback, one that Dave Parks believes

should be in the Hall of Fame?

"Well that's not for me to say," Brodie said. "That's not my nature to talk about my skills. I just played the game and had a lot of fun doing it. I will say I was persistent. That about sums it up, persistence."

Brodie is not one to dwell on the past and his prior accomplishments, but the mention of Kezar Stadium is one thing that raises nostalgic feelings about his prior team.

"My most vivid recol-lections of the 49ers were those days at Kezar Stadium," he said. "That was the place that best represented where foot-ball should be played. That was a real football stadium. The conditions were generally good. The weather was usually workable. The field was nice until it got sloppy near the end of the season.

"It was at Kezar that the 49er spirit really began. They had a great following back then. Those were the 49er faithful. The 49er spirit you see now didn't just get started. It's been around for a while."

Brodie senses that 49er fans may be getting spoiled by the recent success of the team.

"I would say that the 49ers are the best team playing in the 1980s," he said. "It's one of the few teams I have seen that is so good people would be surprised if it didn't win."

Brodie finds it difficult to sum up his 17 years of NFL competition. "There's nothing real deep I can say about my career," he said. "The most important thing is that I survived."

In the fourth period, Detroit held a 27-24 lead and was driving. San Francisco's defense stopped the Lions at their own 40-yard line on fourth-and-one and the offense went to work.

Larry Schreiber gained 10 yards on the ground and another 10 on a Brodie pass. With third-and-eight from the 10-yard line, the Lions sent everyone after Brodie. He spotted a hole through the middle of the blitzing line and ran 10 yards for the score that put San Francisco in front for good, 31-27.

Willard finished the day with 81 yards rushing while Schreiber added another 42 yards on seven carries. Brodie completed 14 of 20 passes for 186 yards.

The win insured San Francisco of a 9-5 record and a match with the Washington Redskins in the NFC playoffs. Former 49er Billy Kilmer would be the starting quarterback for Washington in place of the injured Sonny Jurgensen.

Thunderstorms before the game made the artificial turf at Candlestick hopelessly slick. Winds in excess of 30 mph played havoc with the passing attack of both teams. Nevertheless, the game was a classic cliffhanger.

Washington held a 10-3 lead at the half after both teams spent 30 minutes testing each other. Brodie got things started in the third quarter with a 78-yard scoring pass to Gene Washington that tied the game at 10-10.

Both teams traded points until San Francisco added another touchdown when Washington punter Mike Bragg muffed a punt snap in the end zone and Bob Hoskins pounced on it to put the 49ers in front, 24-13.

But Kilmer still wanted to play. He came right back, moving the Redskins 45 yards for a touchdown that made it 24-20.

Washington got the ball again with only 46 seconds on the clock. That was plenty of time for

TOP: Fullback Ken Willard (40) was the 49ers' first-round pick in 1965 out of the University of North Carolina. In nine seasons with the club, he gained 5,930 yards to rank second behind Joe Perry on the team's all-time rushing list. His best year was 1968 when he was the NFL's second leading rusher with 967 yards. Willard played in four Pro Bowls between 1966 and 1970. BOTTOM: Jimmy Johnson was recognized by his peers as one of the premier defensive backs in the game. For 16 seasons he was the 49ers' left cornerback until his retirement in 1976. He was a unanimous All-Pro selection every year from 1969 to 1973 and holds the team record with 47 interceptions. Johnson was used as a wide receiver in 1962 and caught 34 passes for 627 yards.

LEFT, TOP: Quarterback Tom Owen (14) prepares to take the field with running backs Delvin Williams (24) and Larry Schrieber (35) prior to the start of a 1974 game with Green Bay. LEFT, BOTTOM, LEFT: Gene Washington writhes in agony after injuring his ankle in a 1973 game against the New Orleans Saints. Washington has more receiving yards than any 49er in history with 6,664. LEFT, BOTTOM, RIGHT: Center Forrest Blue played in every Pro Bowl from 1972 to 1975. He was the 49ers' first-round pick in 1968 and spent seven years with the club. RIGHT, TOP: Frank Nunley questions a referee's wisdom from the 49er bench. RIGHT, BOTTOM: Cas Banaszek was drafted in the first round of the 1967 draft as a linebacker. The Northwestern graduate was converted to tackle in 1968 and was a reliable blocker for 10 seasons with the 49ers.

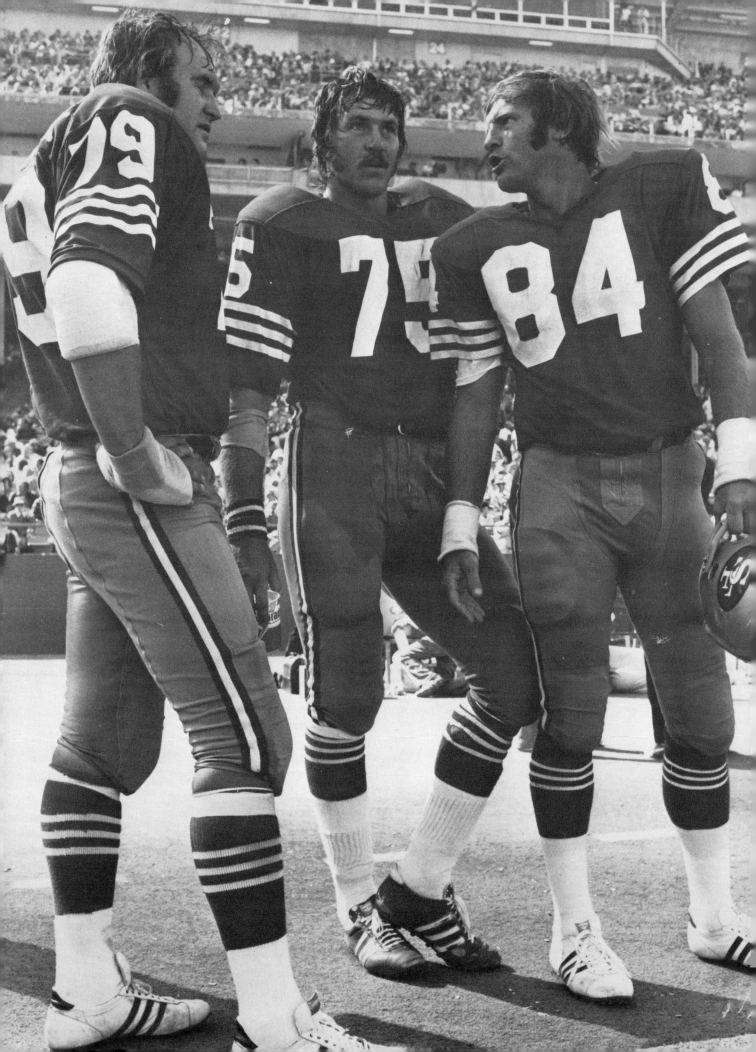

Kilmer. He moved the ball to midfield with 14 seconds left. Then, with six seconds on the clock, and no time outs left, Kilmer dropped back to pass from his 48-yard line. End Cedrick Hardman burst through the line and dropped Kilmer from the blind side to end the game and preserve a 24-20 San Francisco victory.

The Dallas Cowboys were San Francisco's next opponent. The 49ers had not forgotten the championship game of the previous season. Once again rain was to be a factor, but this time it was at Texas Stadium instead of Candlestick Park. The Cowboys were listed as eight-point favorites.

The 49er offense, which was spectacular all season, fizzled in the championship game. It gained just one first down in the first half. A Brodie screen pass that was picked off by lineman George Andrie killed San Francisco. He returned it to the two-yard line and two plays later, Calvin Hill plunged into the end zone for the only touchdown that Dallas needed. The Cowboys' "Doomsday Defense" controlled San Francisco's offense the rest of the way and led Dallas to a 14-3 win.

1972 The quest for a third consecutive Western Division title got underway in 1972 with a 34-3 drubbing of the San Diego Chargers on opening day. Gene Washington had eight receptions, including scoring catches of 13, 23 and 45 yards. Brodie completed 11 of 19 for 156 yards.

Brodie sprained his wrist in the second game of the season against Buffalo and missed part of the action as the Bills won, 27-20.

The 49ers got right back on track the next week as they clubbed New Orleans, 37-2. Brodie returned to form hitting on 18 of 26 passes for 156 yards and two touchdowns.

The offense scored easily in wins over Atlanta, 49-14, Chicago, 34-21, and Dallas, 31-10. Going into

LEFT: Cas Banaszek (79), Forrest Blue (75) and Tom Mitchell (84) watch the clock run out as the 49ers lose to the Cincinnati Bengals, 21-3, in 1974. RIGHT, TOP: Steve Spurrier (11), college football's Heisman Trophy winner in 1966, played nine seasons with the 49ers before being traded to Tampa Bay after the 1975 season. He played behind John Brodie most of his career, but saw action as a starter in 1972 after Brodie was injured. He helped guide the team to an 8-5-1 record that year and a spot in the NFC Championship Game. RIGHT, BOTTOM: Wilbur Jackson (40) was the heart of the 49er backfield from 1974 to 1979 gaining 2,955 yards. He averaged 3.9 yards per carry in a 49er uniform.

The 49ers' defensive unit takes a break during a game with the New Orleans Saints in 1975. From left to right are Mel Phillips, Nate Allen, Bruce Taylor, Cedrick Hardman and Jimmy Johnson.

the final game of the season, the 49ers were 7-5-1. Their opponent at Candlestick was the Minnesota Vikings with a 7-6 record. Once again, a victory was needed on the final day of the season to secure a playoff spot.

San Francisco was a six-point favorite to win it despite the absence of John Brodie who had been sidelined for 10 weeks with a badly injured ankle. Steve Spurrier, who played magnificently in place of Brodie, opened the game at quarterback.

Minnesota jumped out to a 17-6 lead and held it as the fourth quarter began. Under Spurrier, the 49ers were unable to launch any offense. Nolan decided it was time for a change. He motioned to Brodie to begin warming up on the sidelines. The 61,214 fans at Candlestick, who had resigned themselves to defeat, roared their approval as Brodie trotted on the field to begin the last period of play. It was his first appearance for the 49ers in over two months.

It took Brodie nearly half of the fourth quarter to regain his bearings. His first two possessions ended

in interceptions. With eight minutes left in the game, he went to work from his own one-yard line. He hit John Isenbarger for 12 yards, and Gene Washington for 53. Then he found Washington in the end zone on a 24-yard toss. The 99-yard drive brought the 49ers to within four points, at 17-13. They needed one more touchdown.

Minnesota wasn't about to give up the ball. The Vikes worked the clock down to 1:39 and punted. San Francisco took over at its own 35-yard line. But 65 yards of Candlestick turf stood between the 49ers and a playoff spot.

Schreiber picked up nine yards and Vic Washington got eight on two consecutive running plays to move the 49ers past midfield. With a minute to play, Vikes' linebacker Jeff Siemon interfered with Ted Kwalick on a pass play. The 49ers got the ball on the 27-yard line as a result of the penalty. After two running plays picked up six yards, Brodie tossed to Vic Washington who scampered 18 yards to the two with 39 seconds on the clock.

Brodie threw two incomplete passes leaving only 25 seconds to go and the 49ers two yards from the end zone. On third down, Brodie rolled to his right. Several times he pumped the football and motioned to Dick Witcher in the end zone. Witcher broke free, Brodie fired a perfect pass and San

Len Rohde 1960–1974

Len Rohde had a frightening thought on the way to his first 49er training camp. It was 1960, and Rohde, a star tackle at Utah State, had been selected on the fifth round of the college draft.

"Before I left for camp I had read up on the team," he recalled. "I was driving cross country to St. Mary's and I kept thinking about Leo Nomellini, who was a pro wrestler in the off-season and was supposed to have wrestled a bear. Then I started thinking about Bob St. Clair, who was 6' 9" and 270 pounds. I remember reading that he liked to eat raw meat. As I got closer to St. Mary's these guys kept getting bigger and bigger in my mind. I kept wondering how I was going to take a job from them."

It didn't happen over-

night. The 6' 4", 240-pound Rohde payed his dues, waiting for two years in a reserve role before getting a starting assignment at tackle. Those two seasons were spent in the shadow of Bob St. Clair. The waiting period enabled Rohde to learn technique from the veteran linemen on the squad. And it wasn't all related to football.

"Bob St. Clair taught me a few things," Rohde said jokingly. "Most of the technique I learned from Bob couldn't be used on the field though —like how to sneak out of the dorms."

Rohde developed into a solid starter at tackle. He was selected to play in the Pro Bowl in 1971 after anchoring one of the superior lines in football. That line blossomed in 1970 when it allowed only eight quarterback sacks all season, a league

record. In addition to Rohde, the offensive line consisted of Elmer Collett, Cas Banaszek, Woody Peoples, Forrest Blue, Randy Beisler and Bob Hoskins. They became minor celebrities in the area and were nicknamed "The Protectors."

Although Rohde was the veteran in that group, with 11 years of playing experience, he denies that he was their leader.

"We were just good," he said more with honesty than braggadocio. "We were a hard-working bunch of guys. We'd all been together for a while and that helped us. I was the vet of the group, but I don't think that meant anything. It would have been a tough bunch to lead. Everyone was self-motivated.

"Brodie was a big help in getting that sack record. He got rid of the ball quickly. He didn't hang onto it."

The offensive line helped forge the 49ers into near champions in the early 1970s. The teams of 1970, 1971 and 1972 were the best that Rohde played with in his 15 years with the organization. But those years bring mixed emotions to Rohde. Mention "THE" Dallas game and he turns silent. For prior to 1981, when Dwight Clark made "the Catch" that beat Dallas and sent the 49ers to their first Super Bowl, there was only one Dallas game that mattered to 49er fans.

"I don't want to talk about that," he said remembering the team's bitter loss in the 1972 playoffs. But then, as if seeking to purge his feelings, he begins to speak about it.

"That game is still painful to think about. The pain went away and I hadn't thought about it for a while until I saw the team in the Super Bowl the last couple years. Then it came back. I realized how close we had been and what we had missed and it hurt all over again. It was a shock when we lost. All I can say is give credit to Roger Staubach. He brought the Cowboys back."

The near championships of the 1970s offer more than just agony for Rohde. It was particularly sweet for him to play in his first playoff game after suffering through 10 lackluster seasons with the team.

"I remember we had to beat Oakland in 1970 to get into our first playoff game," he said. "We did that. We beat them pretty good (38-7). Then we played against Min-

nesota in the playoffs. That was my biggest thrill from a team standpoint. I remember that game well. We played in the snow back there and were underdogs." San Francisco won, 17-14.

The 49er backfield in those years consisted of two of the team's all-time greats. It was fullback Ken Willard and quarterback John Brodie that made the offense click.

"In the huddle, Brodie was able to communicate just what he wanted to do," Rohde said. "You could tell when we were going to score and when we weren't by the way things were communicated. Brodie knew what he was doing out there. He had a lot of experience. So if he said to the line, 'Give me an extra second here and we'll have six points,' you believed it.

"Willard had a good sense of humor. He was great around the goal line and when a first down was needed, but we used to kid him anyway. We had a saying about him. If we needed two yards, Willard was sure to get us one."

Football in the 1980s has evolved into a highly specialized game. But up front on the offensive line, things have basically remained the same, according to Rohde. The offensive linemen still use brute srength to move their opponents out of position. ·

"The only difference in the linemen today is they are getting bigger," Rohde said. "It doesn't take much to get bigger —just eat. I don't see them as any better than we were. If anything, the

liberal holding rules make it easier for offensive linemen now. You don't have to be as mobile as you used to be."

After 15 years in football, Rohde retired in 1974. He played in the trenches against some of the league's toughest customers. He laughs and scoffs at the generally accepted notion that linebackers are the hatchet men of football.

"The linebackers were nothing," he said with a laugh. "They were little guys who were vocal. They liked to talk to you, but that's about it. They just got in my way."

The defensive linemen were a different story.

"They switched guys around on me quite a bit because I was around 15 years," he said. "But there was a few linemen that were pretty tough to play against. Doug Atkins of the Bears was no fun. He could be devastating."

To round out his top three, Rohde rates Deacon Jones and Coy Bacon, two former Los Angeles Rams, among the defensive linemen he least enjoyed facing.

In 1974, his last season in professional football, Rohde was awarded the Len Eshmont award, the team's most prestigous annual honor.

"That was the biggest personal award I ever received," he said. "As a lineman you don't get many individual awards. That was one of the times I was singled out. It was also voted by the team so it was special. Making the Pro Bowl was a thrill too, but nothing like getting the Len Eshmont Award."

PRECEDING SPREAD: Paul Hofer (36) prepares to hurdle over the Atlanta line on the way to the winning touchdown in a 20-15 win in 1979.

OPPOSITE, TOP: The 49er bench includes, from left to right, Ted Kwalick (82), Gene Washington, Terry Beasley, Bob Penchion, Forrest Blue and Woody Peoples. OPPOSITE, BOTTOM: Ken MacAfee had four touchdown catches in 1979, the ex-Notre Dame star's best year as a professional. LEFT, TOP: Joe Montana in training camp as a rookie in 1979. LEFT, BOTTOM: Keith Fahnhorst, a second-round pick from Minnesota in the 1974 draft, played in his first Pro Bowl in 1985. RIGHT, TOP: Dwaine Board recovered five fumbles and had 13 sacks in 1983 as he helped the 49ers gain a spot in the NFC Championship Game. RIGHT, MIDDLE: Charlie Krueger anchored the 49er defensive line for 15 seasons before retiring in 1973. RIGHT, BOTTOM: John Ayers was an eighth-round draft choice out of West Texas State in 1976, who, prior to the start of the 1985 season, had started 102 of the 49ers' last 105 games.

ABOVE: Delvin Williams (24) bursts through the Miami Dolphins line on the way to a big gain. He set a team single-game record by rushing for 194 yards against the St. Louis Cardinals in 1976. RIGHT, TOP: Dwight Clark races down the sideline on his way to a 41-yard touchdown against the Rams in 1981. RIGHT, BOTTOM: Team owner Edward DeBartolo suffered through four miserable seasons before the 49ers won their first Super Bowl after the 1981 season. OPPOSITE: Roger Craig plows through the Miami Dolphins on the way to one of the three touchdowns he scored in Super Bowl XIX.

FOLLOWING PAGE: Ted Kwalick hauls in a touchdown pass against the Denver Broncos, one of 19 touchdown passes he caught for the 49ers between 1971 and 1973. He led the team in receiving in 1971 with 52 catches and in 1973 with 47.

Larry Schreiber 1971–1975

One of Larry Schreiber's finest games as a 49er occurred on the blackest day in team history.

He scored three touchdowns against Dallas in the 1972 NFC Playoff Game. San Francisco appeared to be on its way to an easy victory. It would have put the 49ers in their third consecutive NFC Championship Game. Schreiber was a hero. But fans don't remember his heroics, they recall the game's tragic outcome. Dallas scored two touchdowns in the last two minutes of the game and won, 30-28.

"The last two games of that season were probably the biggest emotional up and down I ever had," Schreiber recalled. "One week Brodie comes off the bench to beat Minnesota. The next week we had Dallas beat and somehow we blew it."

The 49ers went into the last game of the season needing a win over Minnesota to make the divisional playoffs. An injury to John Brodie had forced the 49ers to use Steve Spurrier at quarterback most of the season. At the start of the fourth quarter, Minnesota held a 17-6 lead. Spurrier was struggling and 61,114

fans at Candlestick Park grew restless.

Coach Dick Nolan decided to use Brodie in the fourth quarter. Brodie calmly entered the game and threw two touchdown passes in the closing minutes to give San Francisco a dramatic 20-17 win.

"We went from one emotional extreme to the other in just a week," Schreiber said. "In the Dallas game, everything happened so fast I didn't really have time to think about it. Of course, I didn't think we could lose it. I just didn't see that coming. It was such

a shock when it was over. I just kind of wandered off the field. Everyone was in shock."

San Francisco wide receiver Preston Riley was considered by many fans to be the goat of the game. He fumbled an onside kick attempt that the Cowboys recovered. Three plays later they scored the winning touchdown with less than a minute to play.

"I really felt sorry for Preston after the game," Schreiber said. "It wasn't really his fault. There was a lot of things that led up to that.

"The 49ers traded him

in the off-season (to New Orleans for a fourth-round draft pick) so I don't know what happened to him. After the game everyone filtered out. No one really said anything about it. I haven't seen him since then. It's funny, 15 years later people still talk about that fumble. At least people remember Preston."

Schreiber was a college sensation at Tennessee Tech before being drafted by the 49ers on the 10th round of the 1970 college draft. He gained 4,421 as an undergraduate. At the time, it ranked him fourth on the all-time collegiate rushing list. A knee injury in his last college game caused him to be passed over on draft day by other teams.

San Francisco had a tough lineup for Schreiber to crack. The 49ers already had Ken Willard, Doug Cunningham, Bill Tucker and John Isenbarger in the backfield. In his rookie season, he waited patiently on the taxi squad. The next year, he played sparingly behind Willard. It was two years before Schreiber got a chance to carry the football with any regularity. It was worth the wait. He gained 1,734 yards in his 49er career, an average of 3.7 yards per carry.

After watching Willard play for two years, Schreiber considers the bruising fullback one of his mentors. John Brodie was the other.

"Brodie had a big influence on me," he said. "In the huddle, he just took command. He had so much experience and knowledge. It made me

feel good when he was in there. He gave us all confidence.

"Ken Willard was a real character. He was the Rodney Dangerfield of the team. He always made us laugh. Him and Doug Cunningham were pretty funny together. As a running back though, there wasn't much those guys could show you. Either you could run with the ball or you couldn't. It's not something you can teach."

The National Football Conference's Western Division had intense intra-divisional rivalries in the early 1970s, Schreiber said. Atlanta and Los Angeles were intimidating teams with bruising hitters on their rosters. As a fullback, it was Schreiber's job to block for halfbacks or protect the quarterback against oncoming linemen.

"Claude Humphrey at Atlanta was the toughest lineman I ever faced," Schreiber said. "He was an outstanding defensive end. The guy that I personally had the worst time with was Ken Geddes from the Rams. He was a linebacker. I don't think he knows I had trouble with him because I always played good against him. I could handle him physically. It's just that I ached afterward. I always had a headache after the Rams games.

"Atlanta was a tough opponent for us. They were just a rough bunch that liked to mix it up. There was always a scuffle in those games, somebody fighting. They came close to beating us a couple times but never could quite do it. I think they only beat us twice while

I played."

Besides the playoff and championship games that Schreiber starred in, he remembers a game at New York's Shea Stadium for its sheer emotional value.

"One game I'll never forget was against the New York Jets in 1971," he said. "We were playing at Shea Stadium and were in a position to make the playoffs if we won our last four games.

"Namath had been hurt and wasn't playing. We were leading about 24-3. I heard this loud cheer and wondered what it was. The fans were cheering for Namath as he came on the field. The place went crazy. It was such an emotional thing. People were on there feet. Well, Namath brings the Jets back to within three points, 24-21, and you have the feeling he is going to pull it out. Fortunately, Johnny Fuller intercepted a pass in the end zone that would have won it for them. We held on and won, 24-21. But I'll never forget the emotion that shot through the stadium when Namath got off the bench."

Schreiber was raised in Kentucky and was eager to play in San Francisco after he was drafted. He looked forward to seeing the city's urban treasures and sophistication. He joined the 49ers in the team's last year at Kezar Stadium and saw first hand the city's feisty football fans.

"The one thing I remember about Kezar is the number of fights there," said Schreiber. "I played at Tennesse Tech and when I was drafted

by San Francisco, I thought how great it would be to play in a sophisticated city. In one of my first games at Kezar, a fight broke out and people were throwing beer all over. A cop trying to break it up had some guy's face mashed against the fence. The fight started in one section and kept spreading. It was probably the original wave. Everyone stood up section by section to see the fight.

"Kezar had real nice turf. It was better to play at than Candlestick. It was a good football stadium. It had a nice football atmosphere about it."

Schreiber was hampered throughout his career with various leg injuries. A torn hamstring ended his playing days after the 1975 season.

"I kind of knew it was over after the hamstring," he said. "I had several knee operations prior to that. I entertained the thought of coming back again but decided against it. When I retired there was no hoopla. It was just over. Going from football to the real world wasn't that bad. There was nothing real emotional. If there's anything I miss, it's the nice paycheck.

"Football was very exciting. I have some injuries I live with. I can't play tennis or racketball, but I'd do it over again. When you look around, everyone wants to be part of football. You talk to successful businessmen and people in large corporations, and they want to talk football. Well, I got to do it. All the work and injury problems were worth it."

Francisco had a dramatic 20-17 win.

In his one quarter of play, Brodie connected on 10 of 15 passes for 165 yards and two touchdowns.

The drama continued the following week as San Francisco faced Dallas in the playoffs. It was a game that still elicits emotion from 49er fans and players.

Vic Washington started the day off right by returning the opening kickoff 97 yards for a touchdown. With only 17 seconds gone, San Francisco had a 7-0 advantage. They gradually padded that lead as Larry Schreiber scored two touchdowns before the half on runs of one and eight yards. In the third period, Schreiber added another touchdown on a one-yard plunge to put San Franciso in front, 28-13.

The Dallas offense was stagnant throughout the third period and coach Tom Landry decided to replace quarterback Craig Morton with Roger Staubach to begin the fourth quarter.

With nine minutes left in the game, Staubach guided the Cowboys into field goal range. Toni Fritsch hit on the three-pointer, cutting the score to 28-16. At the two-minute warning, the score was still 28-16. It looked like the 49ers had shaken the Cowboy jinx that had kept them from the Super Bowl in 1970 and 1971.

With 1:53 to go, the Cowboys took over at their own 45-yard line. Working quickly, Staubach hit Bill Parks on two consecutive passes, the last one a 20-yard scoring strike to make it 28-23 with 1:30 on the clock.

Everyone in Candlestick Park knew that an onside kick was coming. All the 49ers had to do was cover the ball and run out the clock. Fritsch kicked a hard bounder at Preston Riley. The ball bounced off his hands and Mel Renfro recovered on the 50. With just over one minute to play, Staubach was back in business. It took him only three plays to put the Cowboys in the end zone again and give them a 30-28 win. The Cowboys had risen from the dead, scoring two touchdowns in less than a minute. It was a shocking end to an otherwise successful season for the 49ers.

TOP: Delvin Williams (24), receiver Mike Holmes (20) and running back Kermit Johnson rejoice after a 31-3 win over the Chicago Bears in 1975. BOTTOM: Monte Clark guided the 49ers to an 8-6 mark in 1976, his one season as head coach. The following season he resigned after a power struggle with new general manager Joe Thomas. Here, Clark discusses strategy with tackle Keith Fahnhorst.

1973 The 49ers had a difficult time in 1973 trying to rebound from the bitter playoff loss to Dallas. Early in the season, John Brodie announced it would be his final year with the 49ers.

In their first game, the 49ers faced the Super Bowl Champion Miami Dolphins. Miami was coming off the best season in football history winning 17 straight games in 1972 enroute to a perfect season.

The winning streak continued against the 49ers. Brodie had a marvelous first half completing 11 of 14 passes as the 49ers got off to a 10-6 lead, but the heat and humidity, which was over 100 degrees on the field, finally caught up with him. He was replaced by Spurrier in the second half. Spurrier was able to complete only six of his 18 passes and the Dolphins rallied back to win, 21-13.

The 49ers continued to play .500 ball the first half of the season and appeared to be on the right track after beating New Orleans, 40-0. But nothing went right for the 49ers after that. They lost three consecutive games and were 3-6 when they faced Los Angeles in the Coliseum. Joe Reed, who occasionally sang the national anthem prior to the games, was given the starting nod at quarterback for the 49ers. The Rams won easily, 31-13, ending any remote hope of a playoff spot.

It was John Brodie Day at Candlestick on the last day of the season against the Pittsburgh Steelers. Brodie wanted to go out in style. Despite suffering arm problems most of the year, he got the starting call. But there were no miracles this day. His arm obviously was still sore. He completed six of 12 passes, then removed himself in the second period. Pittsburgh won, 37-14. San Francisco finished with a 5-9 record and a tie for last place in the Western Division.

Brodie ended his career with 2,469 completions in 4,491 attempts and 31,548 yards. He threw for 214 touchdown passes. It was also the last season for Ken Willard and Charlie Krueger. Willard gained

The offensive line discusses its game plan. Clockwise are John Watson (67), Cas Banaszek, Bill Reid, Woody Peoples, Jeff Hart, Bob Penchion and Keith Fahnhorst.

Dave Wilcox 1964–1974

Dave Wilcox's best memories of the 49ers involve the crazy pranks they used to play on one another.

"Charlie Krueger was one of the best," Wilcox said. "He liked to pull little tricks on people. He got Howard Mudd good one time.

"Howard used to chew Copenhagen. Somehow, Charlie Krueger found a little tree frog and put it in Howard's Copenhagen before practice. Everyone knew about it but Howard, so we were all wait-ing to see him put it in his mouth. As soon as he did, he knew something was up. But he wouldn't let on. He wouldn't spit the frog out. He didn't want to give everyone the satisfaction of seeing that.

"Ken Willard was another one. One time—I think it was after he had a bad game—he showed up at practice wearing those fake glasses with the big nose and mustache. That really cracked up (Dick) Nolan.

"We were all little kids at heart. But it was the guys that played the hardest that were usually the biggest pranksters."

By all accounts, Dave Wilcox was one of the guys that played the hardest. For 11 years he terrorized opponents from his left side linebacker position. He was a fixture in the Pro Bowl from 1967 to 1974.

"It's hard to say what it takes to become a good linebacker," he said. "I guess the first thing is you have to be a little crazy. You have to be aggressive. You can't be overly aggressive, though, because you have to be able to react to things as they happen."

Mental preparation is also important for a line-backer and it was one of the traits that made Wil-cox a stand out. He constantly reviewed his defensive assignments to ready himself for an upcoming game.

"I didn't like to make mental mistakes," he said. "Once the game started I'd go like hell.

I did everything 100 percent. Even if I made a mistake, I did it at 100 percent.

"I was a perfectionist I guess. I hated to lose. When I went on the field, I thought I could beat anybody. That's the way you have to be when you go out there."

From the outside linebacker spot, Wilcox was often called on to cover running backs on pass patterns. He laughs as he recalls his 235-pound frame trying to keep up with swift backs like Gale Sayers and Jim Brown.

"I was lucky to be in the same neighborhood as those guys," he said. "I saw Gale Sayers at a banquet recently and when I shook his hand I said, 'Geez, its nice to get a hold of you for a change.' "

Sayers tied an NFL record in a 1965 game against the 49ers when he scored six touchdowns. Wilcox was one of the members of the defensive unit that seemed to be constantly chasing Sayers that day.

"I thought that poor guy was going to die of exhaustion," he said jokingly of Sayers' performance. "If he could have gotten some oxygen, he would have scored six more touchdowns. I tell you, that guy was just fantastic."

The 49er defense was molded into a solid outfit in the early 1970s under Coach Dick Nolan. Wilcox teamed up on the left side with All-Pro defensive back Jimmy Johnson, safety Mel Phillips, and linemen Tommy Hart and Charlie Krueger. He says the entire left side worked well together, and as a result,

opposing teams stayed away from them as much as possible.

"That defensive team was a good mix of old and new players," he said. "Cedrick Hardman and Bruce Taylor were rookies in 1970 and Roosevelt Taylor joined us from Chicago. He added a lot of experience."

"From a defensive standpoint, Nolan was good as a coach," Wilcox said. "He was an ex-player. He knew what players thought and how they would react. He had a good feel for defense. If Nolan had a fault, although I wouldn't really call it a fault, it was that he would always talk about Dallas because he had coached there. We got tired of hearing him talk about how Dallas did things. We were the 49ers. We didn't care what Dallas did."

Although Wilcox was part of the 49er teams that lost two NFC championships to Dallas and one playoff game, he feels no animosity toward them. He admits, however, he was crushed when they lost in the 1972 playoff.

"I'll remember that for the rest of my life," he said mournfully. "I remember at halftime someone saying, 'We're doing great.' I thought, this guy must be crazy. We have another half to play. We really hadn't done anything up to that point. We scored on Dallas mistakes.

"I could feel the game slipping away in the second half. The intensity level had dropped off. There was a feeling that we could screw around in the second half and win anyway. Well, we didn't win because we didn't do

our jobs. We had the gates wide open and couldn't get them shut."

One of the most satisfying wins in Wilcox's career came in the 1970 playoff game against the Minnesota Vikings. The 49ers were appearing in their first playoff in 13 years and only the second as a member of the NFL. It was played at Bloomington Stadium in Minneapolis in weather only an Eskimo could enjoy. Temperature at game time was 10 degrees.

"Nobody gave us a chance in that game," he said. "Roman Gabriel was a television announcer at the time and he told Brodie we didn't have a chance. Before the game, we went out there in short sleeves and started jumping around like we were crazy, like we were enjoying the weather. Then we went out and beat them. It was gratifying to go back to Minnesota and win. It shocked everybody."

Minnesota was a tough place to play in the winter due to the nasty weather conditions, but San Francisco's Kezar Stadium had a reputation as a tough park on any given Sunday. Wilcox remembers it as a symbol of history and nostalgia.

"Me and Matt Hazeltine used to drive down Haight Street on the way to the park on Sundays," he said. "That's when all the hippies were hanging around. That was interesting.

"I had some friends who used to come to the games and they always went to the Kezar Club. They didn't think they could drink beer in the stadium, so they did it at the Kezar Club. After-

ward, they would walk right into the locker room and socialize. Nobody stopped them. In fact, a lot of people used to walk in off the street and socialize. They let anybody in the locker room. You couldn't move in there it was so small."

Wilcox finally retired after the 1974 season. He went out in fine fashion playing in the Pro Bowl for his seventh time. Before he retired though, he was party to one of the classic pranks in 49er history, one that is retold by veterans of the team whenever they congregate.

"In 1974, the streakers were going pretty good," he recalled. "We were in training camp going through two-a-day practices. You need something to break up the monotony. We had two go-go dancers come down to practice. We gave them cleats and helmets. It was supposed to be secret but everybody knew what was going to happen. Everybody but Dick Nolan. We were lined up running plays, but no one could concentrate because we were waiting. People were jumping offsides and forgetting the snap count. Finally, they came running across the field with nothing but their helmets on. One of the girls picked up the ball and threw it at Nolan. It hit him right in the chest. We had a cameraman there to film the whole thing."

"That's what I miss the most about football, the crazy things we used to do. I miss some of the other guys. The paycheck wasn't bad either."

6,105 yards in his career and scored 45 touchdowns. Krueger was a fixture on the defensive line for 15 seasons.

1974 The 49ers were fortunate to have four choices in the first two rounds of the 1974 college draft. They used them wisely. Among their picks were Keith Fahnhorst, Wilbur Jackson, Bill Sandifer and Delvin Williams. In addition to the first four choices, Sammy Johnson, Manfred Moore, Tom Owen and Mike Holmes also made the roster, giving the club eight rookies.

In an obvious rebuilding year, Joe Reed and Steve Spurrier battled it out in the preseason for the number-one quarterback position. Spurrier appeared to have the job won until he separated his shoulder in the last exhibition game against the Rams.

In his debut against the New Orleans Saints, Reed didn't remind any fans of John Brodie. He completed seven of 15 passes for only 56 yards. Larry Schreiber was the big gainer for San Francisco, rushing for 75 yards. It was enough to help the 49ers to a 17-13 win.

After beating Atlanta in the second game of the season, the 49ers lack of an experienced signal caller became a serious problem. They dropped seven straight games. During that span they tried five different quarterbacks. In addition to Spurrier and Reed, veteran Norm Snead and rookies Tom Owen, a 13th-round pick from Wichita State, and Dennis Morrison, a free agent from Kansas State, tried their hand at quarterback.

After losing seven in a row, the unexpected happened. San Francisco shutout its opponent in two straight games, beating Chicago, 34-0, and Atlanta, 27-0. It was the first time the 49er defense had shutout two consecutive opponents in 13 years.

The 49ers stumbled to a 6-8 record by beating New Orleans, 35-21, in the final game of the year. Several veterans retired after the 1974 season, including Dave Wilcox and Len Rohde. Tight end Ted Kwalick left the 49ers to play in the World Football League.

1975 Training camp was like a revolving door for quarterbacks in 1975. Norm Snead won the starting job after beating out both Tom Owen and Steve Spurrier.

San Francisco acquired from Dallas a slightly aged Bob Hayes. The former Olympic sprinter was obtained for a third-round draft choice and was intended to give Norm Snead a long ball target.

The 49ers beefed up the defensive line by drafting Jimmy Webb, a tackle from Mississippi, and Cleveland Elam, a defensive end from Tennessee State.

Despite the changes, San Francisco started the 1975 season right where it ended the last one, fumbling away another game. In the opener against Minnesota, Norm Snead completed 10 of 18 but lost the ball twice on fumbles. Minnesota took advantage of the miscues and turned them into touchdowns, winning 27-17.

All season the coaching staff searched for a starting quarterback. Snead, Steve Spurrier and Tom Owen alternated at the position but none of them had much success. The team struggled all year with the high point a 24-23 win over the Rams. They finished the season with four straight defeats.

San Francisco's 5-9 record was good enough for second place in the horribly weak NFC Western Division. There was little room for optimism outside of the 49er running game, which consisted of Delvin Williams, Larry Schreiber and Wilbur Jackson. Williams was the team's leading ground gainer with 631 yards. Schreiber retired at the end of the season having gained 1,734 yards in his five seasons with the 49ers.

1976 The head coaching job was handed to Monte Clark before the start of the 1976 campaign. Clark, formerly a defensive end with the 49ers, was the youngest head coach in the league at 39. He tried to solve the quarterback problem that had plagued the 49ers since John Brodie's retirement by acquiring Jim Plunkett from New England. In what proved to be a costly trade, San Francisco gave up Tom Owen, two number-one picks in 1976, and its first-round and second-round picks in 1977.

Clark and Plunkett made their 49er debuts a memorable one by defeating the Green Bay Packers, 26-14, on opening day of the 1976 season. Plunkett hit on eight of 12 passes for 120 yards. Running back Delvin Williams also showed flashes of brilliance, gaining 121 yards on the ground.

The 49ers staged a remarkable turnaround from the previous season by whipping Los Angeles, 16-0, New Orleans, 33-3, and Atlanta, 15-0. The de-

fense, led by Tommy Hart and Cedrick Hardman, blended into one of the premier outfits in football. In those three games, the defense sacked the quarterback 25 times as the team went on to win six of its first seven games.

The next week, the 49ers lost to St. Louis in overtime, 23-20, and began a four-game slide in which they also lost to Washington, Atlanta and Los Angeles. The possibility of an outstanding season finally ended when they lost to San Diego, 13-7, in their second overtime loss of the year.

Jim Plunkett was benched in the last game of the season and Scott Bull tried his hand at quarterback against New Orleans. Bull guided the team to a 27-7 win and appeared to be the quarterback of the future.

The 8-6 record was the team's first winning season since 1972. The high point of the year was the outstanding work of the defense, which allowed an average of just 13 points per game. Delvin Williams finished the season with a club record 1,203 yards rushing. Jimmy Johnson, a fixture in the 49ers' defensive backfield for 16 seasons, and a five-time Pro Bowl player, retired at the end of the year.

1977 During the off-season there was an unusual amount of activity in the 49er offices. Prior to the start of the season, Edward De-Bartolo Jr. became the new owner of the team. It was the first change of ownership in the franchise's history. Joe Thomas was hired as general manager and the popular Monte Clark resigned after a power squabble with Thomas. Thomas hired Ken Meyer to coach the club.

The team got off to a disastrous start. After losing five of six exhibition games, they were routed in the season opener at Pittsburgh, 27-0. They managed just 101 yards of total offense. For the fourth straight game, including exhibitions, the 49ers failed to score a touchdown. Plunkett completed just three of 13 passes for 30 yards, all to running back Delvin

TOP: Quarterback Steve DeBerg set NFL records in 1979 with 578 pass attempts and 347 completions. The record was broken a year later by San Diego's Dan Fouts. BOTTOM: Coach Bill Walsh considered running back Paul Hofer (36) one of the best all-purpose backs in football. In 1979, he led the 49ers in rushing with 615 yards and averaged five yards a carry. He also topped the club with 58 receptions. Hofer is the only 49er to receive the Len Eshmont Award two consecutive years. An injury cut short his career in 1981.

Delvin Williams 1974–1977

Delvin Williams didn't know what to expect at the start of the 1976 season. The 49ers had finished the previous year with a miserable 5-9 record. In two seasons, they had gone through five quarterbacks. Now there was a new coach in town by the name of Monte Clark and still another quarterback named Jim Plunkett.

It turned out to be quite a year for Williams. His uncertainty was quickly alleviated when he gained 121 yards in the season opening win over Green Bay. It was the first in a series of outstanding games that eventually netted him a club record 1,203 rushing yards.

"We had a lot more fun under Clark," he said. "It was the most fun I had playing football since my senior year in high school. 1976 was prob-ably the peak of my career."

Williams' single-season rushing record was broken in 1984 when Wendell Tyler picked up 1,262 yards rushing. Prior to 1976 the last time a 49er running back had gained over 1,000 yards was in 1959 when J.D. Smith ran for 1,036 yards. Only five times in the team's history has a back gained over 1,000 yards.

"That's definitely a re-flection on the coach," Williams said. "There was a noticeable turn around in the team when he took over. The thing about Clark was that he was able to come in, see where the talent was, and put it to use. He put people in the right posi-tion. Me and Wilbur Jackson had both been playing halfback up until then. He put Wilbur at fullback and me at half-back. It just made for a

better atmosphere. Plus, I was coming of age as a player."

The highlight of the season for Williams was a game against the St. Louis Cardinals when he set the 49er single-game rushing record with 194 yards on 34 carries.

"We lost that game in overtime but it was a good one for me person-ally," he said. "After that game I was just beat but you don't feel it during the game. I was young and I guess I didn't know any better. It sure didn't feel like I had 34 carries, though."

Just one week later, Williams had another big day. He gained 180 yards on 23 carries in a tough 24-21 loss to Washing-ton. His total offensive output running and receiving that day amounted to 279 yards.

"I liked to think of myself as a complete

player," Williams said. "I ran, blocked and caught the ball. I always tried to play intelligently. I always tried to be a student of the game. It's not just athletic skill that is needed in pro football."

The 1976 season was a curious one. The 49ers finished with an 8-6 record but could easily have won 10 or 11 games. They lost twice in overtime and also had a three-point loss to Washington and a five-point loss to Atlanta.

The quarterback situation was unsteady throughout the year, which makes Williams' running achievement even more remarkable. Plunkett was hurt midway through the season, and Clark was forced to use the untested Scott Bull and Marty Domres at quarterback. Wide receiver Willie McGee was also injured, so defensive backfields could double-team Gene Washington, the 49ers' only other deep threat. The passing game was virtually helpless. San Francisco finished the year 11th in the NFC in passing yardage with 1,963 yards. They were second in rushing yardage with 2,447 yards.

Credit for that rushing total obviously goes to the offensive line—which included Randy Cross, Keith Fahnhorst and Cas Banaszek—for its ability to open holes for Williams and Wilbur Jackson. Williams says the ends deserve special mention because it was on sweeps that Williams gained many of his yards.

"Tom Mitchell, our tight end, was a very effective blocker on the run," he said. "He was the one that made it pos-sible to turn the corner. He was underrated."

Williams and Jackson had one of the biggest collective days ever for two running backs on a nationally televised Monday Night Football game. In that contest, against the Minnesota Vikings, they both rushed for more than 150 yards, a rare feat. Williams had 153 yards, while Jackson gained 156.

Things weren't always so good for Williams. In his rookie year with the 49ers, he broke his wrist in a preseason game and wondered if he'd stick with the team. He made the club, but didn't return to action until halfway through the regular season.

It wasn't until his second year with the 49ers that he began to become an effective part of the team's offensive unit. In 1975, he led the team in rushing with 631 yards, averaging 5.4 yards per carry. He caught an additional 34 passes.

"In the second year, I started to become acclimated to pro ball," he said. "The first year did a lot of good though, because I got to play through the pain and the injuries. I got to be part of the team and didn't have to go through the process of being new all over again the next year."

Leaving the relative security of college football for the professional game is often a traumatic experience for a rookie. During his initial season, Williams often looked to backfield coach Doug Scovil or veteran running back Vic Washington for advice.

"It is always a big adjustment for athletes to go from college to pro ball," he said. "In college they take care of everything for you. Suddenly you get to the pros and you have to take care of yourself. The social life is different and, of course, the physical dimension is much more intense on the pro level. They are much bigger and faster than anything you saw in college. You see these guys on TV and now all of a sudden you are playing with them.

"Vic Washington was pretty helpful to me as a rookie," he said. "He was always willing to talk to you. He'd tell you things that made sense. Basically though, it's something you just have to go through. You have to experience it."

Williams had a fruitful career with the 49ers from 1974 to 1977. He ranks fifth on the 49er all-time rushing list with 2,966 yards. He was traded to the Miami Dolphins in 1978 for wide receiver Freddie Solomon and a number-one draft pick. The 49ers used the draft choice to select Dan Bunz. The two players acquired for Williams were instrumental in the 49ers' two Super Bowl victories.

"I'm real happy for the 49ers now," he said. "They have good fans and good people here. They deserve a championship.

"I just wish I could have ended my career here. I enjoyed the time I was with the 49ers. Even when I left for Miami my heart was still in San Francisco."

Tony Bennett couldn't have said it better.

Williams. He also had two passes intercepted.

In the continuing search for an effective quarterback, Scott Bull was sent in to replace Plunkett late in the fourth quarter. He completed just one pass for 26 yards. Prior to that 26-yard pick up, the 49ers biggest gain of the day had been a 15-yard personal foul penalty marched off against Pittsburgh.

The 49ers' ineptitude continued as they lost five straight games. The offense was unable to put together any kind of attack and they were shutout for the second time of the season, 7-0, by Atlanta. In five games they scored 46 points, an average of just nine points per game.

Near midseason, kicker Ray Wersching was signed to replace Steve Mike-Meyer. Wersching immediately made his presence known when he kicked a 50-yard field goal in his first game against the New York Giants. Three weeks later, he kicked a field goal to beat New Orleans, 10-7, in overtime.

At midseason, the 49ers put together a four-game winning streak, mostly through outstanding defensive efforts. Besides the 10-7 overtime win at New Orleans, they won, 10-3, at Atlanta. Although they were winning, the offense was still unable to score consistently.

Before the season was over, Jim Plunkett gave fans hope for the future when he flashed his old form against Dallas on Monday Night Football. He threw four touchdown passes in a 42-35 loss.

It was still a disappointing season. The 49ers finished 5-9. The highlights of the year were the development of a strong defensive line and the improved running game. Delvin Williams had another fine season gaining 934 yards, while fullback Wilbur Jackson added 780.

1978 Something obviously had to be done to rebuild the 49ers. General manager Joe Thomas got started by firing Ken Meyer and the rest of the coaching staff and hiring Pete McCulley. Then,

TOP: Tight end Ken MacAfee (81),dejectedly buries his head as the 49ers lose another game in the miserable 1979 season. They finished the year with a 2-14 record. MacAfee was a first-round choice from Notre Dame in 1978. BOTTOM: Bill Walsh started the 1985 season with a record of 56-41 as head coach of the 49ers. The only San Francisco coach to win more games was Buck Shaw. Shaw had a 72-40-4 record and a .638 winning percentage. Walsh has a .577 winning percentage. PAGES 118-119: Bill Walsh reviews strategy with his troops prior to a game with the Los Angeles Rams in 1979, his first year as head coach.

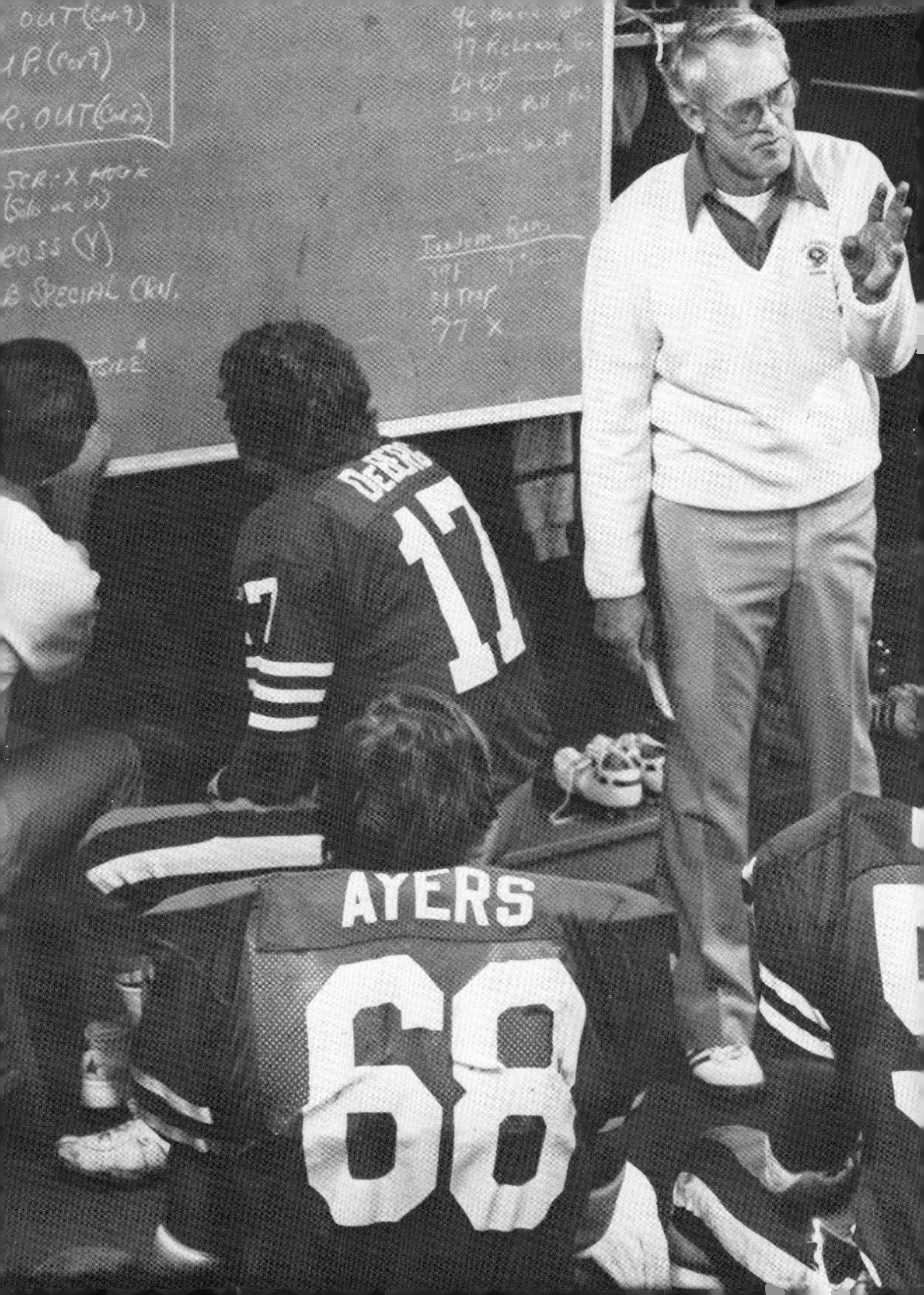
OUT (Cov 9)
R. OUT (Cov 2)
SPECIAL CRV.
77 X
DeBERG
17
AYERS
68

in a bold move, Jim Plunkett was released and the quarterback job was handed to the untested Steve DeBerg. Several other popular veterans were unceremoniously released or traded, including Gene Washington, Bruce Taylor, Skip Vanderbundt, Tommy Hart, Delvin Williams and Woody Peoples.

In the backfield with DeBerg on the opening day of the 1978 season was O.J. Simpson, who was obtained from the Buffalo Bills. The 49ers gambled their future on Simpson, giving up second- and third-round picks in the 1978 draft, first- and fourth-round picks in 1979, and a second-round choice in 1980.

In 1978, the schedule was extended to 16 games. The extra two weeks just added frustration to the longest season in 49er history. The opening game was an indication of things to come when the 49ers turned the ball over six times to Cleveland and were beaten by the Browns, 24-7. DeBerg completed 16 of 32 passes for 174 yards. Simpson gained 78 yards on 22 carries. Ironically, it proved to be one of O.J.'s most fruitful days in a 49er uniform. Before the season was over, he would be sidelined with a separated shoulder.

There wasn't much to cheer about as the team floundered along losing eight of its first nine games. The club's sole win came at the hands of the Cincinnati Bengals. In the ninth week, after suffering a 38-20 beating at the hands of the Washington Redskins, McCulley was fired and Fred O'Connor took over.

O'Connor couldn't do much to change the 49ers' luck in his coaching debut, but then, it's doubtful that Knute Rockne could have redirected the team either. Atlanta beat the 49ers, 21-10, and once again it was turnovers that killed San Francisco.

The 49ers were able to win just one more game all year, a 6-3 yawner over Tampa Bay. But it was the team's final game at Detroit that epitomized the entire frustrating season.

The Lions won the game, 33-14, but it was a comedy of errors from the start as San Francisco fumbled 10 times. Quarterbacks Steve DeBerg and Scott Bull were both injured and wide receiver Freddie Solomon had to be inserted at quarterback.

Solomon never had played the position in the pro ranks. He turned out to be more effective than the regular quarterbacks, completing five of nine passes for 85 yards. He also ran for another 42 yards and a touchdown.

The 49ers finished 2-14 and had the dubious distinction of being only the third team in NFL his-

tory to lose 14 games in a season.

1979 Once again there was considerable activity in the front office during the offseason. Eddie DeBartolo fired Joe Thomas and Fred O'Connor, and hired Bill Walsh as head coach and general manager. The most successful era in the team's history was about to begin.

Walsh got to work immediately, choosing Joe Montana, an unheralded quarterback from Notre Dame, in the third round of the 1979 college draft. With his 10th-round pick, he went after Clemson receiver Dwight Clark. Walsh had set the framework for the 49ers' future success.

Walsh's first season did not go as anticipated, but the 49ers played noticeably better football. The offense moved the ball well as Walsh turned loose DeBerg and put the passing game in high gear.

The losses continued to pile up though, as San Francisco dropped its first seven games. Several were heartbreaking losses including a 28-22 defeat at Minnesota on a disputed touchdown in the last 10 seconds of the game, and a 27-24 loss to the Rams.

Finally, in the eighth week of the season, Walsh got his first 49er victory when the club downed Atlanta, 20-15. The only other win that year came against Tampa Bay. San Francisco's second consecutive 2-14 record placed it in the record books as the losingest team in NFL history over a two-year span.

There were some bright spots. The 49er offense became one of the most productive in football after being virtually last in every offensive category the previous season. Steve DeBerg set new NFL records in pass attempts and completions. He connected on 347 of 578 passes for 3,652 yards to better Fran Tarkenton's single-season marks.

Paul Hofer came into his own as a running back. He gained 615 yards on the ground for a five-yard average and was also the team's leading receiver with 58 catches. He was awarded the Len Eshmont award for the second straight year.

It was also the final time around for the great O.J. Simpson. "The Juice" carried one last time in the season finale against the Atlanta Falcons and picked up 10 yards. It was an insignificant addition to the 11,236 yards he gained in his career.

PAGE 122: Dwight Clark's catch gave the 49ers their first NFC Championship. "It was a perfect pass," Clark said.

1980—1985

CHAPTER FIVE

THE SUPER BOWL YEARS

Walsh continued his rebuilding program in 1980 by trading away veterans Cedrick Hardman and Wilbur Jackson and concentrating on young talent. In the college draft, he selected running back Earl Cooper and defensive end Jim Stuckey on the first round, and linebacker Keena Turner on the second round. By the end of the 1980 season, just 16 of the players that Walsh inherited from Joe Thomas remained with the club.

In preseason, the 49ers looked promising by beating Oakland, San Diego and Kansas City, and losing to Seattle by only three points. They opened the regular season against the New Orleans Saints in the Superdome and carried with them an NFL-record 18-game losing streak on the road.

San Francisco broke the road jinx with the help of New Orleans kicker Russell Erxleben, who missed a 34-yard field goal at the gun. The 49ers held on to win, 26-23. Earl Cooper was the workhorse for San Francisco picking up 77 yards on the ground and catching 10 passes for another 71 yards. He also scored two touchdowns. Paul Hofer added 68 yards on 12 carries and 114 yards with seven receptions. Steve DeBerg also had an outstanding day, completing 21 of 29 passes for 223 yards.

On defense, the club was led by linebacker Scott Hilton, who had made his living as a carpenter just a year earlier. Hilton had a game-high 15 tackles against the Saints, nine of them unassisted.

San Francisco continued its surprising start by beating St. Louis in overtime the following week and then the New York Jets. But after posting a 3-0 record, reality set in. The 49ers were blown out by the Rams, 48-26, and Dallas, 59-14. Then they lost four consecutive heartbreakers, to Tampa Bay, 24-23, Detroit, 17-13, Green Bay, 23-16, and Miami, 17-13, dropping their record to 3-8.

Midway through the season, Paul Hofer, who was off to an outstanding start with a 4.9 yard rushing average, was lost to the club with a knee injury. At quarterback, Joe Montana began alternating with Steve DeBerg and gradually worked his way into the starting lineup.

With three games left to play, the 49ers entertained New Orleans at Candlestick. The Saints were 0-13, but they were able to make the 49ers look pathetic in the first half, jumping out to a 35-7 lead. The 49er offense had gained just 21 yards. As the 49ers left the field at intermission, 37,000 fans at Candlestick booed them unmercifully.

In the second half, Montana caught fire. He threw touchdown passes to Solomon and Clark and scored another on a one-yard run. Suddenly, the 49ers were back in the game. With 1:50 to play, Lenvil Elliott's seven-yard run tied it up. San Francisco won in overtime on a Ray Wersching field goal, and the most remarkable comeback in NFL history was complete.

San Francisco closed out the season with a 6-10 record, but there was evidence that the rebuilding club had a good nucleus upon which to build.

Rookie Earl Cooper led the league in receiving with 83 catches and Clark was second with 82 receptions. Montana won the starting quarterback job in the second half of the season with his intelligent play. He completed 65 percent of his 273 passes for 1,795 yards and 15 touchdowns.

1981 In the 1981 college draft, the 49ers hoped to improve the porous pass defense that plagued them throughout the 1980 season. They selected Ronnie Lott on the first round, Eric Wright on the second round and Carlton Williamson on the third round. The three defensive backs stepped into immediate starting roles. By the end of the 1981 season, the 49ers had the best secondary in football.

To further improve the defense, they obtained linebacker Jack Reynolds from the Rams. He brought leadership and experience to the young defensive unit. Midway through the season, quarterback terrorist Fred Dean was obtained from the Chargers for a second-round draft pick, a trade that was the equivalent of highway robbery.

The start of the 1981 season was less than spectacular. The 49ers lost two of their first three games and seemed headed for a mediocre year. But then things began to happen.

San Francisco squeaked by New Orleans, 21-14, and beat Washington, 30-17, in the nation's capital. They returned home to play the Dallas Cowboys at Candlestick. Just a year earlier, Dallas humiliated San Francisco, 59-14. This time it would be different.

The 49ers jumped off to a 21-0 lead in the first quarter behind the passing of Joe Montana, who sparked the club on touchdown drives of 61 and 68 yards. At the half, San Francisco held a 24-7 advantage.

In the third quarter, Montana hit Clark on a 78-yard scoring pass. Then Lott intercepted a pass and returned it 41 yards for a touchdown. The 49ers were in the driver's seat. But Montana was not finished. He took the 49ers on an 89-yard march to make it 45-7. The rout was complete. Dallas added another

TOP: Archie Reese was an instrumental part of the 49er defense during the 1981 Super Bowl season. The defensive end from Grambling played from 1978 to 1981 with the 49ers. BOTTOM: Linebacker Bobby Leopold (52) returns to the huddle after the 49er defense knocked Cardinal running back Ottis Anderson out of the game in 1980 with a separated shoulder.

Dwight Clark 1979–

The image of Dwight Clark leaping into a darkening sky and snagging a pass to send the 49ers to their first Super Bowl is indelibly etched in the memory of every 49er fan.

No one will forget "the Catch." It is a play that will live on forever. It set the 49ers free from a jinx they could not shake. On three previous occasions in the 1970s, the Dallas Cowboys terminated 49er drives to the Super Bowl. But Clark ended that hex in one electrifying moment when he returned to earth with the pigskin and six points.

"When Joe threw that ball, I thought at first it was a little high," Clark said. "Later, Irv Cross was interviewing me and after I thought about it, I said it was a perfect pass.

He started laughing because he thought I was joking, but it was a perfect pass. There's no other place Joe could have thrown the ball. If it had been anywhere else, Everson Walls would have made a play on it.

"That catch was a big thrill, but what made it exciting was the whole drive and coming back to beat Dallas. Dallas is usually the team that makes the comebacks."

Dwight Clark is painfully modest. He is a master of understatement. He caught 297 passes from 1980 to 1983, more than any other receiver in the NFL, and was *Sports Illustrated's* Player-of-the-Year in 1982. But Clark says it is Bill Walsh's offensive system and Joe Montana's pinpoint passing that have

made him successful.

And he may have a point. He was a 10th-round draft pick out of Clemson in 1979. He caught only 33 passes in his three years of varsity action. He hardly could have expected to be in the NFL Pro Bowl two years into his professional career.

"I don't think I would have this success if I was playing anywhere else," he said. "When I first got here, Sam Wyche (the 49ers' former quarterback and receiver coach) took me aside and worked with me. That helped a lot. But it's Bill's system that makes everything work, not any individual skill of mine.

"Joe makes me play better," he added. "He's good at reading what will happen. He knows

what his receivers will do. He can tell by the way a guy runs downfield which way he will cut."

What is it about Montana and Clark? They have an undefinable mystique, an ability to complement one another in a way that sets them apart from other passing combinations. They may be the most productive aerial duo since Johnny Unitas and Raymond Berry.

"We did have something going that was different," Clark said about their on-field relationship. "But now Joe has that with every receiver on the team."

Clark and Montana have figured prominently in the 49ers' development into an NFL power. When Clark joined the team in 1979, it was coming off a 2-14 season, the worst in its history. In his rookie year, the team did no better, struggling along and finishing again at 2-14. But the pieces were slowly being put into place, Clark says. It took one more season of refinement before San Francisco finally won a championship.

"That first Super Bowl was the culmination of two years of putting the Bill Walsh system into place," Clark said. "I knew we were going to win eventually, but I didn't think we'd win so soon. In 1981, the team wasn't deep. But we were lucky, we didn't have any injuries so things worked out."

Defense became a potent weapon for the 49ers in 1981. The acquisition of Fred Dean solidified the defensive line. But it was in the 1981 college draft that San Fran-

cisco boosted itself into a Super Bowl contender, Clark said. When Ronnie Lott, Eric Wright and Carlton Williamson joined the club, there was a noticeable change in attitude.

"One of the big things that season was all the rookie defensive backs we drafted," he said. "They were not only good, they infected the rest of the team with their college enthusiasm. That really helped spark things."

After the 1984 season, the 49ers' entire defensive backfield was selected to play in the Pro Bowl. Practicing against the best in the business on a daily basis can only be a help, Clark says. "You know if something works against them, it will work against anybody.

"I'm lucky we don't have to play against our defensive backs in a real situation. After watching some of the hits Ronnie Lott has put on people, especially in preseason (1985) when he belted Wes Chandler, I'm glad he's on my side.

"If I was to single out one guy other than our defense that I'd prefer not to play, it would be Mike Haynes from the Raiders. He's given me trouble."

One defensive unit that sticks out in Clark's mind belongs to the Atlanta Falcons. Over the years, the Falcons and 49ers have engaged in physical warfare. Cuts and bruises are the norm after any game that matches the two Western Division rivals.

"Atlanta has a very intense defense," Clark said. "They are like bees.

Everyone swarms to the ball. It's cost them though because they get a lot of people hurt."

One of the most memorable games in Clark's career was played against the San Diego Chargers in the strike-shortened 1982 season. He caught 12 passes, a personal high. The game stands out because it contained the type of football Clark likes to play: lots of passing and plenty of scoring. The Chargers eventually won, 41-37.

Clark has an idyllic life in San Francisco. He cannot envision himself playing for anyone but the 49ers. The combination of Walsh's offensive system, Montana's throwing ability, and the team's camaraderie and spirit, would make it hard for him to play with anyone else. When he was drafted, he had no idea San Francisco would be so good to him.

"I remember when I got drafted by the 49ers, I was really happy and everything but I didn't know that much about them," he said. "I knew John Brodie had been the quarterback for a while, but that's about it. When I got out here, I found out O.J. Simpson was on the team. I was real excited about that. I couldn't wait to meet him. He was my hero as a kid.

"If I played anywhere else I don't think I'd have all these good things happening to me. I was in the right place at the right time. I'm fortunate I was drafted by the 49ers. If I was to be traded or something, I'd probably think about retiring."

touchdown on a fumble recovery to make the final score 45-14, but the damage was done. It became apparent that something special was happening in San Francisco.

Two weeks later, the Los Angeles Rams came to town. The 49ers had a four-game winning streak on the line, their longest in four years, but they had not beaten the Rams at home since 1966. They had never beaten them at Candlestick Park.

Montana moved the club early, connecting with Dwight Clark on a 41-yard touchdown pass and Freddie Solomon on a 14-yard scoring pass. When the Rams had the ball, they advanced at will, but mistakes and tough defense when it counted, kept them out of the end zone. The Rams still managed to put 17 points on the board. Two Wersching field goals gave the 49ers a 20-17 edge in the fourth quarter, but a game between the 49ers and Rams rarely ends without drama, and this was no exception.

With six minutes to play, Rams' kicker Frank Corral tried a 32-yard field goal that would tie up the game. The ball hit the right goal post, then the cross bar, and bounced right back at Corral.

With 2:03 to play, the Rams got the ball again. Quarterback Pat Haden was sacked twice, but on third down he completed a 33-yard pass for a first down at the San Francisco 31-yard line. The Rams moved the ball to the 28 with three more plays. With 17 seconds left on the clock, Corral tried a 45-yard field goal. This one was wide to the left. The 20-17 lead held.

The 49ers were tested again the following week against the Pittsburgh Steelers. The Steelers were the most feared team in football during the 1970s when they won four Super Bowls. The game was played in the hostile environment of Pittsburgh. San

TOP: Defensive end Lawrence Pillers was an instrumental part of both 49er Super Bowl teams. MIDDLE: "Hacksaw was one of the guys that helped turn the team around in 1981," Ronnie Lott says. The 49ers signed Jack Reynolds (64) as a free agent in 1981. He instilled confidence into a young defensive unit and helped guide the 49ers to their two Super Bowl appearances. Here, he discusses strategy with linebacker coach Norb Hecker. BOTTOM: From left to right, Charles Johnson, Charles Cornelius and Charle Young await pre-game taping. Young has a muscle stimulator taped to his thigh. PAGES 128-129: Joe Montana gives encouragement to members of the offense in the closing minutes of a game against the Pittsburgh Steelers in 1981. Clockwise are Montana (16), Eason Ramson (80), Freddie Solomon (88), Randy Cross (51), Charle Young (88), Fred Quillan (56) and Dwight Clark.

In 1984, kicker Ray Wersching became the first 49er to lead the NFL in scoring since Gordy Soltau in 1953.

Francisco was given scant chance of beating the AFC powerhouse. But nobody told Joe Montana.

For Montana it was a homecoming of sorts. He grew up in nearby Monangahela, about 20 miles south of Pittsburgh. He was forced to play the game with a flak jacket because of bruised ribs. The injury did not hamper his performance. He completed 16 of 23 passes in the first half as the 49ers took a 10-0 advantage.

Pittsburgh scored two quick touchdowns in the third period to go in front, 14-10. The 49er offense was unable to generate any momentum after that, but an interception by Carlton Williamson, who ran the ball 28 yards to the Pittsburgh 43, set up their final scoring march. Montana moved the ball into the end zone in nine plays with Walt Easley covering the last yard for the score that made it 17-14. The 49ers had survived another test. They were now 7-2 and had to be considered a legitimate contender.

After beating Atlanta, San Francisco took a seven-game winning streak into Cleveland. The 49ers could put only 12 points on the scoreboard with four Wersching field goals and they lost to the Browns, 15-12.

They rebounded against the Rams, beating them, 33-31, when Wersching kicked a 37-yard field goal with no time on the clock. Then, in the 13th game of the season, the 49ers clinched the NFC Western Division title with a 17-10 win over the New York Giants.

The last three games of the season were anticlimactic. The 49ers beat Cincinnati in a Super Bowl preview, 21-3, eased by Houston, 28-6, and defeated New Orleans, 21-17. San Francisco finished the season 13-3, the best record in the NFL. The 49ers' first opponent in the playoffs would be the New York Giants.

The week before the game, a wild storm made practice at the 49ers' Redwood City training facility impossible. Bill Walsh arranged for the team to practice indoors at a local high school. The rain didn't dampen the 49ers' spirit or effectiveness against the Giants.

San Francisco struck first against New York on an eight-yard pass to tight end Charle Young and never looked back. The 49ers beat the Giants, 38-24. Montana completed 21 of 30 passes for 304 yards including another touchdown pass of 58 yards to Freddie Solomon.

Ronnie Lott 1981–

Pride is the ultimate motivator for Ronnie Lott. The 49er cornerback can think of nothing worse than getting beat on a long pass. To embarrass him is to infuriate him.

But the challenge of stopping the best receivers in football week after week is what makes Lott tick. He loves competition.

"There is no way to describe the feeling of getting beat on a pattern," he said. "It makes you want to come off the field and hide. The only person that can understand that feeling is another defensive back."

Lott is everything you want in a football player. He is a hard-hitting team player who disregards individual awards in favor of collective success.

Such teamwork is evident in the 49er defensive backfield, where working together often means the difference between success and failure. He talks of himself as a member of a unit rather than as an individual cornerback.

"We have a lot of confidence in one another back there," he said. "One person can't do it by himself and we all know that. We know that we can't keep everybody from scoring, but still we compete as best we can at all times. One of the things that makes us good as a unit is we try to get the best out of each other whenever we're on the field."

The 49ers selected Lott, Eric Wright and Carlton Williamson with their first three picks in the 1981 college draft. The year prior to their selection, the 49ers had the worst pass defense in football. Opposing quarterbacks completed 66 percent of their passes against the 49ers, highest in the NFL. The secondary gave up 29 scoring passes, a figure topped only by New Orleans with 30. And they allowed 3,958 yards through the air. Only the Atlanta Falcons gave up more aerial yardage with 3,990.

In 1981, with Dwight Hicks and three rookie starters in the defensive backfield, the 49ers drastically cut those numbers. They allowed only 53 percent of the opposing teams' passes to be completed. They gave up just 16 touchdown passes and 3,135 total passing yards.

The drastic improvement in the defense is a reflection on the talented athletes in the secondary, but Lott thinks credit for the success should go to other people as well.

"In preseason that first year, I remember someone saying it looked like a three-ring circus back there," Lott said. "We were having a tough time because we knew that everyone was watching us. We were concentrating too hard, trying to make the transition to the pros. It was like being under a microscope. George Seifert (the 49er defensive coordinator) took us aside and told us to just relax and have fun. That helped a lot. He wanted us to play hard but have a good time while we were doing it."

The three rookies were looking for an on-field mentor when they reported to the team in 1981, and they got it when the 49ers acquired linebacker Jack Reynolds from the Los Angeles Rams. He instilled a winner's attitude into the entire defense.

"One of the things that turned the team around was the addition of Hacksaw," Lott said. "He knew defense and showed us the little things that made us successful.

"The overall chemistry of that team was good. Everyone started to believe that we could win. There was a lot of fresh people that year who didn't know about the 49ers' past and didn't want to know.

"Bill Walsh was the biggest factor. He is the mainstay of the organization. I'd compare him to Lee Iaccoca. Here's a guy that took over an organization that was down, turned it completely around and made it into

a winner."

The turning point for the 49ers in 1981 was a game against the Dallas Cowboys in the sixth week of the season. Lott intercepted two passes, including one he returned 41 yards for a touchdown. The 49ers came away with a 45-14 win and a 4-2 record. More importantly, the victory gave the team confidence in its ability and proved the 49ers were a competitive team.

"That was a big game for me because I had a lot of admiration for some people on the Dallas team," said Lott. "Not admiration for the team, just some of the players on the team. I was able to pick off a couple of passes and made some tackles. When you play against people you admire, you want to play good against them.

"Whenever I go out on the field, I know there are a lot of people out there watching. I know my family, the fans and people I care about, are watching me and counting on me to play up to their expectations. If I can play up to their expectations, that's what makes it all worthwhile."

Injuries hampered Lott much of the 1984 season. He suffered a twisted ankle in the opening game, a concussion against Houston and a separated shoulder against Tampa Bay. Yet, he remained in the lineup, often switching positions with free safety Dwight Hicks. Lott says he has no preference between safety and cornerback but hints that the one-on-one challenge of the cornerback position is something he enjoys.

"I prefer playing wherever they put me," he said. "Right now it's at the corner so I prefer the corner."

And when he is at the corner, his biggest challenge is Green Bay Packer receiver James Lofton.

"He is such a gifted athlete," said Lott. "He's got good speed and moves. I have to think that he was helped by being coached by Bill Walsh at Stanford.

"At this rank everyone is tough though. Every team gives us some type of problem. One week you think you can relax and the next week you find a receiver that is outstanding."

Lott has been a perennial Pro Bowl selection, appearing in the post-season game every year since joining the NFL. But personal awards mean very little to him. Asked what his biggest thrill has been as a player, he says contributing to a winning team.

"When I retire, I'll be able to look back and say I played with a great bunch of guys," he said. "That I was able to enjoy the game and that I played well with some of the best players around."

"What makes football a thrill for me is that I meet such great people. When people stop me on the street and tell me they enjoy the 49ers, that gives me a big thrill. It's exciting to know that people enjoy watching us play and really care how we do. I know that these people are counting on us to perform our best.

"The only thing that I can promise them is we're going to play our butts off."

Archie Reese celebrates goal line stand in Super Bowl XVI.

Dallas was next. The Cowboys had finished the year with a 12-4 record and were aching for a rematch after their embarrassing defeat at the hands of the 49ers earlier in the season. For the 49ers, it was their first appearance in an NFC Championship Game since 1971 when they played Dallas. The Cowboys were posted as a 2½-point favorite.

Rain pelted the Bay Area the week before the championship game. The Golden Gate Bridge was closed due to high winds for only the third time since its opening. Walsh searched the Peninsula for dry fields to practice on and finally moved the entire organization to Anaheim to practice on the Los Angeles Rams' field.

The 1981 NFC Championship Game was one of the most exciting games in football history. San Francisco scored first on an eight-yard pass from Montana to Solomon, but the two teams exchanged the lead six times before the game was over. The 49ers scored a second quarter touchdown on a 20-yard Montana pass to Dwight Clark. At the intermission, Dallas went into the locker room with a 17-14 lead.

Defense dominated the third quarter. An interception by 49er linebacker Bobby Leopold set up a two-yard touchdown run by Johnny Davis to give the 49ers a 21-17 lead. The Cowboys went back in

front, 27-21, in the fourth quarter after Rafael Septien kicked a 22-yard field goal and Danny White connected with Doug Cosbie on a 21-yard scoring toss.

The best was yet to come. San Francisco's offense took over again on its own 10-yard line with just under five minutes to play. It was do-or-die for the 49ers and they knew it.

Montana moved the ball downfield on short passes to Solomon and Cooper, while Lenvil Elliot picked up yardage on several shifty runs. At the two-minute warning, with the 49ers at midfield, Montana went to the sideline to discuss the situation with Walsh. On the next play, Solomon picked up 14 yards on a reverse, moving the ball to the 35. Montana then threw a 10-yard pass to Clark and a 13-yard pass to Solomon. San Francisco called time out again with 1:13 left to play and the ball on the 12-yard line. Again Walsh and Montana conferred. When play resumed, Montana missed Solomon on a pass to the end zone. Then Elliot rushed for seven more yards to the six.

With 58 seconds to play, Montana dropped back

LEFT: Guard Randy Cross was named to the Pro Bowl following the 1981, 1982 and 1984 seasons. He was the team's top choice in 1976 as a center. RIGHT, TOP: Cornerback Ronnie Lott has appeared in the Pro Bowl every season since joining the 49ers as a first-round pick in 1981. RIGHT, MIDDLE: In one of the great deals of all-time, the 49ers acquired Fred Dean from the San Diego Chargers for a second-round pick and the option to swap first-round picks. In his first season with the 49ers, he was named the NFL's outstanding defensive lineman. RIGHT, BOTTOM: Bill Ring won the Len Eshmont Award in 1983.

135

I WILL NOT BE OUT HIT
ANY TIME THIS SEASON

Bill Walsh fires up his troops at halftme of the 1981 NFC
Championship Game against the Dallas Cowboys.

to pass and was pursued by Ed "Too Tall" Jones and
Larry Bethea. As he was about to be sacked, he
lofted a soaring pass that appeared to be going out
of the end zone. Dwight Clark had other thoughts.
He made a straining leap, grabbed hold of the football and came down near the back of the end zone.
The 49ers were going to the Super Bowl. Their opponent would be the Cincinnati Bengals.

The week before the Super Bowl, Coach Bill
Walsh was honored for transforming the 49ers from
the worst team in the NFL to the top of the heap in
just two years. He received the NFC Coach-of-the-
Year Award at a ceremony in Washington, D.C.

Arriving in Pontiac, Michigan, site of Super
Bowl XVI, Walsh found the temperature at 15 degrees below zero. The wind chill factor made it 51
below zero. His only consolation was the knowledge
that the game was to be played indoors at the
Silverdome.

The 49ers were one-point favorites at game time.
The coaches of the two playoff teams San Francisco
beat to get to the Super Bowl thought differently.
Dallas coach Tom Landry picked the Bengals to win

by seven points. Ray Perkins, coach of the New York
Giants, picked the Bengals by 10 points.

San Francisco won the coin flip and elected to
receive. On the opening kickoff, Amos Lawrence
fumbled the ball and the Bengals recovered on the
26-yard line. It was not the kind of start Walsh had
expected.

Cincinnati immediately drove to the San Francisco five-yard line. On third down, Ken Anderson's
pass to Issac Curtis was intercepted by Dwight Hicks
who returned it to the 32.

Montana didn't waste any time. He drove the
49ers 68 yards in 11 plays and scored the first touchdown himself on a one-yard dive. The big plays in
the drive were a Montana pass to Charle Young for
14 yards and a 14-yard completion to Freddie
Solomon.

In the second quarter, with the 49ers still in front
7-0, Cincinnati threatened again. The Bengals were
on the 49ers' 27-yard line when Anderson completed a 20-yard pass to Cris Collinsworth to the
seven-yard line. As he was hit by Eric Wright, Collinsworth fumbled. The 49ers recovered and stifled
another Bengal scoring opportunity.

Montana went back to work from the eight-yard
line. He completed a 20-yard pass to Solomon and
a 12-yarder to Clark. Cooper picked up 14 yards on

Joe Montana 1979–

There's not much left for Joe Montana to accomplish. He's already at the top. In just his seventh season, he's the NFL's highest rated quarterback of all time. He's been the most valuable player in two Super Bowls. And he's one of the highest paid men in pro football.

But don't get the idea that Montana is content with his past achievements. "I definitely want to go back to the Super Bowl again," he said.

At the start of the 1985 season, the 49ers had won 49 of the 68 games

in which Montana was the starting quarterback, a .721 winning percentage. In his first year as a full-time starter, he led the team to a Super Bowl win over the Cincinnati Bengals. It was the first championship in the team's 36-year history.

Bill Walsh drafted Montana on the third round of the 1979 college draft. He was the 82nd player picked overall. Walsh chose Montana on the strength of a predraft workout he conducted with the Notre Dame star. Walsh left the workout impressed with the

quarterback's quickness. He already had been attracted to Montana because of his competitive play at Notre Dame.

Walsh gingerly introduced Montana to the pro game. In his rookie season, Montana threw only 23 passes, completing 13, as the 49ers suffered through a 2-14 year. During his sophomore season, he was gradually worked into the starting role. The highlight of that year was a victory over the New Orleans Saints in one of the wildest comebacks in NFL history.

In that game, Montana brought the 49ers back from a 35-7 halftime deficit by throwing two touchdown passes and running for another in the second half. The 49ers won in overtime, 38-35.

When the 1981 season started, the quarterback job was handed to Montana. Steve DeBerg, his rival for the position, had been traded in the off-season. Montana responded by leading the 49ers to a championship.

"It was the 49er organization that got this team turned around," Montana said. "It was Bill Walsh and the coaching philosophy he brought with him. Bill installed the system he wanted and had some good drafts to get the players he needed.

"Basically, Bill's philosophy is to attack the defense at its weak spots and make the other team stop us," he said. "We just try to go after a vulnerable area. When I go through the films preparing for games, I try to find those areas."

The Walsh system is repeatedly mentioned as a reason for the team's success. Montana goes one step further, hinting that the system has also contributed to his own good fortune.

"Any quarterback can run this system," he said. "It's made for a quarterback. Anybody would be successful with it. I happen to fit into it well. On pass plays somebody's always open, I just have to find him."

But not just any quarterback could lead his team to two Super Bowl wins in a four-year span. The fact is, Montana has always been a winner. His college career at Notre Dame was like something out of a storybook. He didn't get the starting quarterback assignment until midway through his junior season. At one point, he says, he was the fifth-string quarterback. When he finally was made Notre Dame's number-one signal caller in 1977, he took the Irish to a national championship.

In his senior year, Montana led Notre Dame to a number-seven ranking. But the highlight of the season was the final game of his college career when the Irish played Houston in the Cotton Bowl.

Montana was sick the week of the game. Prior to the opening kickoff, he suffered with the chills. He played anyway. For three periods, Houston was overpowering, building up a 34-12 lead. The Irish seemed doomed, but the thought of losing never entered Montana's mind. He rallied the Irish back to 34-28, and with no time left on the clock, tossed a pass to receiver Kris Haines in the end zone. Final score: Notre Dame 35, Houston 34.

"That was the most exciting comeback I was ever a part of," he said. "It was more satisfying than the New Orleans game. It was the last game I played for Notre Dame."

For pure all-around excitement though, Montana says nothing matches the 1981 NFC Championship Game against the Dallas Cowboys.

"The whole setting of the game made it memorable," he said. "We were playing for the league championship and had to go the length of the field against the Cowboys to win it."

It was Montana's pass to Dwight Clark with 58 seconds to play that clinched it for the 49ers.

"I thought the pass might have been a little high when I threw it, but I really didn't see it," Montana said. "I was knocked to the ground after I threw. I heard the roar of the crowd so I thought Dwight caught it. I didn't know what a great catch it was until I saw it later."

The Montana-to-Clark connection has been a principal part of the 49er offense since Montana took over at quarterback. In 1980 and 1981, Clark caught over 80 passes. In 1984, his reception total dropped to just 52 as Montana started to spread the passes out to all the receivers and backs. But Clark's still the man Montana looks for in the clutch.

"Dwight is good at reading the defense," said Montana. "He can adjust to what's going on as he runs his pattern. It's nice to have a receiver of that size and with that kind of knowledge. I know what he's going to do just by the way he's running a pass route."

Defenses seem to be a minor annoyance to Montana. His ability to scramble and make the big play is one of the elements that sets him apart from other quarterbacks. In that regard, he's a defensive coordinator's nightmare. No planning can stop his impulsiveness. Yet, Montana prefers to avoid certain defenses.

"The Rams' nickel defense has always been tough for me," he said. "Chicago can be a problem, but we don't have to face them as often as the Rams. The thing about the Bears is they do things differently on defense. The Falcons are another one. They are always physical."

Quarterback coach Paul Hackett is responsible for reviewing game plans and upcoming defenses with Montana in preparation for Sunday. Montana credits Hackett and Sam Wyche, the 49ers' former quarterback coach, for helping him blossom into one of the game's stars.

"Paul has been a big help," said Montana. "He points out the little things that make a good quarterback, like feet movement."

Montana was raised in Monongahela, near the coal regions of western Pennsylvania. It was only natural that Joe Namath, who grew up in nearby Beaver Falls, would be Montana's boyhood hero. They are the only two quarterbacks in football history to win a national championship in college, and a Super Bowl as a professional.

"He came from the same area that I grew up in," Montana said. "He had some good years when I was young and went on to win the Super Bowl. I was kind of impressionable as a kid. I guess you could say he was my hero."

Did Montana ever dream he would become as successful as his boyhood idol? Or that he'd be the number-one rated passer in the history of the game?

"I don't think of myself as a great quarterback," he said. "I don't think of my ability or compare it with anyone at all. Maybe when it's all over and I retire I could look back and evaluate it, but I'm not going to do that for quite a while.

"I always wanted to play in a Super Bowl but I wasn't sure I ever would get the chance," he said. "Right now I'm concentrating on going back to the Super Bowl. I want to go again."

a sweep. Then, from the 11-yard line, Montana completed a pass to Cooper for the touchdown that gave San Francisco a 14-0 lead. The 92-yard drive was the longest in Super Bowl history.

On their next possession, the Bengals were unable to move the ball and were forced to punt. San Francisco took the ball on its own 34 and drove to the Bengal's five-yard line. With 18 seconds left in the half, Wersching kicked a 22-yard field goal and the score was 17-0.

On the ensuing kickoff, Wersching booted a deliberate squib kick that bounced into the arms of Archie Griffin. He promptly fumbled and the ball rolled toward the goal line. The 49ers' Milt McColl covered it on the four. The Bengals were stunned. With five seconds left before the intermission, Wersching kicked another field goal and the 49ers had a 20-0 halftime lead.

The second half took on a different tone. The Bengals came out charging and scored on their first possession when Anderson ran five yards to cap an 83-yard drive. The two sides exchanged punts before Cincinnati regained the ball with 6:53 in the third quarter. Anderson completed a 49-yard pass to Collinsworth, and several running plays moved the ball to the three-yard line.

The Bengals had two of football's toughest short-yardage runners in Pete Johnson and Charles Alexander. Johnson, a 250-pound fullback, was considered unstoppable on the goal line. It seemed an impossible task to keep them out of the end zone.

On first down, Johnson gained two yards up the middle. The Bengals had three more downs to pick up one yard and a touchdown that would move them to within six points of San Francisco. On second down, linebacker Dan Bunz plugged a hole over left guard and stopped Johnson for no gain. On third down, Anderson threw a quick swing pass to Alexander. Bunz was ready for it. He flattened Alexander less than a yard from the goal line.

The Bengals were confused. Nobody had stopped Johnson and Alexander on short yardage plays like the 49ers had done. Anderson called a time out to talk things over with Forrest Gregg. The Bengal coach decided to go for the touchdown rather than a certain field goal. They agreed to use the Bengals' best goal line play, a fullback plunge over right guard behind Alexander's lead block. Bunz was there again. He stuffed the hole, slowing down Johnson so that Jack Reynolds and the rest of the defense could make the stop.

After playing in the Pro Bowl for three straight seasons as a member of the New England Patriots, Russ Francis (81) suddenly retired in 1980. He came out of retirement in 1982 and has been in the 49er lineup ever since. An excellent all-around athlete, Francis was drafted by the Kansas City Royals baseball team out of high school. He also set an American prep record by throwing the javelin 259 feet, 9 inches.

The dramatic goal line stand changed the complexion of the game. The momentum swung back to the 49ers. Now the game was clearly in their hands. Ray Wersching added two more field goals and the 49ers held on to win their first Super Bowl, 26-21.

1982 In the off-season, Walsh strengthened his Super Bowl team by coaxing Russ Francis out of retirement. Francis was a former All-Pro tight end with the New England Patriots. He also signed Renaldo Nehemiah, holder of the world record in the 110-meter hurdles, to give the 49ers a deep threat at wide receiver. With the 49ers' first pick in the college draft, Walsh selected Bubba Paris, a massive offensive tackle from the University of Michigan.

The 49ers opened the 1982 season against the Los Angeles Raiders. They needed a victory to vali-

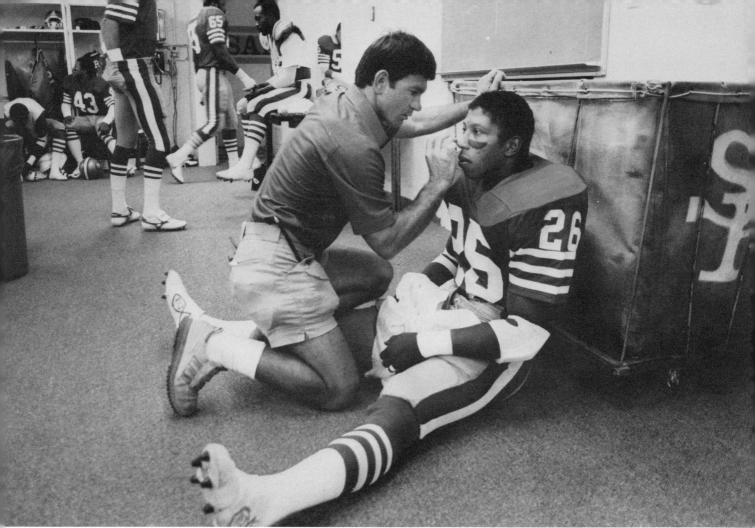

ABOVE: Equipment manager Bronco Hinek applies shadow under the eyes of Wendell Tyler prior to a game. LEFT: Linebacker Riki Ellison, a protege of Jack Reynolds, led the 49ers in tackles in 1984 with 95. He had a career-high 13 tackles in a game against Atlanta. He was named to two All-Rookie teams in 1983. RIGHT: The acquisition of Tyler in 1983, gave the 49ers the running threat they needed to go with their powerful passing attack. Tyler set a team record in 1984 when he rushed for 1,262 yards.

date their Super Bowl victory. Many people still believed it was a fluke. They didn't get it. Sloppy play, turnovers and blown assignments led to a 23-17 loss. More importantly, Dwaine Board, one of the team's best defensive linemen, went down with a knee injury. The loss of Board was noticed immediately as Raiders' running back Marcus Allen ran through the 49er defense for 116 yards.

The 49ers lost their second game of the season at Denver, 24-21, and then the NFL players went on strike. When they returned to action in November, the 49ers won their first game of the year over St. Louis, 31-20. They stumbled through the rest of the season and had a 3-5 record going into their final game against Los Angeles. It was a game the 49ers had to win to gain a playoff spot.

Eric Wright (21) is considered one of the best coverage men in football by defensive coordinator George Seifert. In 1983, he intercepted seven passes and returned them 164 yards. He was selected to play in his first Pro Bowl after the 1984 season.

Los Angeles was one of the worst teams in the league with a 1-7 record. The Ram defense was as solid as a wet soda cracker. The 49ers were favored to beat them by 9½ points.

Somehow the 49ers managed to lose. With 1:50 to go, Ray Wersching could have put San Francisco ahead with an easy 24-yard field goal. The kick was blocked by Ivory Sully, giving the Rams a 21-20 win and capping a dreadful season for San Francisco.

1983 The 49ers had lived and died by the pass for too long. They needed a running game to complement the passing of Joe Montana if they wanted to be successful in the NFL. In 1983, they did just that by selecting Roger Craig, a fullback from Nebraska, in the second round of the college draft, and obtaining halfback Wendell Tyler from the Rams for a second- and fourth-round pick.

Tyler did not endear himself to 49er fans in the 1983 season opener against Philadelphia. With the Eagles leading, 22-17, and 1:19 to play, the 49ers were driving. They had the ball on Philadelphia's 10-yard line when Tyler fumbled it into the end zone, killing the 49ers' scoring chance.

The game was not over yet. Miraculously, the 49ers got another chance when they recovered an Eagle fumble on their 28-yard line. Less than a minute remained when Montana was knocked out of the game on a ferocious hit by linebacker Jerry Robinson. Backup quarterback Guy Benjamin replaced Montana. With 11 seconds to go, he threw a 17-yard touchdown pass to Dwight Clark, but it was negated due to a holding penalty. San Francisco had run out of time.

The 49ers turned things around, winning six of their next seven games. Their only loss was to Los Angeles, 10-7, at Candlestick. A home-field jinx began to haunt them. In addition to the home losses to Philadelphia and Los Angeles, they lost to the New York Jets and Miami Dolphins at Candlestick.

The 49ers ended the season on a Monday night at Candlestick against the Dallas Cowboys. It was their first appearance on Monday Night Football in five years. The 49ers entered the game with a 9-6 record. Dallas was 12-3. The last time the two teams had met was in the 1981 Championship Game.

San Francisco needed a win to clinch the NFC Western Division title. They got it by ripping the Cowboys, 42-17. There was bad news to go with the win, however. Star receiver Dwight Clark was lost

Bubba Paris 1982–

William "Bubba" Paris may be the most important man on the 49ers' offensive line. As the left tackle, it is his job to protect quarterback Joe Montana's blind side.

If Paris misses a block on a passing situation, Montana won't even know what hit him. He'll never see the oncoming rusher.

Paris understands well the role he plays in keeping Montana healthy. And when Montana is healthy, so is the 49er offense.

Since joining the 49ers after being drafted in the second round of the 1982 draft, Paris has steadily improved his pass blocking skills. As

an undergraduate at the University of Michigan, Paris was an overpowering straight-ahead blocker in the Wolverines' running attack.

At 6' 6" and 300 pounds, he was not easily manhandled. The pass was not stressed in the Bo Schembechler system of football, so pass blocking was of little importance to Paris. At Michigan, he was more likely to spot Halley's Comet than a forward pass.

With the 49ers, his role is different. The pass is one of San Francisco's most effective weapons. Paris has had to work on his pass blocking technique from the start. Still, contributing to an effi-

cient running game gives him great satisfaction.

"I've had a history of being able to play with great backs and here at San Francisco is no exception," he said. "Roger Craig is one of the greats in the game. He gives 150 percent on every play. I know if I give him an avenue, he'll just take off.

"Wendell (Tyler) is just naturally blessed. He is an outstanding back, too. He might not have to work as hard as Roger to produce, but he sure gives you results.

"Joe (Montana) can make you look good. If you give him an inch, he'll take five miles. If you miss a block, he can still dodge tacklers and make the play."

The improvement in Paris' pass blocking ability was evident in the 1984 NFC Championship Game when he faced Chicago's Richard Dent. Dent led the NFC with 17½ quarterback sacks during the regular season. Against Paris, Dent made only four tackles and had no sacks.

"We were truly tested in that Chicago game," Paris said candidly. "Going into the game, there was a lot of talk about their defense. I didn't know if we could stop them. I knew it was up to me to stop Dent. It turned out I did, and the team played well, and we won.

"As a team, the Chicago Bears have about the toughest defense I've faced," he said. "I know whenever we play them, I'm going to really have to buckle on my chin strap. They have a good defensive scheme and they have some big hitters. When we play them again, they'll want to show us that they should have been the ones in the 1984 Super Bowl."

Paris got off to a rocky start with the 49ers. In the last preseason game of his rookie year, he injured a knee and was out for the season. Paris came back to play all 16 regular season games in 1983, as well as the playoffs. He had a string of 28 consecutive starts until a bruised knee forced him to miss a game against Cleveland in 1984.

The injury that sidelined Paris for his rookie season had a profound effect on him. He thought his professional career was over before it even began.

"I prepare myself mentally as well as I can," Paris said. "I know as long as my body functions, my mind will take care of the rest. As long as I'm close to God I feel I can perform on the field. When I received that injury my rookie season, I thought I'd never get another chance to perform. I thought it was over."

Paris is a deeply religious man who finds time to do some preaching while he's on the field.

"I have two goals right now," he said. "One is to be an All-Pro, the second is to expand my witness on the field. I talk to people on the line about letting God into their life. I have 20 games in which to witness in 1985. I have nobody particular that I've singled out, but that is one of my goals for the season—to expand my witness."

And what is the reaction of brutes like Richard Dent and Lyle Alzado to Paris' sermons?

"Some people are shocked," he said. "They don't expect that on the line of scrimmage. Some people get irritated and hit you. Others ignore you altogether. But once in awhile someone will say, 'Yeah, maybe you're right.'"

Paris has already checked a schedule and made a list of some of the outstanding ends that he will face in 1985. Among them are Chicago's Dent, Lyle Alzado of the Raiders, Jeff Bryant from the Seahawks, Art Still of the Chiefs and Don Smith of the Atlanta Falcons. But the best defensive lineman in football is not on the 49ers' schedule, Paris says.

The first year he was

in the league he heard rumors about Tampa Bay's Lee Roy Selmon. He was miffed when his fellow linemen voted Selmon to the Pro Bowl. The 49ers had not even played Tampa Bay that year. After facing Selmon for the first time in the 1983 season, Paris was convinced.

"There's no doubt that Lee Roy Selmon is the best I've ever played against," he said. "In practice, I've played against Fred Dean, who is probably in the same league, but I've never had to go against Fred in a game. Lee Roy is big, quick and strong. He's got a good arm-over. I would vote for him to be All-World."

In the 1984 Super Bowl season, a game against the Pittsburgh Steelers, which the 49ers lost, 20-17, was the turning point for Paris.

"It was probably good for us," he said. "After that, we knew we couldn't just show up at the stadium and walk away winners. We knew we had to pull together. It put us all back on earth."

Paris anticipates a successful professional career is still ahead of him and he gives thanks for the natural ability with which he was born.

"So far in my life and my football career I've been blessed," he said. "First of all, there is my size. I'm bigger than people say I should be. I'm an example of what God can do with life. I was able to come back from an injury after I thought I'd never play again. On top of that, I came to a Super Bowl team right out of college. You can't ask for much more than that."

for the playoffs with a torn knee ligament.

The Detroit Lions were the 49ers' opponent in the opening round of the NFC playoffs at Candlestick. San Francisco squeezed by the Lions, 24-23, when Eddie Murray missed a 43-yard field goal attempt with just seconds remaining. The next stop for San Francisco was RFK Stadium, where they would take on the 1983 Super Bowl Champion Washington Redskins for the NFC title.

The first half of the game proved to be a defensive battle. The only scoring came after Washington drove 64 yards and went ahead 7-0 on a four-yard run by John Riggins.

In the third quarter, Washington began to open things up. Joe Theismann directed the Redskins on a 36-yard touchdown drive. On their next possession, he threw a 70-yard scoring pass to Charlie Brown. At the end of the third quarter, Washington had a 21-0 lead.

Joe Montana likes exciting finishes. He earned the nickname "Comeback Kid" at Notre Dame for just that reason. He began another one against Washington by moving the 49ers 79 yards in nine plays. Early in the fourth quarter, he hit Mike Wilson with a five-yard pass to put San Francisco on the scoreboard, 21-7.

After Mosley missed a 41-yard field goal attempt, San Francisco took over on its own 24-yard line. On the first play from scrimmage, Montana hit Freddie Solomon with a 76-yard pass to put San Francisco right back in the game at 21-14. There was still nearly 10 minutes to play.

After the ensuing kickoff, the 49ers held the Redskins and took over at their own 47-yard line. San Francisco again scored quickly. It took the offense just four plays to go 53 yards for a touchdown. Montana was the difference, hitting on passes of 16 yards to Eason Ramson, 22 yards to Mike Wilson and 12 yards to Wilson again for the score.

The 49ers had scored 21 points in seven minutes to tie the game. The momentum was clearly with them. Their biggest enemy now was the clock and, as it turned out, the officials.

There was seven minutes to play after Washington returned the ensuing kickoff to its own 14-yard line. The Redskins used John Riggins and a ball control offense to march down the field. The big plays, however, were two penalties called against the 49er secondary.

With four minutes to play, and the Redskins facing a second and 10, Eric Wright was called for

pass interference on Art Monk. The call was questionable since it did not appear that Monk could have caught the ball anyway. The penalty gave the Redskins a first down and a 27-yard gain.

Three plays later, the Redskins had a third-and-five situation from the 13-yard line. A pass to Alvin Garrett was incomplete. It would have given the Redskins no choice but to try a field goal on fourth down.

However, Ronnie Lott was called for holding on the play. He was covering a man away from the ball and not involved with the pass. Washington had another first down.

The Redskins used three plays to run the clock down to 40 seconds before Mosley attempted his fifth field goal of the day. He already had missed four attempts. This one, from 25 yards, was good.

Super Bowl XIX put Roger Craig (33) into the national spotlight when he set a Super Bowl record with three touchdowns. He led the team in receptions in 1984 with 71 catches good for 675 yards. He also gained 649 yards rushing.

Tackle Keith Fahnhorst tries to relax prior to Super Bowl XVI against the Cincinnati Bengals. PAGE 151: Joe Montana almost turned down a Notre Dame football scholarship to play basketball at North Carolina State. Instead, he led Notre Dame to a National Championship in 1977 and the 49ers to two Super Bowl victories.

The 49ers had 36 seconds left after the ensuing kickoff. A desperate pass by Joe Montana was intercepted and San Francisco's Super Bowl dreams were over.

1984 The 49ers put together the most successful single season in NFL history in 1984. They won 15 games in the regular season and three in post-season play. Their 18-1 record, including a Super Bowl victory, left little doubt around the league that they were the best team in football.

The 49ers started the year off right in the 1984 college draft. Of the nine players chosen, six made the club. Among those who found a place on the roster were linebacker Todd Shell, tight end John Frank, guard Guy McIntyre, defensive tackle Michael Carter, linebacker/safety Jeff Fuller and running back Derrick Harmon.

San Francisco opened the season at Detroit. It

was a good omen. When the 49ers went to the Super Bowl in 1981, they opened the season at Detroit as well. But the Lions were motivated this time. They had been knocked out of the 1983 Super Bowl hunt in the first round of the playoffs by the 49ers.

At the half, San Francisco held a 14-13 lead. The Lions went ahead, 20-14, in the third quarter on a two-yard pass from quarterback Gary Danielson to James Jones. San Francisco came back with two Ray Wersching field goals and Wendell Tyler added a nine-yard run to even up the score at 27-27. With five minutes remaining, Joe Montana started a drive from his own 29-yard line. He worked the ball down to the Detroit 22, and Ray Wersching came on to kick the winning field goal with four seconds remaining.

In the second week of the season, San Francisco had a rematch with the Washington Redskins, runners-up in Super Bowl XVIII. It was the Redskins that prevented San Francisco from playing in the Super Bowl by beating the 49ers in the NFC Championship Game.

The 49ers started with a vengeance. They built up a 27-0 first-half lead before Joe Theismann could spell M-O-N-T-A-N-A. Tyler scored twice in the first quarter on runs of one and five yards. Clark caught a 15-yard touchdown pass from Montana. And Wersching added field goals of 19 and 46 yards.

In the second half the tide changed, but never enough to seriously put the game in doubt. The Redskins scored 14 unanswered points in the third quarter to bring them within 10 points at 27-17. But the 49ers cooly exchanged scores with Washington in the fourth period and walked away with a 37-31 victory.

Montana completed 24 passes for 381 yards, and Tyler gained 96 yards rushing against the Redskins.

The 49ers looked like they were in for an easy one in the third game of 1984 when they jumped out 17-0 against the New Orleans Saints. But then a snake got loose at Candlestick as Ken Stabler replaced Saints' starting quarterback Richard Todd in the second quarter. In one of his last games, "the Snake" rallied New Orleans to four straight scores, putting the Saints in front, 20-17, at the start of the fourth period. He threw touchdown passes of eight and 26 yards, and connected on 14 passes for 157 yards. Just two weeks later, Stabler retired from football.

In the last period, San Francisco took over. Matt Cavanaugh replaced an injured Joe Montana and

Ray Wersching 1977–

It's not easy being a placekicker. The typical kicker plays less than one minute per game, but often, it's his foot that provides the margin between victory and defeat.

Ray Wersching relishes that role with the San Francisco 49ers. His ability in the clutch is taken for granted. Entering the 1985 season, Wersching is second on the team's all-time scoring list with 689 points. That leaves him just 49 points behind Tommy Davis. His field goal accuracy percentage of .739 is far better than any kicker in team history. Bruce Gossett is next with a .641 percentage.

Wersching signed with the 49ers midway through the 1977 season after being released by the San Diego Chargers. He suffered through four dismal years with the 49ers before they won Super Bowl XVI in 1981. Wersching played a major role in the club's turnaround. He led the team in scoring for seven straight seasons from 1978 to 1984. In 1984, he was the leading scorer in the NFL with 131 points.

"I went through those 2-14 seasons and believe me they were no fun," Wersching said. "Actually, there was a lot of spirit on the team when I got here. There was a lot of older vets still around that made you feel comfortable. People like Cedrick Hardman and Jimmy Webb made it easy on newcomers. And it seemed like the 49ers were acquiring a lot of players at that time. The vets were friendly and that filtered down to the rookies, too. We just kept rolling along. Those losing years were no fun though."

Wersching made an immediate impact with the 49ers. In his first game with the club, he made good on a 50-yard field goal attempt against the

New York Giants. Just three weeks later, his 33-yard field goal in overtime beat the New Orleans Saints, 10-7.

Wersching was born in Mondsee, Austria, but grew up in Downey, California, where he became a Los Angeles Rams fan. That affinity quickly changed when Wersching joined the San Francisco 49ers. The intense rivalry between the two clubs helped alter his opinion.

"I was a Rams fan as a kid," Wersching said. "I dislike them a little bit now, but when I lived there I used to follow them closely."

Wersching is particularly delighted by a 33-31 win the 49ers scored over the Rams during the 1981 season. He kicked four field goals that day including the game-winning 37-yard field goal with two seconds to play.

"What happened was the Rams had just scored to go ahead," Wersching said. "They were jumping around thinking they had won the game. There was less than two minutes to play, but Joe (Montana) got hold of the ball and moved us into field goal range. Beating them that day was a pleasure because I'd grown up there."

Super Bowl XVI against the Cincinnati Bengals was another big game for Wersching. In the 49ers' first Super Bowl appearance, Wersching connected on all four of his field goal attempts and scored 14 of the team's 26 points.

His deliberate squib kicks also played an instrumental role in the game's outcome. The Bengals were unable to return any of his kickoffs for sizable gains. One squib kick was fumbled by Bengal return man Archie Griffin just before the first half ended. San Francisco recovered and Wersching kicked another field goal to give the 49ers a 20-0 lead at halftime. The Bengals never regained momentum.

In Super Bowl XIX against the Miami Dolphins, Wersching connected on his only field goal attempt from 27 yards. He added five extra points to give him a total of 22 points scored in his two Super Bowl games. He is ranked second on the Super Bowl scoring list behind Franco Harris, who has 24 points.

The kicker's job has become as much a mental chore as a physical one, Wersching says. Distractions can alter the kicker's timing or affect his confidence. Wersching relies on his holder to take care of the mechanical adjustments that must be made prior to a field goal attempt. As he trots onto the field before an attempt, he never looks at the goal posts. It is the holder's job to guide Wersching to the spot from which he will kick. Prior to the 1985 season, Joe Montana had been the holder, but Matt Cavanaugh has taken over the job.

Wersching says his reluctance to look up at the goal posts is not a conscious action.

"I do that because that's the way I've always done it," he said. "I try to relax as much as possible and just try to remember to keep my head down and follow through.

"Holding is a lot more important than people think. Joe's been great. He gives me a sense of security out there. He's been on the field and he knows the flow of the game. He's not nervous or anything.

"Joe's very fluid. The ball is always there. It gives me one less thing to worry about. All that stuff—the style and rhythm of the holder—is important and Joe does it good. I'm not distracted by anything.

"I'm just starting to work with Matt. I'm sure he'll be just as good."

A common ploy used by opposing coaches is to call a time out prior to a field goal attempt. The added seconds of anticipation are enough to break the concentration of some kickers. Wersching says he is not bothered by such tricks during the course of a game.

"Now it's to the point where I expect a time out," he said. "If they don't call one, it's likely to distract me."

Wersching believes the 49ers are just starting to come into their own as a champion. The team is loaded with talent, he says, and has a good nucleus of veterans.

"Playing together over the last couple years has helped us develop into a solid team," he said. "We are just starting to play our own game.

"I just want to contribute to the team as much as I can. The 49ers changed my career. They gave me a chance. I owe the 49ers. Anything it takes to pay them back and help them win I'm willing to do."

Roger Craig (33) at Super Bowl XIX

threw a 23-yard touchdown pass to Earl Cooper. Tyler picked up 82 yards rushing as the 49ers came out on top, 30-20.

The 49ers' next opponent was the Philadelphia Eagles. This was to be a test of the 49ers' offensive capability without Montana, who was still sidelined. Cavanaugh performed admirably, completing 17 of 34 passes for 252 yards and three touchdowns. Tyler gained 113 yards rushing as San Francisco defeated the Eagles, 21-9.

The 49ers beat Atlanta, 14-5, and the New York Giants, 31-10, before the Pittsburgh Steelers showed up at Candlestick to play football. The 49ers suffered their only defeat of the season against the Steelers, 20-17. Gary Anderson's 21-yard field goal with 1:42 to go proved to be the winning margin.

The 49ers got revenge on the Houston Oilers. They jumped off to a 10-0 lead after the first quarter on an 11-yard Montana pass to Russ Francis and Wersching's field goal. They upped that total to 17-7 at the half on a 26-yard pass from Montana to Tyler.

In all, San Francisco compiled 517 yards of offense as they defeated Houston, 34-21. Wendell Tyler had another 100-yard day, picking up 108 yards on 23 carries.

The highlight of a 35-year rivalry between the Rams and the 49ers was reached on Oct. 28, when the 49ers destroyed Los Angeles, 33-0. Montana completed 21 of 31 passes for 365 yards and three touchdowns. Roger Craig caught a touchdown pass of 64 yards and ran in another from the six.

San Francisco continued its winning streak, rolling up big scores against Cleveland, 41-7, New Orleans, 35-3, and Minnesota, 51-7. The 49ers ended the season five games in front of the second place Rams. Their offense scored 475 points, the most as a member of the NFL, and an average of nearly 30 points a game. On defense, they gave up a league-low 227 points, an average of 14 points per game. In four games the defense didn't allow a touchdown.

The 49ers' first opponent in the NFC playoffs was the New York Giants. Once again the defense prevented a touchdown as San Francisco beat the Giants, 21-10. New York's sole touchdown came on a 14-yard interception return by linebacker Harry Carson.

Montana completed 25 passes for 309 yards and three touchdowns. He also had three passes picked off by the Giants' tough defense. Dwight Clark was the receiving leader with nine catches for 112 yards and one touchdown.

The 49ers now had to prepare for the Chicago Bears, their opponent in the NFC Championship Game. It was the 49ers third appearance in the championship game in four years.

The week of the game, Chicago's unconventional defense was the subject of the media's attention. Many predicted that the Bears' All-Pro pass rushers, Richard Dent and Dan Hampton, would chase Montana out of Candlestick Park.

The largest crowd in Candlestick history, a screaming throng of 61,050, jammed into the stadium. But it wasn't the Bears' defense that was overwhelming, it was the 49ers' pass rushers. The defense sacked Chicago quarterback Steve Fuller nine times, intercepted one of his passes and allowed just 83 yards passing. Walter Payton, the NFL's all-time leading rusher, was held to a harmless 92 yards. The defense prevented a touchdown for the second week in a row, shutting out the Bears, 23-0.

The 49ers scored just six points in the first half on field goals of 21 and 22 yards. In the second half, Montana tossed a 10-yard scoring pass to Freddie Solomon and Tyler ran nine yards for another touchdown to round out the 49ers' scoring.

The Miami Dolphins were all that stood in the way of the San Francisco 49ers' second Super Bowl championship. They were a formidable opponent. They finished the season with a 14-2 record. Quarterback Dan Marino seemed to set new passing records every time he stepped onto the field. The pregame hype centered on Marino, who was said to be unstoppable. In the AFC Championship Game against the Pittsburgh Steelers, Marino completed 21 passes for 421 yards and four touchdowns. The Steelers, the only team to beat San Francisco in the regular season, were picking the Dolphins to win.

San Francisco had the unique advantage of playing the game in its backyard at nearby Stanford University. The overwhelming demand for tickets among 49er fans drove the price of 50-yard-line seats from scalpers above $1,000. A capacity crowd of 84,059 was on hand to witness the event.

The 49ers won the coin toss by President Ronald Reagan but were unable to move the ball on their first possession. Kicker Uwe Von Schamann started the scoring for the Dolphins when he split the uprights with a 37-yard field goal.

San Francisco took the kickoff and drove 78 yards. Montana completed all four of his passes for 50 yards, including a 33-yard touchdown pass to Carl Monroe that put San Francisco back in front, 7-3.

When he regained the football, Marino showed millions of television viewers why he was considered the premier quarterback in the game. He completed all five of his pass attempts and the Dolphins scored in just six plays to go in front, 10-7. The pregame hype appeared to be correct. Marino looked superb.

Then the 49ers scrapped their three-man defensive line and went to a nickel defense with four down linemen. The defensive line had a field day after that. Dwaine Board, Fred Dean and Gary "Big Hands" Johnson were on top of Marino the rest of the afternoon. He was sacked four times, threw two interceptions and hurried countless passes. Miami didn't score another touchdown.

Meanwhile, Roger Craig was busy crossing the goal line three times as the 49ers routed Miami, 38-16. He scored on an eight-yard pass from Montana, a 16-yard pass and a two-yard run. Craig caught eight passes in all for 82 yards.

Montana was putting on quite a show himself and was named the game's most valuable player. He set Super Bowl records for passing, with 331 yards on 24 completions, and rushing by a quarterback, with 59 yards. It marked the second time he had been honored as the Super Bowl MVP, a distinction held by only two other players, Green Bay's Bart Starr and Pittsburgh's Terry Bradshaw. Bradshaw led the Steelers to four Super Bowl victories. Montana could well do the same.

RECORDS

The 49ers' all-time records are constantly evolving and changing. The records and club career leaders listed in this section, include only those statistics compiled since 1950, when the 49ers joined the National Football League. Team leaders in catagories such as passing, rushing and receiving are provided for the years 1946-1949, however. In addition, statistics compiled since the start of the 1985 season are not included.

A complete list of the team's draft choices helps chronicle the team's growth during its 40 years of operation. The all-time roster will keep readers abreast of the years each player was with the club and the college which he attended.

49ERS' ALL-TIME NFL DRAFT

1950
(Drafted Alternately 9-10)
1. **NOMELLINI, LEO**
T, 6-3, 260, Minnesota
2. **CAMPORA, DON**
T, 6-3, 270, Pacific
3. **COLLINS, RAY**
T, 6-0, 230, LSU
4. **BAILEY, MORRIS**
E, 6-2, 215, Texas Christian
5. **KANE, HARRY**
C, 6-1, 215, Pacific
6. **VAN POOL, DON**
E, 6-3, 225, Oklahoma
7. **BERRY, LINDY**
B, 6-0, 180, Texas Christian
8. **WILLIAMS, ELLERY**
E, 6-2, 200, Santa Clara
9. **ZINACH, PETE**
B, 6-0, 190, West Virginia
10. **CELERI, BOB**
B, 5-10, 175, California
11. **DOW, HARLEY**
T, 6-2, 220, San Jose State
12. **BURKE, DON**
B, 6-0, 235, Southern Cal
13. **CECCONI, LOU**
B, 5-8, 171, Pittsburgh
14. **PAYNE, TOM**
E, 6-2, 200, Santa Clara
15. **GRAMPSEY, LEO**
E, 6-1, 195, St. Bonaventure
16. **SHAW, CHARLEY**
G, 6-3, 195, Oklahoma A&M
17. **VAN METER, CLIFF**
B, 6-1, 198, Tulane
18. **GENITO, RALPH**
B, 5-11, 180, Kentucky
19. **KLEIN, FORREST**
G, 6-0, 205, California
20. **NIX, JACK**
E, 6-2, 205, Southern Cal
21. **ALKER, GUERIN**
C, 6-1, 207, Loyola
†22. **WILSON, BILLY**
E, 6-3, 198, San Jose State
23. **WILLIAMS, JIM**
E, 6-2, 185, Rice
24. **WYMAN, BILL**
T, 6-2, 220, Rice
25. **DUNN, BOB**
G, 6-2, 200, Dayton
26. **POWERS, JIM**
B, 6-0, 183, Southern Cal
27. **JOHNSON, KEN**
G, 6-3, 200, Pacific
28. **HALL, CHARLEY**
B, 6-1, 190, Arizona
29. **WHELAN, BOB**
B, 5-11, 175, Boston U.
30. **STILLWELL, BOB**
E, 6-0, 200, Southern Cal

1951
(Drafted Alternately 2-3)
1. **TITTLE, Y.A.**
QB, 6-0, 190, LSU
2. **SCHABARUM, PETE**
HB, 5-11, 185, California
3. **MIXON, BILL**
HB, 5-11, 197, Georgia
4. **Choice To Cleveland**
5. **STEERE, DICK**
T, 6-3, 225, Drake
6. **STRICKLAND, BISHOP**
HB, 5-10, 195, Southern Cal
7. **FORBES, DICK**
E, 6-2, 215, St. Ambrose
8. **ARENAS, JOE**
HB, 5-11, 180, Omaha
9. **VAN ALSTYNE, BRUCE**
E, 6-3, 205, Stanford
10. **FEHER, NICK**
G, 6-0, 220, Georgia
11. **JESSUP, BILL**
E, 6-1, 195, Southern Cal
12. **MONACHINO, JIM**
HB, 5-10, 190, California
13. **MARVIN, DICK**
E, 6-3, 190, Georgia Tech
14. **BERRY, REX**
B, 5-11, 180, Brigham Young
15. **SPARKS, DAVE**
G, 6-1, 228, South Carolina
16. **WHITE, BOB**
B, 5-11, 174, Stanford
17. **MICHALIK, ART**
G, 6-2, 225, St. Ambrose
18. **MURPHY, JIM**
T, 6-3, 240, Xavier
19. **PHILLIPS, JOHN**
B, 6-0, 178, Mississippi State
20. **TATE, AL**
T, 5-11, 210, Illinois
21. **BROWN, HARDY**
B, 6-0, 195, Tulsa

1952
(Drafted Alternately 8-9)
22. **WINSLOW, DWIGHT**
B, 6-3, 205, Boise J.C.
23. **BRUNSWALD, WALLY**
HB, 6-0, 170, Gustavus Adolphus
24. **KINSFORD, TOM**
B, 5-11, 180, Montana
25. **PETERSON, MIKE**
E, 6-1, 201, Denver
26. **CARPENTER, KEITH**
T, 6-3, 226, San Jose State
27. **LUNG, RAY**
G, 5-9, 209, Oregon
28. **ROHAN, JACK**
HB, 6-0, 185, Loras College
29. **GARNETT, S.P.**
T, 6-3, 215, Kansas
30. **FASKE, JERRY**
HB, 5-9, 190, Iowa

1952
(Drafted Alternately 8-9)
1. **McELHENNY, HUGH**
HB, 6-1, 198, Washington
2. **TONEFF, BOB**
T, 6-2, 252, Notre Dame
3. **TIDWELL, BILLY**
HB, 5-9, 178, Texas A&M
4. **CAMPBELL, MARION**
T, 6-3, 245, Georgia
5. **O'DONAHUE, PAT**
E, 6-1, 205, Wisconsin
6. **BEASLEY, JIM**
C, 6-4, 215, Tulsa
7. **ROBISON, DON**
B, 6-1, 190, California
8. **SMITH, JERRY**
T, 6-1, 230, Wisconsin
9. **CHRISTIAN, GLEN**
HB, 5-10, 180, Idaho
10. **WEST, CARL**
B, 6-2, 214, Mississippi
11. **KIMMEL, J.D.**
T, 6-4, 245, Army–Houston
12. **SNYDER, FRED**
E, 6-1, 180, Loyola
13. **YEAGER, RUDY**
T, 6-3, 210, LSU
14. **SIMONS, FRANK**
E, 6-3, 195, Nebraska
15. **NORMAN, HALDO**
E, 6-3, 200, Gustavus Adolphus

16. **MYERS, BOB**
B, 6-2, 185, Stanford
17. **BALDOCK, AL**
E, 6-2, 200, Southern Cal
18. **CAREY, BILL**
E, 6-4, 219, Michigan State
19. **TALARICO, SAM**
T, 6-0, 207, Indiana
20. **YATES, JESS**
E, 6-2, 190, LSU
21. **OFFIELD, GENE**
E, 5-11, 195, Hardin-Simmons
22. **COZAD, JIM**
T, 6-2, 215, Santa Clara
23. **GLAZIER, BILL**
E, 6-1, 189, Arizona
24. **KRUEGER, RALPH**
T, 6-3, 225, California
25. **LAUGHLIN, HENRY**
B, 6-1, 200, Kansas
26. **KANE, DICK**
G, 6-3, 215, Cincinnati
27. **SCHAFF, WALDO**
T, 6-3, 210, Oklahoma A&M
28. **PALUMBO, JOE**
G, 5-10½, 205, Virginia
29. **MOSHER, CHUCK**
E, 6-3, 200, Colorado
30. **PATRICK, DICK**
C, 6-2, 215, Oregon

1953
(Drafted Alternately 9-8-7)
1. **(A) Bonus Choice:
BABCOCK, HARRY**
E, 6-2, 196, Georgia
1. **(B) STOLHANDSKE, TOM**
E, 6-2, 210, Texas
2. **MORRIS, GEORGE**
C, 6-3, 235, Georgia Tech
3. **ST. CLAIR, BOB**
T, 6-7, 250, Tulsa–USF
4. **FULLERTON, ED**
B, 6-0, 205, Maryland
5. **MILLER, HAL**
T, 6-4, 249, Georgia Tech
6. **Choice to Chicago Bears**
7. **CARR, PAUL**
B, 6-0, 205, Houston
8. **HOGLAND, DOUG**
T, 6-3, 225, Oregon State
9. **LEDYARD, HAL**
QB, 6-0½, 185, Chattanooga

† Future Arrival (Redshirt)

10. **BROWN, PETE**
G, 6-2, 217, Georgia Tech
11. **CHARLTON, AL**
B, 5-11, 185, Washington State
12. **LEACH, CARSON**
G, 5-10, 218, Duke
13. **EARLEY, BILL**
B, 6-1, 198, Washington
14. **FLETCHER, TOM**
B, 6-0, 195, St. Mary's & Arizona State
15. **GENTHNER, CHARLEY**
T, 6-2, 225, Texas
16. **DURIG, FRED**
B, 6-1, 200, Bowling Green
17. **LATHAM, HUGH**
T, 6-3, 225, San Diego State
18. **WACHOLZ, STAN**
E, 6-3½, 200, San Jose State
19. **DuCLOS, KING**
E, 6-3, 218, Texas Western
20. **HUIZINGA, RAY**
T, 6-5, 230, Northwestern
21. **BAHNSEN, KEN**
B, 5-10, 200, North Texas State
22. **ROBBINS, LAVERNE**
G, 5-11½, 225, Midwestern
23. **HUNT, TRAVIS**
T, 6-1, 220, Alabama
24. **MORGAN, ED**
B, 6-1, 195, Tennessee
25. **STOCKERT, ERNIE**
E, 6-6, 220, UCLA
26. **COOPER, HARLEY**
B, 6-1, 195, Arizona State
27. **McCLEOD, RALPH**
E, 6-4, 205, LSU
28. **NOVIKOFF, TOM**
B, 6-0, 195, Oregon
29. **STILLWELL, DON**
E, 6-1, 180, Southern Cal
30. **No pick as result of BONUS CHOICE**

1954
(Drafted 10th)
1. **FALONEY, BERNIE**
QB, 6-1, 190, Maryland
2. **RUCKA, LEO**
G, 6-3, 225, Omaha
3. **KORCHECK, STEVE**
C, 6-1, 205, George Washington
4. **BOXHOLD, CHARLIE**
HB, 5-11, 186, Maryland
5. **MINCEVICH, FRANK**
G, 6-2, 245, South Carolina
6. **SAGELY, FLOYD**
E, 6-1, 187, Arkansas
7. **YOUNGELMAN, SID**
T, 6-3, 247, Alabama
8. **Choice to Cleveland**
9. **CONNOLLY, TED**
G, 6-3, 230, Santa Clara—Tulsa
10. **GOSS, DON**
T, 6-5, 260, SMU
11. **SKOCKO, JOHN**
E, 6-3, 220, Southern Cal
12. **EASTERWOOD, HAL**
C, 6-0, 195, Mississippi State
13. **WILLIAMS, MORGAN**
G, 6-1½, 195, Texas Christian

14. **WILLIAMS, SAM**
HB, 6-1, 190, California
15. **PALUMBO, SAM**
G, 6-2, 220, Notre Dame
16. **FIVEASH, BOBBY**
HB, 5-11, 185, Florida State
17. **KAUTZ, KARL**
T, 6-2, 245, Texas Tech
18. **KAY, MORRIS**
E, 6-2, 204, Kansas
19. **EDMISTON, BOB**
T, 6-2, 255, Temple–Michigan State
20. **DiPIETRO, FRANK**
B, 6-1, 197, Georgia
21. **ALSUP, HOWARD**
T, 6-4, 230, Middle Tennessee State
22. **REYNOLDS, RALPH**
B, 6-0, 186, North Texas State
23. **FENSTEMAKER, LEROY**
QB, 6-2, 205, Rice
24. **DANIELS, JERRY**
T, 6-1, 230, Tennessee Tech
25. **PLATT, JOHN**
FB, 6-2, 215, Elon–Kentucky
26. **BELLO, PETE**
C, 6-0, 205, Pasadena City College
27. **BAKER, ED**
G, 6-1½, 225, Omaha
28. **GARBRECHT, BOB**
FB, 6-1, 205, Rice
29. **DUNN, BILL**
B, 6-1, 200, Murray State–Washington (Missouri)
30. **FOLKS, DON**
E, 6-2, 210, Houston

1955
(Drafted Alternately 8-9)
1. **MOEGLE, DICK**
HB, 6-0, 180, Rice
2. **MORZE, FRANK**
T, 6-4, 245, Boston College
3. **HARDY, CARROLL**
HB, 6-0, 185, Colorado
4. **HAZELTINE, MATT**
C, 6-2, 201, California
5. **KRAEMER, ELDRED**
T, 6-3, 235, Pittsburgh
6. **LUNA, BOBBY**
HB, 5-11, 183, Alabama
7. **DEAN, JOHN**
QB, 6-1, 195, VPI
† 8. **MEYERS, FRED**
QB, 6-2, 205, Oklahoma
† 9. **PREZIOSIO, FRED**
QB, 6-2, 245, Purdue
10. **ASHBACHER, RON**
E, 6-3, 220, Oregon State
11. **RATELLA, RUDY**
E, 6-3½, 215, Omaha
†12. **PALATELLA, LOU**
T, 6-2, 230, Pittsburgh
13. **GASKELL, RICHIE**
E, 6-2, 195, George Washington
14. **McKEITHAN, NICK**
HB, 6-1, 195, Duke
15. **HESS, BURDETTE**
G, 6-0, 220, Idaho

16. **HALL, JIM**
E, 6-2, 195, Auburn
17. **NEWTON, BOB**
G, 6-2, 220, San Diego State
18. **PHEISTER, RON**
E, 6-2, 210, Oregon
19. **GARZOLI, JOHN**
T, 6-7, 265, California
20. **DYER, GLEN**
QB, 6-5, 200, Texas
21. **MADEROS, GEORGE**
E, 6-1, 195, Chico State
22. **VANN, PETE**
QB, 6-1, 189, Army
†23. **GUNNARI, TOM**
T, 6-2, 220, Washington State
24. **HEASTON, BOB**
G, 6-2, 222, Cal Poly–SLO
25. **WADE, DEWEY**
E, 6-1, 225, Kansas State
26. **KERR, JOHNNY**
E, 6-0, 170, Purdue
†27. **SHOCKEY, DICK**
QB, 6-3, 210, Marquette
28. **SANDERS, DON**
HB, 6-0, 185, Stanford
†29. **KNIEDINGER, OTTO**
T, 6-2, 230, Penn State
†30. **GONGOLA, BOB**
QB, 6-3, 180, Illinois

1956
(Drafted Alternately 1-2)
1. **MORRALL, EARL**
QB, 6-1, 190, Michigan State
2. **BOSLEY, BRUCE**
T, 6-2, 240, West Virginia
3. **HERCHMAN, BILL**
T, 6-2, 249, Texas Tech
4. **PAJACZKOWSKI, FRANK**
HB, 6-0, 187, Richmond
5. **Choice to Los Angeles**
6. **SARDISCO, TONY**
G-LB, 6-2, 210, Tulane
† 7. **BARNES, LARRY**
FB, 6-1, 215, Colorado A&M
8. **SMITH, CHARLES**
E, 6-2, 200, Abilene Christian
9. **COX, JIM**
E, 6-3, 190, Cal Poly–SLO
10. **ZALESKI, JERRY**
HB, 5-10, 195, Colorado A&M
11. **PELL, STEWART**
T, 6-4, 225, North Carolina
12. **SWEDBERG, ROGER**
TE, 6-1, 220, Iowa
13. **MOODY, RALPH**
HB, 6-0, 195, Kansas
†14. **OWENS, R.C.**
E, 6-3, 205, College of Idaho
15. **(A) HENDERSON, REED**
G-T, 6-2, 235, Utah State
15. **(B) BOYD, GENE (Choice from Pittsburgh)**
HB, 6-0, 200, Abilene Christian
16. **HERRING, GEORGE**
QB, 6-3, 200, Mississippi Southern
17. **WEIS, RICHARD**
T, 6-1, 230, Mississippi
†18. **YELVERTON, BILLY**
TE, 6-4, 215, Mississippi

19. **ARRIGONI, PETE**
HB, 6-0, 185, Arizona
20. **SCARBROUGH, BOB**
C-G, 6-1, 210, Auburn
21. **JOYNER, L.C.**
HB-E, 6-1, 185, Contra Costa J.C.
22. **WESSMAN, CLARENCE**
E, 6-3, 235, San Jose State
23. **MONROE, MIKE**
HB, 6-1, 205, Washington
24. **WALLACE, ED**
G, 6-3, 260, San Diego J.C.
25. **GOAD, PAUL**
HB, 6-0, 200, Abilene Christian
26. **LOUDD, ROMMIE**
E, 6-0, 215, UCLA
27. **GUSTAFSON, JERRY**
QB, 6-2, 190, Stanford
†28. **DREW, JERRY**
FB, 5-10, 195, California
29. **BENSON, DEAN**
E, 6-3, 195, Willamette
†30. **MITCHELL, BOB**
G-t, 6-0, 204, Puget Sound

1957
(Drafted 2nd)
1. **BRODIE, JOHN**
QB, 6-1, 195, Stanford
2. **WOODSON, ABE**
HB, 5-11, 188, Illinois
3. **Choice to Los Angeles**
4. **(A) RIDLON, JIM**
HB, 6-1, 195, Syracuse
4. **(B) SANDUSKY, MIKE (Choice from Chicago Cardinals)**
G, 5-11, 228, Maryland
5. **RUBKE, KARL**
C, 6-4, 235, Southern Cal
6. **(A) HUNTER, JIM**
HB, 6-0, 195, Missouri
6. **(B) RHODES, BILL (Choice from Philadelphia)**
HB, 6-0, 200, Western State
† 7. **DUGAN, FRED**
E, 6-3, 195, Dayton
8. **PITTS, ERNIE**
E, 6-2, 190, Denver
† 9. **BRUECKMAN, CHARLES**
C-LB, 6-2, 218, Pittsburgh
†10. **HURST, JERRY**
T, 6-7, 240, Middle Tennessee
†11. **DAVIS, TOM**
HB, 6-2, 205, LSU
†12. **SINGTON, FRED**
T-G, 6-1, 225, Alabama
13. **MACKEY, CHARLES**
E, 6-4, 190, Arizona State
14. **WARZEKA, RON**
T, 6-3, 235, Montana State
†15. **KAISER, EARL**
HB, 6-0, 190, Houston
16. **KRISTOPAITIS, VIC**
FB, 6-2, 205, Dayton
17. **KUHN, DAVE**
C-LB, 6-1, 220, Kentucky
†18. **GUY, RICHARD**
G, 6-3, 225, Ohio State
19. **BABB, GENE**
FB, 6-2, 210, Austin

† Future Arrival (Redshirt)

20. **DeLOACH, SID**
G, 6-1, 220, Duke
21. **WILCOX, FRED**
HB, 6-1, 185, Tulane
22. **TRIPP, PAUL**
T, 6-3, 240, Idaho State
23. **THOMAS, JOHN**
E, 6-5, 215, Pacific
24. **LADNER, JOHN**
E, 6-2, 205, Wake Forest
25. **MEYER, RAY**
FB, 5-11, 210, Lamar Tech
†26. **TOPPING, TOM**
T-G, 6-2, 215, Duke
27. **VICIC, DON**
FB, 6-1, 210, Ohio State
28. **CURTIS, BILL**
HB, 6-3, 180, TCU
29. **HALLBECK, VERN**
LB, 6-2, 213, TCU
30. **PARKS, GEORGE**
QB, 6-2, 205, Lamar Tech

1958
(Drafted Alternately 8-9)
1. (A) **PACE, JIM**
(Choice from Pittsburgh)
HB, 6-0, 195, Michigan
1. (B) **KRUEGER, CHARLES**
T, 6-4, 230, Texas A&M
† 2. **NEWMAN, BOB**
QB, 6-2, 190, Washington State
3. **HOPPE, BOB**
HB, 6-0, 190, Auburn
4. **VARONE, JOHN**
HB, 5-11, 190, Miami
5. **ATKINS, BILL**
HB, 6-1, 200, Auburn
6. **SCHMIDT, HENRY**
T, 6-4, Trinity College
7. **Choice traded to Detroit**
8. (A) **MILLS, RON**
HB, 6-1, 180, West TexasState
† 8. (B) **BURTON, LEON**
(Choice from Chicago Cardinals)
HB, 5-9, 170, Arizona State
9. **TROUTMAN, GEORGE**
C, 6-4, 260, Capitol (Ohio)
†10. **HECKMAN, VEL**
T, 6-0, 230, Florida
†11. **WHARTON, ROBERT**
T, 6-2, 238, Houston
12. **WILLIAMS, PETE**
T, 6-1, 225, Lehigh
13. (A) **DUKES, HAROLD**
E, 6-2, 225, Michigan State
13. (B) **YORE, JAMES**
(Choice from Pittsburgh)
FB, 6-2, 225, Indiana
14. **FIELDS, MAX**
HB, 5-10, 185, Whittier College
15. **Choice traded to Detroit**
16. **SHIRKEY, GEORGE**
T, 6-4, 250, Stephen F. Austin
17. **WHITTENBORN, JOHN**
T, 6-2, 238, SE Missouri St.
18. **MORRIS, DENNIT**
G-LB, 6-1, 230, Oklahoma
19. **MUSHATT, RANNIE**
G, 6-4, 244, Grambling

20. **MERTENS, JERRY**
E, 6-0, 185, Drake
21. **CHRISTIAN, DON**
HB, 6-0, 190, Arkansas
22. **HARTMAN, BRUCE**
T, 6-0, 245, Luther College
23. **FIELDS, LARRY**
HB, 6-0, 200, Utah
†24. **MACKEY, DEE**
E, 6-5, 227, E. Texas St.
25. **KAUZMAREK, BILL**
C, 6-0, 225, SW Missouri St.
†26. **HILL, HILLARD**
E, 6-1, 188, Southern Cal
27. **WITUCKI, BOB**
E, 6-3, 225, Notre Dame
28. **WARREN, GARLAND**
C, 6-1, 225, No. Texas St.
29. **HODGES, HERMAN**
HB, 6-2, 210, Sam Houston
†30. **STAHURA, TED**
T, 6-0, 250, Pittsburgh State

1959
(Drafted 6th)
1. (A) **BAKER, DAVE**
HB, 6-0, 190, Oklahoma
1. (B) **JAMES, DAN**
(Choice from Pittsburgh)
C, 6-2, 250, Ohio State
2. **HARRISON, BOB**
LB, 6-2, 227, Oklahoma
3. **DOVE, EDDIE**
HB, 6-2, 183, Colorado
4. **CLARK, MONTE**
DT, 6-6, 260, Southern Cal
5. **GEREMIA, FRANK**
T, 6-3, 245, Notre Dame
6. **BAVARO, WALLY**
T, 6-4, 245, Holy Cross
† 7. (A) **COLCHICO, DAN**
E, 6-4, 225, San Jose State
7. (B) **ROGERS, DON**
(Choice from Chicago Cardinals)
LB, 6-2, 245, South Carolina
8. **AKIN, LEWIS**
E, 6-4, 210, Vanderbilt
9. **GREEN, ROBERT**
HB, 5-11, 175, Florida
10. **NAGURSKI, BRONKO**
T, 6-2, 225, Notre Dame
11. **HAYS, JACK**
HB, 6-2, 190, Trinity College
12. **KORUTZ, BILL**
C, 6-2, 250, Dayton
13. **LOPASKY, BILL**
G, 6-2, 235, West Virginia
14. **DUKES, MICHAEL**
FB-LB, 6-3, 218, Clemson
15. **BELLAND, JOE**
HB, 5-10, 182, Arizona State
16. **COOK, BOB**
HB, 6-3, 185, Idaho State
17. **JURCZAK, JEROME**
C, 6-2½, 220, St. Benedict's
18. **COWLEY, JACK**
T, 6-2, 210, Trinity College
†19. **OSBORNE, TOM**
HB, 6-3, 195, Hastings (Nebraska)
†20. **DEESE, TOBY**
T, 5-10, 185, Georgia Tech

21. **CARR, LUTHER**
HB, 5-10, 185, Washington
22. **McQUEEN, BURNIO**
E, 6-3, 200, North Carolina A&T
23. **DOLLAHAN, BRUCE**
T, 6-3, 225, Illinois
24. **CHUDY, CRAIG**
E, 6-3, 200, UCLA
†25. **GEE, ROY**
G, 6-2, 200, Trinity College
26. **YOUNG, ED**
E, 6-2, 215, Louisville
27. **SEMENKO, MEL**
T, 6-2, 200, Colorado
28. **McCLUSKEY, MIKE**
HB, 6-0, 185, Washington
29. **BOLTON, JACK**
T, 6-3, 235, Puget Sound
30. **CARTER, LOWELL**
E-LB, 6-3, 230, Denver

1960
(Drafted Alternately 10-11)
1. **STICKLES, MONTY**
E, 6-3, 232, Notre Dame
† 2. (A) **KAMMERER, CARL**
LB, 6-3, 237, Pacific
2. (B) **MAGAC, MIKE**
(Choice from Washington)
G, 6-2, 225, Missouri
3. **BREEDLOVE, ROD**
C-LB, 6-2, 215, Maryland
4. **NORTON, RAY**
HB, 6-2, 184, San Jose State
5. **ROHDE, LEN**
T, 6-4, 235, Utah State
6. **MURCHISON, OLA**
E, 6-3, 211, Pacific
7. **WATERS, BOB**
QB, 6-2, 188, Presbyterian
8. (A) **MATHIS, BILL**
(Choice from Washington)
HB, 6-1, 200, Clemson
6. (B) **FUGLER, MAX**
C-LB, 6-2, 224, LSU
9. **WASDEN, BOB**
C-LB, 6-2, 220, Auburn
10. **BRANCH, MEL**
E, 6-2, 220, LSU
11. (A) **PITTS, ED**
(Choice from Pittsburgh)
T, 6-2, 230, South Carolina
†11. (B) **HANSEN, ERNEST**
C, 6-4, 250, Arizona State
12. **WILLIAMS, JIM**
T, 6-1, 255, North Carolina College
†13. **HINSHAW, DEAN**
T, 6-6, 240, Idaho State
14. **CAMPBELL, GARY**
QB, 6-0, 199, Whittier
15. **DOWDLE, MIKE**
FB-LB, 6-4, 225, Texas
16. **HEINEKE, JIM**
TB, 6-2, 230, Wisconsin
17. **GONSOULIN, AUSTIN**
HB, 6-3, 205, Baylor
18. **ROBINSON, CARL**
T, 6-5, 245, South Carolina State
19. **PATE, BOBBY**
HB, 6-0, 175, Presbyterian

20. **WOODWARD, JIM**
T, 6-5, 228, Lamar Tech

1961
1. (A) **JOHNSON, JIM**
(Choice from Pittsburgh)
HB, 6-2, 184, UCLA
1. (B) **CASEY, BERNIE**
(Choice from Baltimore)
FB, 6-4, 215, Bowling Green
1. (C) **KILMER, BILL**
QB, 6-0, 190, UCLA
2. **LAKES, ROLAND**
C-T, 6-4, 245, Wichita
3. **COOPER, BILL**
FB, 6-2, 215, Muskingum
4. (A) **THOMAS, AARON**
(Choice from Pittsburgh)
E, 6-3, 208, Oregon
4. (B) **MESSER, DALE**
HB, 5-10, 175, Fresno
5. (A) **McCREARY, BOB**
T, 6-5, 250, Wake Forest
† 5. (B) **MILLER, CLARK**
(Choice from Dallas)
T, 6-5, 245, Utah State
† 6. **McCLELLAN, MIKE**
HB, 6-0, 185, Oklahoma
7. **PURDIN, RAY**
HB, 6-0, 185, Northwestern
8. **PLUMLEY, NEILL**
T, 6-6, 240, Oregon State
† 9. (A) **DONOHUE, LEON**
(Choice from Pittsburgh)
T, 6-4, 245, San Jose State
9. (B) **NINO, EVERISTO**
T, 6-4, 243, E. Texas State
10. **HYNES, PAUL**
HB, 6-0, 210, Louisiana Tech
11. **PARRILLI, TONY**
LB, 6-1, 220, Illinois
†12. **COFFEY, DON**
E, 6-2, 190, Memphis State
12. (A) **HACKLER, TOMMY**
(Choice from Pittsburgh)
E, 6-4, 217, Tennessee
†13. (B) **FINCKE, JULIUS**
T, 6-3, 260, McNeess State
14. **WORRELL, BILL**
T, 6-2, 240, Georgia
†15. **SAMS, BOB**
T, 6-2, 250, Central State (Oklahoma)
16. **FULLER, CHARLIE**
HB, 5-11, 170, San Francisco State
17. **JEWELL, TOM**
G, 6-1, 240, Idaho State
†18. **McFARLAND, KAY**
E-HB, 6-2, 180, Colorado State
19. **SIMPSON, TOM**
C-OT, 6-3, 245, Davidson
20. **PEERY, JERRY**
G-DT, 6-3, 245, Central State (Oklahoma)

1962
(Drafted 8th)
1. **ALWORTH, LANCE**
HB, 6-0, 180, Arkansas
2. **PINE, ED**
LB, 6-4, 230, Utah

3. **ADAMS, BILLY RAY**
FB, 6-2, 215, Mississippi

† 4. **(A) DEAN, FLOYD**
LB, 6-4, 245, Florida

† 4. **(B) SIEMINSKI, CHARLIE**
(Choice from Dallas)
DT, 6-4, 245, Penn State

5. **(A) WOODS, TED**
(Choice from St. Louis
Cardinals)
HB, 6-1, 194, Colorado

† 5. **(B) LIND, MIKE**
FB, 6-2, 215, Notre Dame

6. **(A) LUHNOW, KEITH**
(Choice from Washington)
FB, 6-3, 220, Santa Ana J.C.

6. **(B) BROWN, JERRY**
(Choice from Pittsburgh)
G, 6-1, 230, Mississippi

6. **(C) WINTER, BILL**
G, 6-1, 235, West Virginia

7. **BURRELL, JOHN**
E, 6-3, 190, Rice

8. **VOLLENWEIDER, JAMES**
HB-FB, 6-1, 210, Miami (Fla.)

9. **ROBERTS, JIM**
T, 6-3, 240, Mississippi

10. **COUSTILLAC, REGIS**
C, 6-2, 224, Pittsburgh

11. **JEPSON, LARRY**
C, 6-5, 230, Furman

12. **McPIKE, MILTON**
E, 6-2, 225, Kirksville
Teachers

13. **PIEROVICH, GEORGE**
LB-FB, 6-2, 225, California

14. **EASTERLY, DICK**
DB, 5-11, 185, Syracuse

15. **OSBORNE, RAY**
T, 6-6, 235, Mississippi State

16. **FRANK, RON**
T, 6-6, 232, So. Dakota State

17. **FOLTZ, WALLY**
E, 6-3, 218, De Pauw

18. **BROWN, GARY**
T, 6-2, 239, Illinois

19. **BURTON, BOB**
T, 6-2, 250, Murray State

20. **McFARLAND, RODGER**
DB, 6-1, 183, Kansas

1963
(Drafted Alternately 8-7)

1. **ALEXANDER KERMIT**
HB, 5-11, 186, UCLA

2. **ROCK, WALTER**
OT-DT, 6-5, 240, Maryland

3. **LISBON, DON**
HB, 6-0, 190, Bowling Green

4. **Choice to Chicago**

† 4. **(A) ROSDAHL, HARRISON**
(Choice from Philadelphia)
G, 6-4, 245, Penn State

4. **(B) CAMPBELL, HUGH**
(Choice from Washington)
E, 6-1, 184, Washington State

† 5. **(A) BURKE, VERN**
E, 6-4½, 201, Oregon

† 5. **(B) PILOT, JIM**
(Choice from Pittsburgh)
FB, 6-1, 205, New Mexico
State

5. **(C) MOELLER, GARY**
(Choice from Chicago)
LB, 6-1, 224, Ohio State

6. **EMERICK, PAT**
LG, 6-2, 238, Western
Michigan

7. **DeCOURLEY, ERNEST**
DT, 6-6, 250, Moorehead
State

† 8. **LOCKE, ROGER**
E, 6-2, 185, Arizona State

† 9. **MACZUZAK, JOHN**
T, 6-5, 245, Pittsburgh

10. **LOPOUR, DICK**
HB, 6-2, 214, Huron

11. **SHAFER, STEVE**
QB, 6-0, 185, Utah State

12. **DENTON, ROBERT**
T, 6-2, 240, Mississippi State

13. **SHULTZ, DICK**
T, 6-3, 240, Ohio University

14. **TOBIN, BILL**
HB, 5-11, 210, Missouri

†15. **ROSS, OLLIE**
FB, 6-0, 215, West Texas
State

16. **BOGDALEK, JIM**
DT, 6-4, 245, Toledo

17. **REED, KEN**
G, 6-0, 230, Tulsa

†18. **SELLERS, JOHN**
T, 6-2, 220, Bakersfield J.C.

19. **PRICE, BOB**
G, 6-1, 230, North Texas
State

20. **DAVIS, DON**
B, 5-11, 220, McMurry

1964
(Drafted 1st)

1. **PARKS, DAVE**
E, 6-2, 195, Texas Tech

2. **MIRA, GEORGE**
QB, 5-11, 183, Miami (Fla.)

3. **WILCOX, DAVE**
LB, 6-3, 230, Oregon

† 4. **WILSON, JAMES**
G, 6-3, 244, Georgia

5. **JOHNSON, RUDY**
FB, 5-11, 200, Nebraska

† 6. **LEWIS, GARY**
FB, 6-2½, 227, Arizona State

7. **CLARKE, HAGWOOD**
DB, 6-0, 196, Florida

† 8. **(A) DAUGHERTY, BOB**
HB, 6-2, 185, Tulsa

8. **(B) POOOLE, BOB**
(Choice from Washington)
TE, 6-4, 216, Clemson

9. **MUDD, HOWARD**
G, 6-3, 237, Hillsdale

†10. **POLSER, FRED**
T, 6-5, 235, East Texas State

11. **ALMQUIST, DENNIS**
G, 6-1, 218, Idaho

†12. **LONG, JIM**
FB, 6-1, 202, Fresno State

13. **BROWN, ROBERT**
DT, 6-5, 263, Arkansas A&M

14. **BEARD, ED**
T, 6-2, 235, Tennessee

15. **GRIFFIN, JAMES**
E, 6-3½, 230, Grambling

†16. **GORDON, CORNELL**
DB, 5-11, 180, North Carolina
A&T

†17. **BRUSVAN, KEN**
T, 6-4, 223, Oregon State

†18. **COLE, JERRY**
E, 6-4, 215, Southwest Texas
State

19. **RAWSON, LARRY**
B, 5-11, 209, Auburn

20. **BAKER, GENE**
G, 6-1, 235, Whitworth

1965
(Drafted 2nd)

1. **(A) WILLARD, KEN**
FB, 6-2, 230, North Carolina

1. **(B) DONNELLY, GEORGE**
(Choice from Cleveland)
DB, 6-3, 202, Illinois

2. **CERNE, JOE**
C, 6-2, 237, Northwestern

3. **(A) SCHWEICKERT, BOB**
(Choice from N.Y. Giants)
HB, 6-1, 191, Virginia Poly

3. **(B) NORTON, JIM**
T, 6-4, 247, Washington

3. **(C) CHAPPLE, JACK**
(Choice from Baltimore)
LB, 6-2, 225, Stanford

† 4. **TODD, LARRY**
FL, 6-1, 190, Arizona State

† 5. **McCORMICK, DAVE**
T, 6-6, 250, LSU

6. **Choice to Cleveland**

7. **Choice to Green Bay**

8. **Choice to Minnesota**

9. **SWINFORD, WAYNE**
DB, 6-0½, 185, Georgia

†10. **CAPPADONA, ROBERT**
HB, 6-2, 225, Northeastern

†11. **MASS, STEVE**
T, 6-2, 270, Detroit

†12. **PLUMP, DAVE**
HB, 6-0, 190, Fresno State

13. **SCHUMACHER, GREG**
LB, 6-3, 230, Illinois

14. **ANDRUSKI, FRANK**
DB, 6-0, 185, Utah

15. **PABIAN, JOE**
T, 6-3, 270, West Virginia

†16. **HETTEMA, DAVE**
T, 6-3½, 230, New Mexico

17. **FRKETICH, LEN**
E, 6-3, 220, Oregon State

†18. **STANDRIDGE, LEON**
E, 6-3, 220, San Diego State

19. **FORD, DALE**
QB-DB, 6-1, 200, Washington
State

†20. **DUNCAN, DENNIS**
HB, 6-1, 200, Louisiana College

1966
(Drafted Alternately 10-11)

1. **HINDMAN, STAN**
DE-G, 6-3, 235, Mississippi

† 2. **WINDSOR, BOB**
E, 6-4, 224, Kentucky

3. **(A) RANDOLPH, ALVIN**
(Choice from Dallas)
DB, 6-2, 193, Iowa

3. **(B) BLAND, DAN**
DB, 5-11, 190, Mississippi
State

† 4. **PARKER, DON**
G, 6-3, 240, Virginia

5. **(A) PHILLIPS, MEL**
(Choice from Dallas)
DB, 6-0, 190, North Carolina
A&T

5. **(B) SMITH, STEVE**
TE, 6-5, 240, Michigan

6. **JOHNSON, CHARLES**
DT, 6-2, 266, Louisville

7. **Choice to Baltimore**

8. **WITCHER, DICK**
E, 6-3, 210, UCLA

9. **KRAMER, KENT**
TE, 6-5, 235, Minnesota

10. **SBRANTI, RON**
LB, 6-2, 228, Utah

11. **RIDLEHUBER, PRESTON**
DB, 6-2, 195, Georgia

12. **LOEBACH, LYALL**
T, 6-5, 248, Simpson

†13. **JACKSON, JIM**
DB, 5-11, 185, Western
Illinois

†14. **COLLETT, ELMER**
G, 6-4, 225, San Francisco
State

†15. **SAFFOLD, S.T.**
E, 6-3, 205, San Jose State

16. **LeCLAIR, JIM**
QB, 6-1, 195, C.W. Post

17. **BRELAND, JIM**
G, 6-2, 230, Georgia Tech

†18. **PARSON, RON**
E, 6-5, 240, Austin Peay

†19. **FITZGERALD, DICK**
T, 6-1, 250, Nebraska

20. **WALKER, WILLIE**
LB, 6-3, 220, Baylor

1967
(Drafted Alternately 11-13)

1. **(A) SPURRIER, STEVE**
(Choice from Atlanta)
QB, 6-2, 203, Florida

1. **(B) BANASZEK, CAS**
LB, 6-3, 245, Northwestern

2. **HOLZER, TOM**
T, 6-4, 248, Louisville

3. **(A) NUNLEY, FRANK**
(Choice from Pittsburgh)
LB, 6-2, 230, Michigan

3. **(B) TUCKER, BILL**
HB, 6-2, 232, Tennessee A&I

4. **TRIMBLE, WAYNE**
DB, 6-3, 205, Alabama

5. **Choice to Atlanta**

6. **CUNNINGHAM, DOUG**
HB, 5-11, 185, Mississippi

7. **JACKSON, MILT**
DB, 6-3, 185, Tulsa

8. **JOHNSON, WALTER**
LB, 6-4, 235, Tuskegee

9. **BRIGGS, BOB**
T, 6-3, 248, Heidelberg

10. **MYERS, PHIL (Chip)**
FL, 6-4, 185, Northwest
Oklahoma

11. **CARMANN, KEN**
DT, 6-4, 265, Kearney
(Nebraska)

12. **HALL, JAMES**
LB, 6-3, 230, Tuskegee

13. **GIBBS, RICH**
DB, 6-1, 187, Iowa

† Future Arrival (Redshirt)

159

14. **LeBLANC, DALTON**
FL, 5-11, 175, Northeast Louisiana
15. **SPENCER, CLARENCE**
FL, 6-4, 200, Louisvile
16. **TEMPLEMAN, BART**
C, 6-3, 248, Eastern Montana
17. **TALBOTT, DAN**
QB, 6-0, 180, North Carolina

1968
(Drafted Alternately 14-15)
1. **BLUE, FORREST**
C, 6-5, 248, Auburn
2. **Choice traded to St. Louis**
3. (A) **OLSSEN, LANCE**
(Choice from Detroit)
T, 6-5, 267, Purdue
3. (B) **VANDERBUNDT, SKIP**
LB, 6-3, 234, Oregon
4. **FULLER, JOHN**
E, 6-0, 175, Lamar Tech
5. **LEE, DWIGHT**
RB, 6-2, 190, Michigan State
6. (A) **JOHNSON, LEO**
(Choice from New Orleans)
FL, 6-2, 185, Tennessee State
6. (B) **BELK, BILL**
DE, 6-3, 240, Maryland State
7. **RICHARDSON, JERRY**
LB, 6-2, 218, Mississippi
8. (A) **BROWN, CHARLES**
(Choice from N.Y. Giants)
T, 6-5, 246, Augustana
8. (B) **GRAY, TOM**
FL, 5-9, 174, Morehead State
9. **BOYETT, CASEY**
E, 6-1, 188, Brigham Young
10. **HART, TOMMY**
LB, 6-3, 215, Morris Brown
11. **FITZGIBBONS, DENNIS**
G, 6-1, 260, Syracuse
12. **JOHNSON, HENRY**
QB, 6-0, 180, Fisk
13. **MITRAKOS, TOM**
C, 6-4, 220, Pittsburgh
14. **MOORE, ALEX**
RB, 6-1, 200, Norfolk State
15. **SPENCER, CLARENCE**
FL, 6-2, 188, Louisville
16. **ROSENOW, TOM**
DT, 6-3, 250, Northern Illinois
17. **PATERA, DENNIS**
K, 6-0, 214, Brigham Young

1969
(Drafted 16th)
1. (A) **KWALICK, TED**
(Choice from New Orleans)
TE, 6-4, 230, Penn State
1. (B) **WASHINGTON, GENE**
FL, 6-1, 186, Stanford
2. **Choice to Pittsburgh via Cleveland**
3. **Choice to Dallas**
4. (A) **SNIADECKI, JIM**
(Choice from Detroit)
LB, 6-2, 220, Indiana
4. (B) **MOORE, GENE**
RB, 6-1, 200, Occidental
5. **EDWARDS, EARL**
DT, 6-6, 276, Wichita State

6. **THOMAS, JIM**
RB, 6-1, 216, Texas-Arlington
7. **VAN SINDEREN, STEVE**
T, 6-4, 255, Washington State
8. **LOPER, MIKE**
T, 6-4, 230, Brigham Young
9. **CRAWFORD, HILTON**
DB, 6-1, 195, Grambling
10. **CHAPPLE, DAVE**
K, 6-1, 180, Santa Barbara
11. **PEAKE, WILLIE**
T, 6-3, 260, Alcorn A&M
12. **O'MALLEY, JACK**
T, 6-4, 250, Southern Cal
13. **CHAMPLIN, PAUL**
DB, 6-0, 194, Eastern Montana
14. **BLACK, TOM**
FL, 6-1, 192, East Texas State
15. **GOLDEN, GARY**
DB, 6-0, 179, Texas Tech
16. **HOSKINS, BOB**
LB, 6-2, 235, Wichita State
17. **RUSHING, JOE**
LB, 6-2, 216, Memphis State

1970
(Drafted 9th)
1. **HARDMAN, CEDRICK**
DE, 6-3, 250, North Texas State
1. (B) **TAYLOR, BRUCE**
(Choice from Washington)
DB, 6-0, 180, Boston U.
2. **Choice to Los Angeles**
2. **ISENBARGER, JOHN**
(Choice from Philadelphia via Los Angeles)
RB, 6-3, 205, Indiana
3. **Choice to Kansas City**
4. **WASHINGTON, VIC**
WR, 5-11, 180, Wyoming
5. **McARTHUR, GARY**
T, 6-5, 247, Southern Cal
6. **CLARK, RUSTY**
QB, 6-2, 212, Houston
7. **STRONG, JIM**
RB, 6-2, 204, Houston
8. **CAMPBELL, CARTER**
LB, 6-3, 214, Weber State
9. **RILEY, PRESTON**
WR, 6-1, 180, Memphis State
10. **SCHREIBER, LARRY**
RB, 6-0, 193, Tennessee Tech
11. **CROCKETT, DANNY**
WR, 6-1, 170, Toledo
12. **TANT, BILL**
T, 6-4, 245, Dayton
13. **VANDERSLICE, JIM**
LB, 6-3, 220, Texas Christian
14. **KING, JACK**
G, 6-2, 245, Clemson
15. **DELSIGNORE, DAVE**
WR, 6-0, 175, Youngstown State
16. **PERKINS, PRODUS**
WR, 6-0, 178, Livingstone College
17. **CULTON, MIKE**
P, 5-11, 195, LaVerne College

1971
(Drafted Alternately 18-19)
1. **ANDERSON, TIM**
CB, 5-11, 201, Ohio State

2. (A) **JANET, ERNIE**
(Choice from Green Bay)
G, 6-4, 243, Washington
2. (B) **ORDUNA, JOE**
RB, 6-0, 194, Nebraska
3. (A) **DICKERSON, SAM**
(Choice from Philadelphia)
WR, 6-2, 196, Southern Cal
3. (B) **PARKER, WILLIE**
C, 6-3, 238, North Texas State
4. **HARRIS, TONY**
RB, 6-3, 191, Toledo
5. (A) **SHATERNICK, DEAN**
(Choice from Chicago)
T, 6-5, 244, Kansas State
5. (B) **WELLS, GEORGE**
(Choice from N.Y. Giants)
LB, 6-1, 240, New Mexico State
5. (C) **HUFF, MARTY**
LB, 6-2, 239, Michigan
6. **BRESLER, AL**
WR, 6-1, 185, Auburn
7. **WATSON, JOHN**
T, 6-4, 251, Oklahoma
8. **McCANN, JIM**
P, 6-2, 170, Arizona State
9. **COUCH, THERMAN**
LB, 6-2, 218, Iowa State
10. (A) **CARDO, RON**
(Choice from New Orleans)
RB, 6-3, 254, Wisconsin State
10. (B) **JENNINGS, ERNIE**
WR, 6-0, 170, Air Force
11. **REED, JOE**
QB, 6-1, 196, Mississippi State
12. **BUNCH, JIM**
DT, 6-3, 254, Wisconsin State
13. **BULLOCK, JOHN**
RB, 5-11, 216, Purdue
14. **DUNSTAN, BILL**
LB, 6-4, 217, Utah State
15. **LENNON, JOHN**
DE, 6-3, 221, Colgate
16. **PURCELL, DAVE**
DT, 6-4, 260, Kentucky
17. **CHARLTON, LEROY**
CB, 6-2, 180, Florida A&M

1972
(Drafted Alternately 19-18)
1. **BEASLEY, TERRY**
WR, 5-11, 186, Auburn
2. (A) **McGILL, RALPH**
(Choice from N.Y. Giants)
CB, 6-0, 181, Tulsa
2. (B) **BARRETT, JEAN**
T, 6-6, 253, Tulsa
3. **DUNBAR, ALLEN**
WR, 6-0, 196, Southern
4. **HALL, WINDLAN**
CB, 5-11, 170, Arizona State
5. **GREENE, MIKE**
LB, 6-4, 233, Georgia
6. **WALKER, JACKIE**
SS, 6-0, 186, Tennessee
7. **HARDY, EDGAR**
G, 6-4, 233, Jackson State
8. **WITTUM, TOM**
P, 6-1, 185, Northern Illinois
9. **BROWN, JERRY**
CB, 5-10, 170, Northwestern
10. **WILLIAMS, STEVE**
DT, 6-4, 251, Western Carolina

11. **LAPUTKA, TOM**
DE, 6-4, 235, Southern Illinois
12. **SETZLER, STEVE**
DE, 6-3, 232, St. Johns
13. **PETTIGREW, LEON**
T, 6-5, 228, San Fernando Valley State
14. **GUTHRIE, ERIC**
QB, 6-0, 200, Boise State
15. **MADDOX, BOB**
DE, 6-6, 235, Frostburg State
16. **DAVIS, RON**
G, 6-2, 235, Virginia State
17. **ALEXANDER, TED**
RB, 6-0, 192, Langston

1973
(Drafted Alternately 18-19)
1. **HOLMES, MIKE**
CB, 6-1, 180, Texas Southern
2. **HARPER, WILLIE**
(Choice from N.Y. Giants)
LB, 6-2, 205, Nebraska
2. **Choice to St. Louis**
3. **Choice to Denver via Washington**
4. **Choice to San Diego via Washington**
5. (A) **FULK, MIKE**
(Choice from Chicago)
LB, 6-3, 229, Indiana
5. (B) **BEVERLY, ED**
WR, 5-11, 172, Arizona State
6. **MOORE, ARTHUR**
DT, 6-5, 253, Tulsa
7. **MITCHELL, JOHN**
LB, 6-3, 229, Alabama
8. **ATKINS, DAVID**
RB, 6-1, 202, Texas-El Paso
9. **PRAETORIUS, ROGER**
RB, 6-3, 228, Syracuse
11. **HUNT, CHARLIE**
LB, 6-3, 218, Florida State
11. **DAHLBERG, TOM**
RB, 6-2, 209, Gustavus Adolphus
12. **PETTUS, LARRY**
T, 6-4, 228, Tennessee State
13. **KELSO, ALAN**
C, 6-6, 244, Washington
14. **MORRISON, DENNIS**
QB, 6-3, 207, Kansas State
15. **BETTIGA, MIKE**
WT, 6-3, 181, Humbolt State
16. **OVEN, MIKE**
TE, 6-4, 205, Georgia Tech
17. **ERICKSON, BOB**
G, 6-3, 240, North Dakota State

1974
(Drafted 10th)
1. (A) **JACKSON, WILBUR**
RB, 6-1, 205, Alabama
1. (B) **SANDIFER, BILL**
(Choice from New England)
DT, 6-6, 278, UCLA
2. (A) **FAHNHORST, KEITH**
OT, 6-6, 248, Minnesota
2. (B) **WILLIAMS, DELVIN**
(Choice from Washington)
RB, 6-1, 197, Kansas
3. **Choice to St. Louis**

4. **(A) HASLERIG, CLINT**
(Choice from N.Y. Jets via
New Orleans)
WR, 6-0, 189, Michigan
4. **Choice to New Orleans**
4. **(B) JOHNSON, SAMMY**
(Choice from Green Bay)
RB, 6-1, 217, North Carolina
5. **Choice to New Orleans**
6. **RAINES, MIKE**
DT, 6-6, 255, Alabama
7. **JOHNSON, KERMIT**
RB, 5-11, 189, UCLA
8. **SCHNEITZ, JIM**
T, 6-3, 253, Missouri
9. **MOORE, MANFRED**
RB, 6-1, 190, Southern Cal
10. **GASPARD, GLEN**
LB, 6-1, 210, Texas
11. **BATTLE, GREG**
S, 5-11, 188, Colorado State
12. **HULL, TOM**
LB, 6-3, 229, Penn State
13. **OWEN, TOM**
QB, 6-1, 195, Wichita State
14. **WILLIAMSON, WALT**
DE, 6-4, 225, Michigan
15. **GRAY, LEONARD**
TE, 6-8, 240, Long Beach State
16. **CONNORS, JACK**
DB, 5-11, 185, Oregon
17. **STANLEY, LEVI**
G, 6-2, 250, Hawaii

1975
(Drafted Alternately 10-9)
1. **WEBB, JIMMY**
DT, 6-5, 248, Mississippi State
2. **COLLINS, GREG**
LB, 6-3, 228, Notre Dame
3. **Choice to N.Y. Giants**
3. **(A) HART, JEFF**
(Choice from Buffalo)
T, 6-5, 266, Oregon State
3. **(B) MIKE-MAYER, STEVE**
(Choice from Washington)
K, 6-0, 180, Maryland
3. **(C) BAKER, WAYNE**
(Choice from St. Louis)
DT, 6-6, 260, Brigham Young
4. **(A) ELAM, CLEVELAND**
(Choice from New Orleans)
DE, 6-3, 240, Tennessee State
4. **(B) OLIVER, FRANK**
DB, 6-1, 189, Kentucky State
5. **BULLOCK, WAYNE**
RB, 6-0, 232, Notre Dame
6. **Choice to Kansas City**
7. **Choice to Buffalo**
8. **KENDRICK, PRESTON**
LB, 6-1, 217, Florida
9. **(A) JOHNSON, JAMES**
DB, 6-2, 195, Tennessee State
9. **(B) NATALE, DAN**
(Choice from Philadelphia)
TE, 6-3, 223, Penn State
9. **(C) DOUGLAS, CEASER**
(Choice from St. Louis)
T, 6-5, 272, Illinois Wesleyan
10. **LAYTON, DONNIE**
RB, 6-0, 190, South Carolina
State
11. **HERNANDEZ, GENE**
DB, 6-2, 173, Texas Christian

12. **WORLEY, RICK**
QB, 6-1, 195, Howard Payne
13. **MITCHELL, DALE**
LB, 6-3, 211, Southern Cal
14. **HENSON, DAVID**
WR, 6-3, 173, Abilene Christian
15. **LAVIN, RICH**
TE, 6-5, 223, Western Illinois
16. **& 17. Choices to Baltimore**
for Colts' 15th & 16th in 1976

1976
(Drafted Alternately 4 & 3)
1. **Choice to New England**
1. **(Choice from Houston to**
New England)
2. **(A) CROSS, RANDY**
C, 6-3, 245, UCLA
2. **(B) LEWIS, EDDIE**
(Choice from Tampa Bay)
CB, 6-0, 172, Kansas
3. **(Choice from New Orleans**
to Kansas City)
3. **Choice to Dallas**
4. **RIVERA, STEVE**
(Choice from Philadelphia)
WR, 5-11, 190, California
4. **Choice to N.Y. Giants**
5. **Choice to Cincinnati**
5. **LEONARD, ANTHONY**
(Choice from Detroit)
CB, 5-11, 170, Virginia Union
6. **(A) PENNYWELL, ROBERT**
LB, 6-1, 222, Grambling
6. **(B) BULL, SCOTT**
(Choice from St. Louis)
QB, 6-5, 209, Arkansas
7. **CHESLEY, JAY**
DB, 6-1, 184, Vanderbilt
8. **AYERS, JOHN**
T, 6-5, 238, West Texas State
9. **HARRISON, KENNY**
WR, 6-0, 179, Southern
Methodist
10. **ROSS, ROBIN**
T, 6-4, 248, Washington State
11. **HOFER, PAUL**
RB, 6-0, 186, Mississippi
12. **LOPER, GERALD**
G, 6-2, 245, Florida
13. **BRUMFIELD, LARRY**
CB, 6-0, 171, Indiana State
14. **MILLER, JOHNNY**
G, 6-1, 241, Livingstone
15. **STIDHAM, HOWARD**
LB, 6-2, 214, Tennessee Tech
16. **LEWIS, REGGIE**
DE, 6-1, 215, San Diego State
17. **JENKINS, DARRYL**
RB, 6-2, 235, San Jose State

1977
(Drafted 16th)
1. **Choice to New England**
2. **Choice to New England**
3. **BOYD, ELMO**
(Choice from Houston)
WR, 5-11, 185, Eastern
Kentucky
3. **Choice to N.Y. Jets**
4. **BLACK, STAN**
S, 6-0, 204, Mississippi State

5. **Choice to Buffalo**
6. **(A) BURNS, MIKE**
(Choice from Buffalo)
CB, 6-0, 184, Southern Cal
6. **(B) HARLAN, JIM**
C, 6-5, 241, Howard Payne
7. **VAN WAGNER, JIM**
RB, 6-0, 202, Michigan Tech
8. **Choice to New York Giants**
9. **POSEY, DAVID**
K, 5-11, 167, Florida
10. **Choice to Tampa Bay**
11. **BILLICK, BRIAN**
TE, 6-5, 232, Brigham Young
12. **MARTIN, SCOTT**
T, 6-4, 257, North Dakota

1978
(Drafted 7th)
1. **(A) MacAFEE, KEN**
TE, 6-4, 250, Notre Dame
1. **(B) BUNZ, DAN**
(Choice from Miami)
LB, 6-4, 230, Long Beach State
2. **Choice to Buffalo**
2. **DOWNING, WALT**
(Choice from Chicago)
G, 6-3, 254, Michigan
3. **Choice to Buffalo**
3. **HUGHES, ERNIE**
(Choice from Baltimore)
G, 6-3, 253, Notre Dame
4. **LeCOUNT, TERRY**
WR, 5-10, 172, Florida
5. **Choice to Baltimore**
5. **(A) REESE, ARCHIE**
(Choice from Houston via
Kansas City and Chicago)
DT, 6-3, 263, Clemson
5. **(B) THREADGILL, BRUCE**
(Choice from Miami)
DB, 6-0, 190, Mississippi State
6. **Choice from Minnesota to**
Washington
6. **WALKER, ELLIOTT**
RB, 5-11, 193, Pittsburgh
7. **QUILLAN, FRED**
C, 6-5, 240, Oregon
8. **Choice to Washington**
9. **(A) REDDEN, HERMAN**
DB, 6-2, 190, Howard
9. **(B) MOORE, DEAN**
(Choice from Detroit)
LB, 6-2, 210, Iowa
9. **(C) McDANIELS, STEVE**
(Choice from Denver)
T, 6-6, 276, Notre Dame
10. **CONNELL, MIKE**
P, 6-1, 200, Cincinnati
11. **McCRAY, WILLIE**
DE, 6-5, 234, Troy State
12. **(A) IRONS, DAN**
T, 6-7, 260, Texas Tech
12. **(B) CONNORS, ROD**
(Supplemental Draft)
RB, 6-2, 190, Southern Cal

1979
(Drafted 1st)
1. **Choice to Buffalo**
2. **OWENS, JAMES**
RB, 5-11, 188, UCLA

3. **Choice to Seattle**
3. **MONTANA, JOE**
(Choice from Dallas via
Seattle)
QB, 6-2, 200, Notre Dame
4. **Choice to Buffalo**
5. **(A) SEABRON, TOM**
LB, 6-3, 209, Michigan
5. **(B) ALDRIDGE, JERRY**
(Choice from Detroit)
RB, 6-2, 220, Angelo State
6. **VAUGHAN, RUBEN**
DT, 6-2, 264, Colorado
7. **FRANCIS, PHIL**
FB, 6-1, 205, Stanford
8. **Choice to Green Bay**
9. **HAMILTON, STEVE**
DE, 6-3, 240, Missouri
10. **(A) CLARK, DWIGHT**
WR, 6-3, 204, Clemson
10. **(B) BALLAGE, HOWARD**
(Choice from Tampa Bay)
CB, 6-1, 182, Colorado
11. **McBRIDE, BILLY**
DB, 6-1, 187, Tennessee State
12. **Forfeited choice via**
supplemental draft of 1978.

1980
(Drafted Alternately 2 & 1)
1. **Choice to N.Y. Jets**
1. **(A) COOPER, EARL**
(Choice from New York Jets)
RB, 6-2, 227, Rice
1. **(B) STUCKEY, JIM**
(Choice from Denver via N.Y.
Jets)
DE, 6-4, 245, Clemson
2. **Choice to Buffalo**
2. **Choice from Detroit**
to Minnesota
2. **TURNER, KEENA**
(Choice from Minnesota)
LB, 6-2, 219, Purdue
3. **Choice to Los Angeles**
3. **(A) MILLER, JIM**
(Choice from Minnesota)
P, 5-11, 183, Mississippi
3. **(B) PUKI, CRAIG**
(Choice from Washington
via
Los Angeles)
LB, 6-1, 231, Tennessee
4. **(A) CHURCHMAN, RICKY**
SS, 6-1, 193, Texas
4. **(B) HODGE, DAVID**
(Choice from New England
via
Los Angeles)
LB, 6-2, 221, Houston
5. **TIMES, KEN**
DT, 6-2, 246, Southern
6. **WILLIAMS, HERB**
CB, 6-0, 198, Southern
7. **Choice to Cincinnati**
8. **Choice to Oakland**
8. **LEOPOLD, BOBBY**
(Choice from Oakland)
LB, 6-1, 215, Notre Dame
9. **Choice to Detroit via**
Kansas City
9. **HARTWIG, DAN**
(Choice from Oakland)
QB, 6-3, 212, Cal Lutheran

10. Choice to Pittsburgh
11. Choice to Miami
12. Choice to Pittsburgh

1981
(Drafted Alternately 8-10)
1. LOTT, RONNIE
   DB, 6-0, 199, Southern Cal
2. (A) HARTY, JOHN
   (Choice from Washington)
   DT, 6-4, 253, Iowa
2. Choice to Chicago
2. (B) WRIGHT, ERIC
   (Choice from Chicago)
   DB, 6-1, 180, Missouri
3. WILLIAMSON, CARLTON
   DB, 6-0, 204, Pittsburgh
4. Choice to Dallas
5. (A) THOMAS, LYNN
   DB, 5-11, 181, Pittsburgh
5. (B) JONES, ARRINGTON
   (Choice from Chicago)
   FB, 6-0, 230, Winston-Salem
6. KUGLER, PETE
   DT, 6-4, 255, Penn State
7. Choice to Philadelphia
8. WHITE, GARRY
   RB, 5-11, 201, Minnesota
9. Choice to Cincinnati
10. Choice to Baltimore
11. DeBOSE, RON
    TE, 6-5, 229, UCLA
12. (A) OGLIVIE, MAJOR
    RB, 5-11, 202, Alabama
12. (B) ADAMS, JOE
    (Choice from Pittsburgh)
    QB, 6-3, 185, Tennessee State

1982
(Drafted 27th)
1. Choice to New England

2. PARIS, WILLIAM "BUBBA"
   (Choice from New England)
   T, 6-6, 293, Michigan
2. Choice from Washington
   to New England
2. Choice to New England
3. Choice to San Diego
4. Choice to New England
5. WILLIAMS, NEWTON
   RB, 5-10, 204, Arizona State
6. WILLIAMS, VINCE
   (Choice from Oakland)
   FB, 6-0, 231, Oregon
6. Choice to New Orleans
7. FERRARI, RON
   LB, 6-0, 212, Illinois
8. Choice to New Orleans
9. CLARK, BRYAN
   QB, 6-2, 196, Michigan State
10. (A) McLEMORE, DANA
    (Choice from Tampa Bay)
    DB, 5-10, 183, Hawaii
10. (B) BARBIAN, TIM
    DT, 6-3, 230, Western Illinois
11. GIBSON, GARY
    LB, 6-1, 215, Arizona
12. WASHINGTON, TIMOTHY
    CB, 5-9, 184, Fresno State

1983
(Drafted Alternately 5-8)
1. Choice to San Diego
2. Choice to L.A. Rams
2. CRAIG, ROGER
   (Choice from San Diego)
   RB, 6-0, 222, Nebraska
3. MONTGOMERY,
   BLANCHARD
   (Choice from L.A. Rams)
   LB, 6-2, 236, UCLA
3. Choice to L.A. Rams
4. (Choice from Denver to L.A.
   Rams)

4. HOLMOE, TOM
   DB, 6-2, 180, Brigham Young
5. ELLISON, RIKI
   LB, 6-2, 220, Southern Cal
6. Choice to Tampa Bay
7. MOTEN, GARY
   LB, 6-1, 210, Southern
   Methodist
8. Choice to San Diego
9. MULARKEY, MIKE
   TE, 6-4, 245, Florida
9. (Choice from Cleveland to
   Chicago)
10. MERRELL, JEFF
    NT, 6-4, 264, Nebraska
11. SAPOLU, JESSE
    G-C, 6-4, 260, Hawaii
12. Choice to Chicago

1984
(Drafted Alternately 23-24)
1. SHELL, TODD
   LB, 6-4, 225, Brigham Young
2. Choice to L.A. Raiders
2. FRANK, JOHN
   (Choice from L.A. Raiders)
   TE, 6-3, 225, Ohio State
3. McINTYRE, GUY
   (Choice from St. Louis)
   G, 6-3, 271, Georgia
3. Choice to St. Louis
4. Choice from Tampa Bay to
   Seattle
4. Choice to San Diego
5. (A) CARTER, MICHAEL
   (Choice from Atlanta)
   DT, 6-2, 281, Southern
   Methodist
5. Choice from Denver to
   Atlanta
5. Choice to St. Louis
5. (B) FULLER, JEFF
   (Choice from Washington,

via L.A. Raiders)
   LB-S, 6-2, 216, Texas A&M
6. Choice to Atlanta
7. Choice to New England
8. Choice to San Diego
9. (A) MILLER, LEE
   (Choice from Chicago)
   DB, 6-1, 186, Cal State-
   Fullerton
9. (B) HARMON, DERRICK
   RB, 5-10, 202, Cornell
10. MORITZ, DAVE
    WR, 6-0, 181, Iowa
11. PENDLETON, KIRK
    WR, 6-3, 191, Brigham Young
12. Choice from Chicago to
    Miami
12. Choice to San Diego

1985
(Drafted 16th in 1st; 28th 2-12)
1. RICE, JERRY
   WR, 6-2, 220, Mississippi
   Valley State
1. Choice to New England
2. Choice to New England
3. MOORE, RICKY
   (Choice from New England)
   RB, 6-11, 236, Alabama
3. Choice to New England
4. Choice to Buffalo
5. COLLIE, BRUCE
   OT, 6-6, 275, Texas Arlington
6. BARRY, SCOTT
   QB, 6-2, 190, UC-Davis
7. Choice to San Diego
8. Choice to New England
9. Choice to San Diego
10. Choice to Seattle
11. WOOD, DAVID
    DE, 6-4, 250, Arizona
12. CHUMLEY, DONALD
    DT, 6-4, 259, Georgia

49ers' All-Time Roster—1946–84

—A—
Abramowicz, Danny, WR, Xavier (Ohio), 1973-74
Albert, Frank, QB, Stanford, 1946-52
Aldridge, Jerry, RB, Angelo State, 1980
Alexander, Kermit, HS, UCLA, 1963-69
Allen, Nate, CB, Texas Southern, 1975
Anderson, Terry, WR, Bethune-Cookman, 1980
Anderson, Tim, S, Ohio State, 1975
Arenas, Joe, HB, Omaha, 1951-57
Atkins, Bill, HB, Auburn, 1958-59
Atkins, Dave, RB, Texas-El Paso, 1973
Audick, Dan, T-G, Hawaii, 1981-82
Ayers, John, G, West Texas State, 1976-84

—B—
Babb, Gene, FB, Austin, 1957-58
Babcock, Harry, E, Georgia, 1953-55
Bahnsen, Ken, FB, North Texas State, 1953
Bahr, Matt, K, Penn State, 1981
Baker, Dave, HB, Oklahoma, 1959-61
Baker, Wayne, DT, BYU, 1975
Balatti, Ed, E, Oakland High (Calif.), 1946-48
Baldassin, Mike, LB, Washington, 1977-78
Baldwin, John, C, Centenary, 1947
Banaszek, Cas, T, Northwestern, 1968-77
Banducci, Bruno, G, Stanford, 1946-54
Barnes, Larry, FB, Colorado, 1957
Barrett, Jean, T, Tulsa, 1973-80
Bassi, Dick, G, Santa Clara, 1946-47

Beals, Alyn, E, Santa Clara, 1946-51
Beard, Ed, LB, Tennessee, 1965-72
Beasley, Terry, WR, Auburn, 1972-75
Beatty, Ed, C, Mississippi, 1955-56
Beeson, Terry, LB, Kansas, 1982
Beisler, Randy, T, Indiana, 1969-74
Belser, Ceaser, LB, Arkansas AM&N, 1974
Belk, Bill, DE, Maryland State, 1968-74
Benjamin, Guy, QB, Stanford, 1981-83
Bentz, Roman, T, Tulane, 1948
Berry, Rex, HB, BYU, 1951-56
Bettiga, Mike, WR, Humboldt State, 1973
Beverly, Ed, WR, Arizona State, 1973

Black, Stan, DB, Mississippi State, 1977
Blackmore, Richard, CB, Mississippi State, 1983
Blue, Forrest, C, Auburn, 1968-74
Board, Dwaine, DE, North Carolina A&T, 1979-84
Boone, J.R., HB, Tulsa, 1952
Bosley, Bruce, C-G, West Virginia, 1956-68
Bouza, Matt, WR, California, 1981
Boyd, Elmo, WR, Eastern Kentucky, 1978
Boykin, Greg, FB, Northwestern, 1978
Bradley, Ed, LB, Wake Forest, 1977-78
Braggonier, Dennis, DB, Stanford, 1974
Bristor, John, S, Waynesburg, 1979
Britt, Charlie, HB, Georgia, 1964
Brock, Clyde, T, Utah State, 1963

Odom, Ricky, DB, USC, 1978
O'Donahue, Pat, E, Wisconsin, 1952
Olerich, Dave, E, San Francisco, 1967-68, 1972-73
Olssen, Lance, T, Purdue, 1968-69
Orosz, Tom, P, Ohio State, 1983
Osborne, Clancy, LB, Arizona State, 1959-60
Owen, Tom, QB, Wichita State, 1974-75
Owens, James, WR, UCLA, 1979-80
Owens, R.C., HB, College of Idaho, 1957-61

—P—

Pace, Jim, HB, Michigan, 1958
Palatella, Lou, G, Pittsburgh, 1955-58
Paris, Bubba, T, Michigan, 1982-84
Parker, Don, G, Virginia, 1967
Parks, Dave, E, Texas Tech, 1964-67
Parsons, Earle, HB, USC, 1946-47
Patera, Dennis, K, BYU, 1968
Patton, Ricky, RB, Jackson State, 1980-82
Pavlich, Chuck, G, Muskegon High (Mich.), 1946
Peets, Brian, TE, Pacific, 1981
Penchion, Bob, T, Alcorn A&M, 1974-75
Peoples, Woody, G, Grambling, 1968-77
Perry, Joe, FB, Compton J.C., 1948-60, 1963
Perry, Scott, S, Williams, 1980
Phillips, Mel, DB, North Carolina A&T, 1966-76
Pillers, Lawrence, DE, Alcorn A&M, 1980-84
Pine, Ed, LB, Utah, 1962-64
Plunkett, Jim, QB, Stanford, 1976-77
Poole, Bob, E, Clemson, 1964-65
Powell, Charles, E, San Diego High (Calif.), 1952-53, 1955-57
Powers, Jim, HB, USC, 1950-53
Puddy, Harold T, Oregon, 1948
Puki, Craig, LB, Tennessee, 1980-81

—Q—

Quillan, Fred, C, Oregon, 1978-84
Quilter, Chuck, T, Tyler J.C., 1949

—R—

Raines, Mike, DT, Alabama, 1974
Ramson, Eason, TE, Washington State, 1979-83
Randle, Sonny, E, Virginia, 1967
Randolph, Alvin, DB, Iowa, 1966-70, 1974
Rasley, Rocky, G, Oregon State, 1976
Reed, Joe, QB, Mississippi State, 1972-74
Reese, Archie, DE, Grambling, 1978-81
Reid, Bill, C, Stanford, 1975
Remington, Bill, C, Washington State, 1946
Renfro, Dick, FB, Washington State, 1946

Reynolds, Jack, LB, Tennessee, 1981-84
Rhodes, Bruce, DB, San Francisco State, 1976
Rhodes, Ray, CB, Tulsa, 1980
Ridion, Jim, HB, Syracuse, 1957-1962
Ring, Bill, RB, BYU, 1981-84
Rivera, Steve, WR, California, 1976
Roberson, Vern DB, Grambling, 1978
Roberts, C.R., FB, USC, 1959-62
Robinson, Jimmy, WR, Georgia Tech, 1980
Robnett, Ed, HB, Texas Tech, 1947
Rock, Walter, T. Maryland, 1963-67
Rohde, Len, T. Utah State, 1960-74
Roskie, Ken, FB, South Carolina, 1946
Rubke, Karl, C, USC, 1957-60, 1962-63, 1965
Rucka, Leo, C, Rice, 1956
Runager, Max, P, South Carolina, 1984

—S—

Sabuco, Tino, C, San Francisco, 1949
Sagely, Floyd, E, Arkansas, 1954-56
Salata, Paul, E, USC, 1949-50
Sandifer, Bill, DT, UCLA, 1974-76
Sandifer, Dan, HB, LSU, 1950
Sapolu, Jesse, G, Hawaii, 1983
Sardisco, Tony, G, Tulane, 1956
Saunders, John, DB, Toledo, 1974-75
Satterfield, Alf, T, Vanderbilt, 1947
Schabarum, Pete, HB, California, 1951, 1953-54
Schiechl, John, C, Santa Clara, 1947
Schmidt, Henry, T, USC-Trinity (Tex.), 1959-60
Schreiber, Larry, RB, Tennessee Tech, 1971-75
Scoggins, Eric, LB, USC, 1982
Scotti, Ben, HB, Maryland, 1964
Seabron, Thomas, LB, Michigan, 1979-80
Seal, Paul, TE, Michigan, 1977-79
Sharkey, Ed, G, Duke-UN-Reno, 1955-56
Shaw, Charles, G, Oklahoma State, 1950
Shell, Todd, LB, BYU, 1984
Sheriff, Stan, LB, Cal Poly-SLO, 1956-57
Shields, Billy T, Georgia Tech, 1984
Shoener, Hal, E, Iowa, 1948-50
Shumann, Mike R, Florida, 1978-79, 1981
Shumon, Ron, LB, Wichita State, 1979
Sieminski, Charlie, T, Penn State, 1963-65
Silas, Sam, DE, Southern Illinois, 1969-70
Simpson, Mike, DB, Houston, 1970-72

Simpson, O.J., RB, USC, 1978-79
Singleton, Ron, T, Grambling, 1977-80
Sitko, Emil, H B, Notre Dame, 1950
Skaugstad, Daryle, DT, California, 1983
Smith, Charles, E, Abilene Christian, 1956
Smith, Ernie, HB, Compton J.C., 1955-56
Smith, George, C, California, 1947
Smith, J.D., HB, North Carolina A&T, 1956-64
Smith, Jerry, G, Wisconsin, 1952-53
Smith, Noland, RB, Tennessee State, 1969
Smith, Steve, E, Michigan, 1966-67
Snead, Norman, QB, Wake Forest, 1974-75
Sniadecki, Jim, LB, Indiana, 1969-73
Solomon, Freddie, WR, Tampa, 1978-84
Soltau, Gordy, E, Minnesota, 1950-58
Sparks, Dave, G, South Carolina, 1951
Spence, Julian, HB, Sam Houston, 1957
Spurrier, Steve, QB, Florida, 1967-75
Standlee, Norm, FB, Stanford, 1946-52
St. Clair, Bob, T, San Francisco-Tulsa, 1953-64
Steptoe, Jack, WR, Utah, 1978
Stickles, Monty, E, Notre Dame, 1960-67
Stidham, Howard, LB, Tennessee Tech, 1977
Stits, Bill, HB, UCLA, 1957-58
Stolhandske, Tom, LB, Texas, 1955
Stover, Jeff, DE, Oregon, 1982-84
Strickland, Bishop, FB, South Carolina, 1951
Strong, Jim, RB, Houston, 1970
Strzykalski, John, HB, Marquette, 1946-52
Stuckey, Jim, DE, Clemson, 1980-84
Sullivan, Bob, HB, Holy Cross, 1948
Susoeff, Nick, E, Washington State, 1946-49
Sutro, John, T, San Jose State, 1962
Swinford, Wayne, DB, Georgia, 1965-67

—T—

Tanner, Hamp, T, Georgia, 1951
Tautolo, Terry, LB, UCLA, 1980-81
Taylor, Bruce, CB, Boston U, 1970-77
Taylor, Roosevelt, S, Grambling, 1969-71
Teresa, Tony, HB, San Jose State, 1958
Thomas, Aaron, E, Oregon State, 1961

Thomas, Jimmy, RB, Texas-Arlington, 1969-73
Thomas, John, T, Pacific, 1958-67
Thomas, Lynn, DB, Pittsburgh, 1981-82
Thornton, Rupe, G, Santa Clara, 1946-47
Threadgill, Bruce, S, Mississippi State, 1978
Tidwell, Billy, HB, Texas A&M, 1954
Times, Ken, DT, Southern (La), 1980
Titchenal, Bob, E, San Jose State, 1946
Tittle, Y.A., QB, LSU, 1951-60
Toneff, Bob, T, Notre Dame, 1952, 1954-59
Trimble, Wayne, DB, Alabama, 1967
Tubbs, Jerry, LB, Oklahoma, 1958-59
Tucker, Bill, RB, Tennessee A&I, 1967-70
Tuiasosopo, Manu, DT, UCLA, 1984
Turner, Keena, LB, Purdue, 1980-84
Tyler, Wendell, RB, UCLA, 1983-84

—U—
None

—V—

Van Doren, Bob, E, USC, 1953
Vanderbundt, Skip, LB, Oregon State, 1969-77
Vaughan, Ruben, DT, Colorado, 1979
Vaught, Ted, E, Texas Christina, 1953
Vetrano, Joe, HB, Southern Mississippi, 1946-49
Vincent, Ted, DT, Wichita State, 1979-80
Visger, George, DT, Colorado, 1980
Vollenweider, Jim, FB, Miami (Fla.), 1962-63

—W—

Wagner, Lowell, HB, USC, 1949-53, 1955
Wallace, Bev, QB, Compton J.C., 1947-49
Walker, Elliott, RB, Pittsburgh, 1978
Walker, Val Joe, HB, SMU, 1957
Walter Michael LB, Oregon 1984
Washington Dave, LB, Alcorn A&M 1975-76
Washington Gene WR, Stanford 1969-76
Washington, Tim, CB, Fresno State, 1982
Washington, Vic, RB, Wyoming, 1971-73
Waters, Bob, QB, Presbyterian, 1960-64
Watson, John, T, Oklahoma, 1971-76
Webb, Jimmy, DT, Mississippi State, 1975-80
Wersching, Ray, K, California, 1977-84

West, Robert, WR, San Diego State, 1974
White, Bob, HB, Stanford, 1951-52
Wilcox, Dave, LB, Oreon, 1964-74
Wilkerson, Jerry, DE, regon State, 1980
Willard, Ken, FB, North Carolina, 1965-73
Williams, Dave, RB, Colorado, 1977
Williams, Delvin, RB, Kansas, 1974-77
Williams, Gerard, DB, Langston, 1979-80
Williams, Herb, CB, Southern (La,), 1980

Williams, Howie, HB, Howard, 1963
Williams, Joel, C, Texas, 1948
Williams, John, HB, USC, 1954
Williams, Vince, FB, Oregon, 1982-83
Williamson, Carlton, S, Pittsburgh, 1981-84
Wilson, Billy, E, San Jose State, 1951-60
Wilson, Jerry, LB, Auburn, 1960
Wilson, Jim, G, Georgia, 1965-66
Wilson, Mike, WR, Washington State, 1981-84
Windsor, Bob, E, Kentucky, 1967-71
Winston, Lloyd, FB, USC, 1962-63

Wismann, Pete, LB, St. Louis, 1949-52, 1954
Witcher, Dick, E, UCLA, 1966-73
Wittenborn, John, G, Southeast Missouri, 1958-60
Wittum, Tom, P, Northern Illinois, 1973-77
Woitt, John, DB, Mississippi State, 1968-69
Wondolowski, Bill, WR, Eastern Montana, 1969
Woods, Don, RB, New Mexico, 1980
Woodson, Abe, HB, Illinois, 1958-64
Woudenberg, John, T, Denver, 1946-49

Wright, Eric, CB, Missouri, 1981-84

—X—
None
—Y—
Yonamine, Wally, HB, Farrington High (Hi.), 1947
Young, Charle, TE, USC, 1980-82
Youngelman, Sid, T, Alabama, 1955
Yowarsky, Walt, C, Kentucky, 1958

—Z—
Zamlynsky, Zigmond, HB, Villanova, 1946

All-Time 49ers' Coaches

Frank C. (Frankie) Albert (Stanford)
Head Coach–1956-58
Assistant–1955
Ed Alsman (Washington)
Assistant–1976-77
Bill Atkins (Auburn)
Assistant–1976-77
Jerry Attaway (Cal State-Sacramento)
Assistant–1983- Current
Cas Banaszek (Northwestern)
Assistant–1981
Ed Beard (Tennessee)
Assistant–1974-78
Phil Bengston (Minnesota)
Assistant–1951-58
Rich Brooks (Oregon State)
Assistant–1975
Jimmy Carr (Morris Harvey)
Assistant–1978
Jack Christiansen (Colorado State)
Head Coach–1963-67
Assistant–1959-63
Monte Clark (Southern Cal)
Head Coach–1976
Dan Colchico (San Jose State)
Assistant–1967
Jim David (Colorado State)
Assistant–1964-66
Mark Duncan (Denver)
Assistant–1955-62
Dick Enright (Southern Cal)
Assistant–1976-77
Lew Erber (Montana State)
Assistant–1975
Eddie Erdelatz (St. Mary's)
Assistant–1948-49
Chet Franklin (Utah)
Assistant–1971-74
Frank Gansz (Navy)
Assistant–1978
Doug Gerhart (Occidental)
Assistant–1976-77
Mike Giddings (California)
Assistant–1968-73
Dennis Green (Iowa)
Assistant–1979
Paul Hackett (UC-Davis)
Assistant–1983-Current

Tommy Hart (Morris Brown)
Assistant–1983- Current
Norb Hecker (Baldwin-Wallace)
Assistant–1979-Current
Don Heinrich (Washington)
Assistant–1971-75
Howard W. (Red) Hickey (Arkansas)
Head Coach–1959-63
Assistant–1955-58
Bob Hollway (Michigan)
Assistant–1975
Mike Holovak (Boston College)
Assistant–1969
Ed Hughes (Tulsa)
Assistant–1968-70
Milt Jackson (Tulsa)
Assistant–1980-1982
Bill Johnson (Tyler JC)
Assistant–1955-67
Jim Lawson (Stanford)
Assistant–1946-54
Earl Leggett (LSU)
Assistant–1978
Sherman Lewis (Michigan State)
Assistant–1983- Current
Billie Matthews (Southern)
Assistant–1979-1982
Pete McCulley (Louisiana Tech)
HeadCoach–1978
Bobb McKittrick (Oregon State)
Assistant–1979-Current
Bill McPherson (Santa Clara)
Assistant–1979-Current
Ken Meyer (Denison)
HeadCoach–1977
Assistant–1968
Burnie Miller (Wofford)
Assistant–1970
Howard Mudd (Hillsdale)
Assistant–1977
Jack Myers (UCLA)
Assistant–1963
Dick Nolan (Maryland)
Head Coach–1968-75
Fred O'Connor (East Stroudsburg State)
Head Coach–1978
Assistant–1978

Joe Perry (Compton JC)
Assistant–1968-69
Floyd Peters (San Francisco State)
Assistant–1976-77
Dan Radakovich (Penn State)
Assistant–1978
Jimmy Raye (Michigan State)
Assistant–1977
Ray Rhodes (Tulsa)
Assistant–1981- Current
Al Ruffo (Santa Clara)
Assistant–1946-47
Jim Shofner (TCU)
Assistant–1977 & 1967-73
Doug Scovil (Pacific)
Assistant–1970-75
George Seifert (Utah)
Assistant–1980- Current
Bob Shaw (Ohio State)
Assistant–1959
Lawrence T. (Buck) Shaw (Notre Dame)
Head Coach–1946-54
Jim Spavital (Oklahoma State)
Assistant–1976-77
Dick Stanfel (San Francisco)
Assistant–1971-75
Les Steckel (Kansas)
Assistant–1978
Norman P. (Red) Strader (St. Mary's)
Head Coach–1955
Assistant–1952
Chuck Studley (Illinois)
Assistant–1979-1982
Chuck Taylor (Stanford)
Assistant–1950
Y. A. Tittle (LSU)
Assistant–1965-69
Al Vermeil (Utah State)
Assistant–1979-1982
Joe Vetrano (Southern Mississippi)
Assistant–1953-56
Fred vonAppen (Linfield)
Assistant–1983-Current
Dick Voris (San Jose State)
Assistant–1963-67
Bill Walsh (San Jose State)
Head Coach–1979-Current

Mike White (California)
Assistant–1978-79
Billy Wilson (San Jose State)
Assistant–1961-62 & 1964-67 & 1980
Paul Wiggin (Stanford)
Assistant–1968-74
Sam Wyche (Furman)
Assistant–1979-1982
Ernie Zwahlen (Oregon State)
Assistant–1968-70

Dick Nolan

49ers' Year-By-Year Scores
ALL-AMERICA FOOTBALL CONFERENCE

1946 (9-5)
Lawrence T. Shaw, Coach

L	7 New York Yankees/S-8	21
W	21 Miami Seahawks/S-15	14
W	32 Brooklyn Dodgers/S-22	13
L	7 At Chicago Rockets/S-29	21
W	34 At Miami Seahawks/0-7	7
W	23 At Los Angeles Dons/0-12	14
L	14 At Buffalo Bills/0-18	17
W	34 At Cleveland Browns/0-27	20
W	27 Buffalo Bills/N-2	14
L	7 Cleveland Browns/N-10	14
L	9 At New York Yankees/N-17	10
W	30 At Brooklyn Dodgers/N-24	14
W	14 Chicago Rockets/N-30	0
W	48 Los Angeles Dons/0-8	7
	307	189

1947 (8-4-2)
Lawrence T. Shaw, Coach

W	23 Brooklyn Dodgers/A-31	7
W	17 Los Angeles Dons/S-7	14
W	14 Baltimore Colts/S-14	7
L	16 New York Yankees/S-21	21
W	41 At Buffalo Bills/S-28	24
T	28 At Baltimore Colts/0-5	28
W	42 Chicago Rockets/0-12	28
L	7 Cleveland Browns/0-26	14
W	26 At Los Angeles Dons/N-2	16
L	16 At New York Yankees/N-9	24
L	14 At Cleveland Browns/N-16	37
W	41 At Chicago Rockets/N-21	16
W	21 At Brooklyn Dodgers/N-27	7
T	21 Buffalo Bills/D-7	21
	327	264

1948 (12-2)
Lawrence T. Shaw, Coach

W	35 Buffalo Bills/A-29	14
W	36 Brooklyn Dodgers/S-5	20
W	41 New York Yankees/S-12	0
W	36 Los Angeles Dons/S-19	14
W	38 At Buffalo Bills/S-26	28
W	31 At Chicago Rockets/0-1	14
W	56 At Baltimore Colts/0-10	14
W	21 At New York Yankees/0-17	7
W	21 Baltimore Colts/0-24	10
W	44 Chicago Rockets/N-7	21
L	7 At Cleveland Browns/N-14	14
W	63 At Brooklyn Dodgers/N-21	40
L	28 Cleveland Browns/N-28	31
W	38 At Los Angeles Dons/D-5	21
	495	248

1949 (9-3/10-4)
Lawrence T. Shaw, Coach

W	31 Baltimore Colts/A-28	1/
W	42 Chicago Hornets/S-4	7
W	42 Los Angeles Dons/S-18	14
L	17 At Buffalo Bills/S-25	28
W	42 At Chicago Hornets/S-30	24
W	56 Cleveland Browns/0-9	28
W	51 Buffalo Bills/0-16	7
L	3 At New York Yankees/0-23	24
L	28 At Cleveland Browns/0-30	30

W	28 At Baltimore Colts/N-6	10
W	41 At Los Angeles Dons/N-13	24
W	35 New York Yankees/N-27	14
	416	227

Playoff Game–Dec. 4
(At San Francisco–Kezar)

W	I7 New York Yankees	7

Championship Game–Dec. 11
(At San Francisco–Kezar)

L	7 Cleveland Browns	21

49ers' Year-By-Year Scores, Dates, Attendance
NATIONAL FOOTBALL LEAGUE

1950 (3-9)
Lawrence T. Shaw, Coach

L	17 New York Yankees (29,600)/S-17	21
L	20 Chicago Bears (35,558)/S-24	32
L	14 Los Angeles Rams (27,262)/0-1	35
L	7 At Detroit (17,337)/0-8	24
L	24 At New York Yankees (5,740)/0-12	29
W	28 Detroit (27,350)/0-22	27
W	17 Baltimore (14,800)/0-29	14
L	21 At Los Angeles Rams (15,952)/N-5	28
L	14 At Cleveland (28,786)/N-12	34
L	0 At Chicago Bears (35,105)/N-19	17
L	21 At Green Bay (13,186)/N-26	25
W	30 Green Bay (19,204)/D-10	14
	213	300

1951 (7-4-1)
Lawrence T. Shaw, Coach

W	24 Cleveland (48,263)/S-30	10
L	14 At Philadelphia (23,827)/0-6	21
W	28 At Pittsburgh (27,124)/0-14	24
L	7 At Chicago Bears (42,296)/0-21	13
W	44 Los Angeles Rams (49,538)/0-28	17
L	16 At Los Angeles Rams (54,346)/N-4	23
W	19 New York Yankees (25,538)/N-11	14
L	21 Chicago Cards (19,658)/N-18	27
T	10 At New York Yankees (10,184)/N-25	10
W	20 At Detroit (46,467)/D-2	10
W	31 Green Bay (15,121)/D-9	19
W	21 Detroit (27,276)/D-16	17
	255	205

1952(7-5)
Lawrence T. Shaw, Coach

W	17 Detroit (52,750)/S-28	3
W	37 At Dallas Texans (12,566)/0-5	14
W	28 At Detroit (48,842)/0-12	0
W	40 At Chicago Bears (46,338)/0-19	16
W	48 Dallas Texans (26,887)/0-26	21
L	17 Chicago Bears (58,255)/N-2	20
L	14 At New York Giants (54,230)/N-9	23
W	23 At Washington (30,863)/N-16	17
L	9 At Los Angeles Rams (64,450)/N-23	35
L	21 Los Angeles Rams (49,420)/N-30	34
L	7 Pittsburgh (13,886)/D-7	24
W	24 Green Bay (17,579)/D-14	14
	285	221

1953 (9-3)
Lawrence T. Shaw, Coach

W	31 Philadelphia (25,000)/S-27	21
W	31 Los Angeles Rams (41,446)/O-4	30
L	21 At Detroit (56.080)/O-11	24
W	35 At Chicago Bears (36,909)/O-18	28
L	10 Detroit (52,300)/O-25	14
W	24 Chicago Bears (26,308)/N-1	14
W	31 At Los Angeles Rams (85,856)/N-8	27
L	21 At Cleveland (80,698)/N-15	23
W	37 At G.B. in Milwaukee (16,378)/N-22	7
W	38 At Baltimore (26,005)/N-29	21
W	48 Green Bay (31,337)/D-6	14
W	45 Baltimore (23,932)/D-13	14
	372	237

1954 (7-4-1)
Lawrence T. Shaw, Coach

W	41 Washington (32,085)/S-26	7
T	24 At Los Angeles Rams (79,208)/O-3	24
W	23 At G.B. in Milwaukee (15,571)/O-10	17
W	27 At Chicago Bears (42,935)/O-17	24
W	37 Detroit (58,891)/O-24	31
L	27 Chicago Bears (49.833)/O-31	31
L	34 Los Angeles Rams (58,758)/N-7	42
L	7 At Detroit (58,431)/N-14	48
W	31 At Pittsburgh (37,001)/N-20	3
L	13 At Baltimore (23,875)/N-28	17
W	35 Green Bay (32,012)/D-5	0
W	10 Baltimore (25,456)/D-1	17
	313	251

1955 (4-8)
Norman P. Strader, Coach

L	14 Los Angeles Rams (58,772)/S-25	23
L	3 Cleveland (43,595)/O-2	38
W	20 At Chicago Bears (41,651)/O-9	19
W	27 At Detroit (50,179)/O-16	24
L	23 Chicago Bears (56,350)/O-23	34
W	38 Detroit (44,831)/O-30	21
L	14 At Los Angeles Rams (71,832)/N-6	27
L	0 At Washington (25,112)/N-13	7
L	21 At G.B. in Milwaukee (19,099)/N-20	27
L	14 At Baltimore (33,485)/N-27	26
L	7 Green 8ay (32,897)/D-4	28
W	35 Baltimore (33,471)/D-11	24
	216	308

1956 (5-6-1)
Frank C. Albert, Coach

L	21 New York Giants (41,751)/S-30	38
W	33 Los Angeles Rams (56,489)/O-7	30
L	7 At Chicago Bears (47,526)/O-14	31
L	17 At Detroit (55,662)/O-21	20
L	21 Chicago Bears (52,612)/O-28	38
L	13 Detroit (46,708)/N-4	17
L	6 At Los Angeles Rams (69,828)/N-11	30
W	17 At Green Bay (17,986)/N-18	16
T	10 At Philadelphia (19,326)/N-25	10
W	20 At Baltimore (37,227)/D-2	17
W	38 Green Bay (32,433)/D-8	20
W	30 Baltimore (43,791)/D-16	17
	233	284

1957 (8-4/8-5)
Frank C. Albert, Coach

L	10 Chicago Cards (35,7431/S-29	20
W	23 Los Angeles Rams (59,637)/O-6	20
W	21 At Chicago Bears (45,310)/O-13	17
W	24 At G.B. in Milwaukee (18,919)/O-20	14
W	21 Chicago Bears (56,693)/O-27	17
W	35 Detroit (59.702)/N-3	31
L	24 At Los Angeles Rams (102,368)/N-10	37
L	10 At Detroit (56.915)/N-17	31
L	21 At Baltimore (50,073)/N-24	27
W	27 At New York Giants (54,121)/D-1	17
W	17 Baltimore (59,950)/D-8	13
W	27 Green Bay (59,100)/D-15	20
	287	295

Playoff Game–Dec. 22
(At San Francisco–Kezar)

L	27 Detroit (60,118)	31

1958 (6-6)
Frank C. Albert, Coach

W	23 Pittsburgh (51,856)/S-28	20
L	3 Los Angeles Rams (59,826)/O-5	33
L	6 At Chicago Bears (45,310)/O-12	28
W	30 At Philadelphia (33,1 10)/O-19	24
L	14 Chicago Bears (59,441)/O-26	27
W	24 Detroit (59,350)/N-2	21
L	7 At Los Angeles Rams (95,082)/N-9	56
L	21 At Detroit (54,523)/N-16	35
W	33 At G.B. in Milwaukee (43,819)/N-23	12
L	27 At Baltimore (57,557)/N-30	35
W	48 Green Bay (50,793)/D-7	21
W	21 Baltimore (58,334)/D-14	12
	257	324

1959 (7-5)
Howard W. Hickey, Coach

W	24 Philadelphla (41,697)/S-27	14
W	34 Los Angeles Rams (56,028)/O-4	0
L	20 At Green Bay (32,150)/O-11	21
W	34 At Detroit (52,585)/O-18	13
W	20 Chicago Bears (59,045)/O-25	17
W	33 Detroit (59,064)/N-1	7
W	24 At Los Angeles Rams (94,276)/N-8	16
L	3 At Chicago Bears (42,157)/N-15	14
L	14 At Baltimore (56,007)/N-22	45
W	21 At Cleveland (53,763)/N-29	20
L	14 Baltimore (59,075)/D-5	34
L	14 Green Bay (55,997)/D-13	36
	255	237

1960 (7-5)
Howard W. Hickey, Coach

L	19 New York Giants (44,598)/S-25	21
W	13 Los Angeles Rams (53,633)/O-2	9
L	14 At Detroit (49,825)/O-9	10
L	10 At Chicago Bears (48,226)/O-16	27
L	14 At G.B. in Milwaukee (39,914)/O-23	41
W	25 Chicago Bears (55,071)/O-30	7
L	0 Detroit (48,447)/N-6	24
W	26 At Dallas (10,000)/N-20	14
W	30 At Baltimore (57,808)/N-27	22
W	23 At Los Angeles Rams (77,254)/D-4	7
L	0 Green Bay (53,612)/D-10	13
W	34 Baltimore (57,269)/D-18	10
	208	205

1961 (7-6-1)
Howard W. Hickey

W	35 Washington (43,412)/S-17	3
L	10 At Green Bay (38,624)/S-24	30
W	49 At Detroit (53,155)/O-1	0
W	35 Los Angeles Rams (59,004)/O-8	0

W	38 At Minnesota (34,415)/O-15	24
L	0 At Chicago Bears (49,070)/O-22	31
L	10 At Pittsburgh (19,686)/O-29	20
T	20 Detroit (56,878)/N-5	20
L	7 At Los Angeles Rams (63,766)/N-12	17
W	41 Chicago Bears (52,972)/N-19	31
W	38 Minnesota (43,905)/N-26	28
L	17 At Baltimore (57,641)/D-8	20
W	22 Green Bay (55,722)/D-10	21
L	24 Baltimore (45,517)/D-16	27
	346	143

1962 (6-8)
Howard W. Hickey, Coach

L	14 Chicago (46,052)/S-16	30
L	24 At Detroit (51,032)/S-23	45
W	21 Minnesota (38,407)/S-30	7
W	21 At Baltimore (54,148)/O-7	13
W	34 At Chicago (48,902)/O-14	27
L	13 At G.B. in Milwaukee (46,012)/O-21	31
L	14 Los Angeles Rams (51,033)/O-28	28
L	3 Baltimore (44,875)/N-4	22
L	24 Detroit (43,449)/N-11	38
W	24 At Los Angeles Rams (42,554)/N-18	17
W	24 At St. Louis (17,532)/N-25	17
W	35 At Minnesota (33,076)/D-2	12
L	21 Green Bay (53,769)/D-9	31
L	10 Cleveland (35,274)/D-15	13
	282	331

1963 (2-12)
Coach*

L	20 Minnesota (30,781)/S-15	24
L	14 Baltimore (31,006)/S-22	20
L	14 At Minnesota (28,567)/S-29	45
L	3 At Detroit (44,088)/O-6	26
L	3 At Baltimore (56,962)/O-13	20
W	20 Chicago (35,837)/O-20	14
L	21 At Los Angeles Rams (45,532)/O-27	28
L	7 Detroit (33,511)/N-3	45
W	31 Dallas (29,563)/N-10	24
L	14 At New York Giants (62,982)/N-17	48
L	10 At G.B. in Milwaukee (45,905)/N-24	28
L	17 Los Angeles Rams (33,321)/D-1	21
L	7 At Chicago (46,994)/D-8	27
L	17 Green Bay (31,031)/D-14	21
	198	391

*Coach Red Hickey resigned after third league game and Jack Christiansen was appointed his successor.

1964 (4-10)
Jack Christiansen, Coach

L	17 Detroit (33,204)/S-13	26
W	28 At Philadelphia (57,352)/S-20	24
L	13 St. Louis (30,969)/S-27	23
W	31 Chicago (33,132)/O-4	21
L	14 At G.B. in Milwaukee (47,380)/O-11	24
L	14 At Los Angeles Rams (54,355)/O-18	42
L	22 Minnesota (31,845)/O-25	27
L	7 At Baltimore (60,213)/N-1	37
L	7 At Minnesota (40,408)/N-8	24
W	24 Green Bay (38,483)/N-15	14
L	21 At Chicago (46,772)/N-22	23
L	3 Baltimore (33,642)/N-29	14
W	28 Los Angeles Rams (31,791)/D-6	7
L	7 At Detroit (41,854)/D-13	24
	236	330

1965 (7-6-1)
Jack Christiansen. Coach

W	52 Chicago (31,211)/S-19	24

W	27 Pittsburgh (28.161)/S-26	17
L	24 At Baltimore (57,342)/O-3	27
L	10 At Green Bay (50.858)/O-10	27
W	45 At Los Angeles Rams (34.703)/O-17	21
L	41 Minnesota (40,673)/O-24	42
L	28 Baltimore (43,575)/O-31	34
L	31 At Dallas (30,531)/N-7	39
W	27 At Detroit (52,570)/N-14	21
W	30 Los Angeles Rams (39,253)/N-21	27
W	45 At Minnesota (36,748)/N-28	24
W	17 Detroit (38,483)/D-5	14
L	20 At Chicago (43,400)/D-12	61
T	24 Green Bay (45,710)/D-19	24
	421	402

1966 (6-6-2)
Jack Christiansen, Coach

T	20 Minnesota (29,312)/S-11	20
L	14 At Baltimore (56,715)/S-25	36
L	3 At Los Angeles Rams (45,642)/S-30	34
W	21 Green Bay (39,290)/O-9	20
W	44 At Atlanta (54,788)/O-16	7
W	27 Detroit (36,745)/O-23	24
L	3 At Minnesota (45,007)/O-30	28
W	21 Los Angeles Rams (35,372)/N-6	13
T	30 At Chicago (47,079)/N-13	30
L	34 Philadelphia (31,993)/N-20	35
W	41 At Detroit (53,189)/N-24	14
L	7 At G.B. in Milwaukee (48,725)/D-4	20
W	41 Chicago (37,170)/D-11	14
L	14 Baltimore (40,005)/D-18	30
	320	325

1967 (7-7)
Jack Christiansen, Coach

W	27 At Minnesota (39,638)/S-17	21
W	38 Atlanta (30,207)/S-24	7
L	7 At Baltimore (60,238)/O-1	41
W	27 At Los Angeles Rams (60,424)/O-8	24
W	28 At Philadelphia (60,825)/O-15	27
W	27 New Orleans (34,285)/O-22	13
L	3 Detroit (37,990)/O-29	45
L	7 Los Angeles Rams (53,194)/N-5	17
L	28 At Washington (50,326)/N-12	31
L	0 At Green Bay (50,861)/N-19	13
L	9 Baltimore (44,815)/N-26	26
L	14 Chicago (25,613)/D-3	28
W	34 At Atlanta (51.798)/D-10	28
W	24 Dallas (27,182)/D-16	16
	273	337

1968 (7-6-1)
Dick Nolan, Coach

L	10 At Baltimore (56,864)/S-15	27
W	35 St. Louis (27,557)/S-22	17
W	28 Atlanta (27,477)/S-29	13
L	10 At Los Angeles Rams (69,520)/O-6	24
L	14 Baltimore (32,822)/O-13	42
W	26 At New York Giants (62.958)/O-20	10
W	14 At Detroit (53,555)/O-27	7
L	21 Cleveland (31,359)/N-3	33
L	19 At Chicago (46,978)/N-10	27
T	20 Los Angeles Rams (41,815)/N-17	20
W	45 At Pittsburgh (21,408)/N-24	28
W	27 Green Bay (47,218)/D-1	20
L	20 Minnesota (29,049)/D-8	30
W	14 At Atlanta (44,977)/D-15	12
	303	310

1969 (4-8-2)
Dick Nolan, Coach

L	12 At Atlanta (45,940)/S-21	24
L	7 At G.B. in Milwaukee (48,184)/S-28	14
T	17 Washington (35,184)/O-5	17
L	21 Los Angeles Rams (45,995)/O-12	27
L	7 Atlanta (28,684)/O-19	21
W	24 At Baltimore (60,23B)/O-26	21
L	14 Detroit (35,100)/N-2	26
L	30 At Los Angeles Rams (73,975)/N-9	41
W	20 Baltimore (38,472)/N-16	17
L	38 At New Orleans (71,448)/N-23	43
T	24 At Dallas (62,348)/N-27	24
W	42 Chicago (32,826)/D-6	21
L	7 At Minnesota (43,028)/D-14	10
W	14 Philadelphia (25,391)/D-21	13
	277	319

1970 (10-3-1/11-4-1)
Dick Nolan, Coach

W	26 Washington (34,984)/S-20	17
W	34 Cleveland (37,502)/S-27	31
L	20 At Atlanta (58,850)/O-4	21
W	20 At Los Angeles Rams (77,272)/O-11	6
T	20 New Orleans (39,446)/O-18	20
W	19 Denver (39,515)/O-25	14
W	26 Green Bay (59,335)/N-1	10
W	37 At Chicago (45,607)/N-8	16
W	30 At Houston (43,040)/N-15	20
L	7 At Detroit (56,232)/N-22	28
L	13 Los Angeles Rams (59,602)/N-29	30
W	24 Atlanta (41,387)/D-6	20
W	38 At New Orleans (61,940)/D-13	27
W	38 At Oakland Raiders (54,535)/D-20	7
	352	267

NFC PLAYOFF—DEC. 27
(At Bloomington–Metropolitan)

W	17 Minnesota (45,103)	14

NFC CHAMPIONSHIP—JAN. 3
(At San Francisco–Kezar)

L	10 Dallas (59,364)	17

1971 (9-6/10-6)
Dick Nolan, Coach

L	17 At Atlanta (56,990)/S-19	20
W	38 At New Orleans (81,595)/S-26	20
W	31 At Philadelphia (65,358)/O-3	3
L	13 Los Angeles Rams (44,000)/O-10	20
W	13 Chicago (44,133)/O-17	0
W	26 At St. Louis (50,419)/O-24	14
W	27 New England (45,092)/O-31	10
W	13 At Minnesota (49,784)/N-7	9
L	20 New Orleans (45,138)/N-14	26
L	6 At Los Angeles Rams (80,050)/N-21	17
W	24 At New York Jets (62,936)/N-28	21
L	17 Kansas City (45,306)-**MN**/D-6	26
W	24 Atlanta (44,584)/D-12	3
W	31 Detroit (45.580)/D-19	27
	300	216

NFC PLAYOFF—DEC. 26
(At San Francisco–Candlestick)

W	24 Washington (45,327)	20

NFC CHAMPIONSHIP—JAN. 2
(At Irving–Texas)

L	3 Dallas (63,409)	14

1972 (8-5-1/8-6-1)
Dick Nolan, Coach

W	34 San Diego (56,906)*/S-17	3
L	20 At Buffalo (45,825)/S-24	27
W	37 At New Orleans (69,840)/O-1	2
L	7 At Los Angeles Rams (77,382)/O-8	31
L	17 New York Giants (53,284)/O-15	23
T	20 New Orleans (53,571)/O-22	20
W	49 At Atlanta (58,850)/O-29	14
L	24 At G.B. in Milwaukee (47,897)/N-5	34
W	24 Baltimore (57,225)/N-12	21
W	34 At Chicago (65,201)/N-19	21
W	31 At Dallas (65,214)/N-23	10
L	16 Los Angeles Rams (60,175)-**MN**/D-4	26
W	20 Atlanta (57,523)/D-10	0
W	20 Minnesota (58,502)/D-16	17
	353	249

NFC PLAYOFF—DEC. 23
(At San Francisco–Candlestick)

L	28 Dallas (59,746)	30

*Attendance from 1972 on is actual, does not include "no-shows".

1973 (5-9)
Dick Nolan, Coach

L	13 At Miami (68,275)/S-16	21
W	36 At Denver (50,966)/S-23	34
L	20 Los Angeles Rams (57,487)/S-30	40
W	13 At Atlanta (58,850)/O-7	9
L	13 Minnesota (56,438)/O-14	17
W	40 New Orleans (52,881)/O-21	0
L	3 Atlanta (56,825)/O-28	17
L	20 At Detroit (49,531)/N-4	30
L	9 At Washington (54,381)/N-11	33
L	13 At Los Angeies Rams (78,358)/N-18	31
W	20 Green Bay (49,244)-**MN**/N-26	6
W	38 Philadelphia (51,155)/D-2	28
L	10 At New Orleans (62,490)/D-9	16
L	14 Pittsburgh (52,752)/D-15	37
	262	319

1974 (6-8)
Dick Nolan, Coach

W	17 At New Orleans (65,071)/S-15	13
W	17 At Atlanta (47,686)/S-22	10
L	3 Cincinnati (49,895)/S-29	21
L	9 St. Louis (47,675)/O-6	34
L	13 At Detroit (45,199)-**MN**/O-14	17
L	14 At Los Angeles Rams (74,070)/O-20	37
L	24 Oakland Raiders (58,524)/O-27	35
L	13 Los Angeles Rams (57,526)-**MN**/N-4	15
L	14 At Dallas (50,018)/N-10	20
W	34 At Chicago (42,731)/N-17	0
W	27 Atlanta (45,435)/N-24	0
L	0 At Cleveland (24,559)/D-1	7
L	7 Green Bay (45,475)/D-8	6
W	35 New Orleans (40,418)/D-15	21
	226	236

1975 (5-9)
Dick Nolan, Coach

L	17 At Minnesota (48,418)/S-21	27

L	14 Los Angeles Rams (55,072)/S-28	23
W	20 At Kansas City (54,490)/O-5	3
L	3 Atlanta (43,719)/O-12	17
W	35 New Orleans (39,654)/O-19	21
L	16 At New England (60,358)/O-26	24
L	17 Detroit (42,683)/N-2	28
W	24 At Los Angeles Rams (78,995)/N-9	23
W	31 Chicago (41,319)/N-16	3
W	16 At New Orleans (40,328)/N-23	6
L	17 At Philadelphia (56,694)/N-30	27
L	13 Houston (43,767)/D-7	27
L	9 At Atlanta (38,501)/D-14	31
L	23 New York Giants (33,939)/D-21	26
	255	286

1976 (8-6)
Monte Clark, Coach

W	26 At Green Bay (54,628)/S-12	14
L	12 Chicago (44,158)/S-19	19
W	37 At Seattle (59,108)/S-26	21
W	17 New York Jets (42,961)/O-3	6
W	16 At Los Angeles Rams (84,483)-**MN**/O-11	0
W	33 New Orleans (43,160)/O-17	3
W	15 Atlanta (50,240)-SN/O-23	0
L	20 At St. Louis (50,365)/O-31	(OT)-23
L	21 Washington (56,134)/N-7	24
L	16 At Atlanta (20,058)/N-14	21
L	3 Los Angeles Rams (57,909)/N-21	23
W	20 Minnesota (56,775)-**MN**/N-29	16
L	7 At San Diego (33,539)/D-5	(OT)-13
W	27 At New Orleans (42,536)/D-12	7
	270	190

1977 (5-9)
Ken Meyer, Coach

L	0 At Pittsburgh (48,046)-**MN**/S-19	27
L	15 Miami (40,503)/S-25	19
L	14 At Los Angeles Rams (55,466)/O-2	34
L	0 Atlanta (38,009)/O-9	7
L	17 At New York Giants (70,366)/O-16	20
W	28 Detroit (39,392)/O-23	7
W	20 Tampa Bay (34,750)/O-30	10
W	10 At Atlanta (46,577)/N-6	3
W	10 At New Orleans (41,564)/N-13	(OT)-7
L	10 Los Angeles Rams (56,779)/N-20	23
W	20 New Orleans (33,702)/N-27	17
L	27 At Minnesota (40,745)/D-4	28
L	35 Dallas (55,848)-**MN**/D-12	42
L	14 At G.B. in Milwaukee (44,902)/D-18	16
	220	260

1978 (2-14)
Coach*

L	7 At Cleveland (68,973)/S-3	24
L	14 Chicago (49,502)/S-10	16
L	19 At Houston (46,161)/S-17	20
L	10 At New York Giants (71,536)/S-24	27
W	28 Cincinnati (41,107)/O-1	12
L	10 At Los Angeles Rams (59,337)/O-8	27
L	7 New Orleans (37,671)/O-15	14
L	17 Atlanta (34,133)/O-22	20
L	20 At Washington (53,706)/O-29	38
L	10 At Atlanta (55,468)/N-5	21
L	10 St. Louis (33,155)/N-12	16
L	28 Los Angeles Rams (45,022)/N-19	31
L	7 Pittsburgh (51,657)-**MN**/N-27	24
L	13 At New Orleans (50,068)/D-3	24
W	6 Tampa Bay (30,931)/D-10	3
L	14 At Detroit (56,674)/D-17	33
	219	350

* Pete McCulley was fired after 9 games and Fred O'Connor was appointed his successor.

1979 (2-14)
Bill Walsh, Coach

L	22 At Minnesota (46,539)/S-2	28
L	13 Dallas (56.728)/S-9	21
L	24 At Los Angeles Rams (44,303)/S-16	27
L	21 New Orleans (39.727)/S-23	30
L	9 At San Diego (50,893)/S-30	31
L	24 Seattle (44.592)/O-7	35
L	16 At New York Giants (70,352)/O-14	32
W	20 Atlanta (33,952)/O-21	15
L	27 Chicago (42,773)/O-28	28
L	10 At Oakland Raiders (52,764)/N-4	23
L	20 At New Orleans (65,551)/N-11	31
L	28 Denver (42,910)/N-18	38
L	20 Los Angeles Rams (49,282)/N-25	26
L	10 At St. Louis (41,593)/D-2	13
W	23 Tampa Bay (44,506)/D-9	7
L	21 At Atlanta (37,211)/D-16	31
	308	416

1980 (6-10)
Bill Walsh, Coach

W	26 At New Orleans (58,621)/S-7	21
W	24 St. Louis (49,999)/S-14	(OT)-21
W	37 At New York Jets (50,608)/S-21	27
L	17 Atlanta (56,518)/S-28	20
L	26 At Los Angeles Rams (62,188)/O-5	48
L	14 At Dallas (63,399)/O-12	59
L	17 Los Angeles Rams (55,360)/O-19	31
L	23 Tampa Bay (51,925)/O-26	24
L	13 At Detroit (78,845)/N-2	17
L	16 At G.B. in Milwaukee (54,475)/N-9	23
L	13 At Miami (45.135)/N-16	17
W	12 New York Giants (38,574)/N-23	0
W	21 New England (45,254)/N-30	17
W	38 New Orleans (37,949)/D-7	(OT)-35
L	10 At Atlanta (55,767)/D-14	35
L	13 Buffalo (37,476)/D-21	18
	320	415

1981 (13-3/16-3)
Bill Walsh, Coach

L	17 At Detroit (62,123)/S-6	24
W	28 Chicago (49,520)/S-13	17
L	17 At Atlanta (56,653)/S-20	34
W	21 New Orleans (44,433)/S-27	14
W	30 At Washington (51.843)/O-4	17
W	45 Dallas (57,574)/O-11	14
W	13 At G.B. in Milwaukee (50,171)/O-18	3
W	20 Los Angeles Rams (59.190)/O-25	17
W	17 At Pittsburgh (52,878)/N-1	14
W	17 Atlanta (59.127)/N-8	14
L	12 Cleveland (52,445)/N-15	15
W	33 At Los Angeles Rams (63,456)/N-22	31
W	17 New York Giants (57,186)/N-29	10
W	21 At Cincinnati (56,796)/D-6	3
W	28 Houston (55,707)/D-13	6
W	21 At New Orleans (43,639)/D-20	17
	357	250

NFC PLAYOFF—JAN. 3
(At San Francisco–Candlestick)

W	38 New York Giants (58,360)	24

NFC CHAMPIONSHIP—JAN. 10
(At San Francisco–Candlestick)

W	28 Dallas (60,525)	27

SUPER BOWL XVI—JAN. 24
(At Pontiac, Michigan–Silverdome)

W	26 Cincinnati (81,270)	21

1982 (3-6)
Bill Walsh, Coach

L	17 Los Angeles Raiders (59,748)/S-12	23
L	21 At Denver (73,899)/S-19	24
W	31 At St. Louis (38.064)/N-21	20
L	20 New Orleans (51.611)/N-28	23
W	30 At Los Angeles Rams (58,574)-**THN**/D-2	24
L	37 San Diego (51,988)-**SA**/D-11	41
L	7 Atlanta (53,234)-**SUN**/D-19	17
W	26 At Kansas City (24,319)/D-26	13
L	20 Los Angeles Rams (54,256)/J-2	21
	209	206

1983 (10-6/11-7)
Bill Walsh, Coach

L	17 Philadelphia (55,775)-**SA**/S-3	22
W	48 At Minnesota (58,167)-**THN**/S-8	17
W	42 At St. Louis (38,130)/S-18	27
W	24 Atlanta (57,814)/S-25	20
W	33 At New England (54,293)/O-2	13
L	7 Los Angeles Rams (59,119)/O-9	10
W	32 At New Orleans (68.134)/O-16	13
W	45 At Los Angeles Rams (66,070)/O-23	35
L	13 New York Jets (54,796)/O-30	27
L	17 Miami (57,832)/N-6	20
W	27 New Orleans (40.022)/N-13	0
L	24 At Atlanta (32,782)/N-20	28
L	3 At Chicago (40.483)/N-27	13
W	35 Tampa Bay (49,773)/D-4	21
W	23 At Buffalo (38,039)/D-11	10
W	42 Dallas (59,957)-**MN**/D-19	17
	432	293

NFC PLAYOFF—DEC. 31
At San Francisco–Candlestick)

W	24 Detroit (58,386)-**SA**	23

NFC CHAMPIONSHIP—JAN. 8
(At Washington, DC–RFK)

L	21 Washington (55.363)	24

1984 (15-1/18-1)
Bill Walsh, Coach

W	30 At Detroit (56,782)/S-2	27
W	37 Washington (59,707)-**MN**/S-10	31
W	30 New Orleans (57,611)/S-16	20
W	21 At Philadelphia (62,771)/S-23	9
W	14 Atlanta (57,990)/S-30	5
W	31 At New York Giants (76,112)-**MN**/O-8	10
L	17 Pittsburgh (59,110)/O-14	20
W	34 At Houston (39,900)/O-21	21
W	33 At Los Angeles Rams (65,481)/O-28	0
W	23 Cincinnati (58,234)/N-4	17
W	41 At Cleveland (60,092)/N-11	7
W	24 Tampa Bay (57,704)/N-18	17
W	35 At New Orleans (65,177)/N25	3
W	35 At Atlanta (29,644)/D-2	17
W	51 Minnesota (56,670)/D-8	7
W	19 Los Angeles Rams (59,743)-**MN**/DI4	16

NFC PLAYOFF—DEC. 29
(At San Francisco–Candlestick)

W	21 New York Giants (60,303)-**SA**	10

NFC CHAMPIONSHIP—JAN. 6
(At San Francisco–Candlestick)

W	23 Chicago (61.040)	0

SUPER BOWL XIX—JAN. 26
(At Palo Alto, California–Stanford Stadium)

W	38 Miami (84,059)	16

Records For 49ers' Coaches

Coach	Yrs	Dates	Games	W	L	T	Winning Percentage
Lawrence T. (Buck) Shaw	9	1946-54	116#	72	40	4	.638
Norman P. (Red) Strader	1	1955	12	4	8	0	.333
Frank C. (Frankie) Albert	3	1956-58	37#	19	17	1	.527
Howard W. (Red) Hickey	5*	1959-63	55	27	27	1	.500
Jack Christiansen	5*	1963-167	67	26	38	3	.411
Dick Nolan	8	1968-75	117#	56	56	5	.500
Monte Clark	1	1976	14	8	6	0	.571
Ken Meyer	1	1977	14	5	9	0	.357
Pete McCulley	1+	1978	9	1	8	0	.111
Fred O'Connor	1+	1978	7	1	6	0	.143
Bill Walsh	6	1979-present	97#	56	41	0	.577
TOTAL	**39**	**1946-present**	**545†**	**275**	**256**	**14**	**.518**

*Hickey coached the first 3 games of 1963/Christiansen the final 11.
+ McCulley coached the first 9 games of 1978/O'Connor the final 7.
#Includes postseason record

Club Career Leaders

Rushing (Yards)

Player	No.	Yds.	Avg.	Long	TD
1. Perry, Joe (1950-60, 1963)	1,475	7,344	4.9	78t	50

2. Willard, Ken (1965-73)	1,582	5,930	3.7	69t	45
3. Smith, J.D. (1956-64)	1,007	4,370	4.3	80t	37
4. McElhenny, Hugh (1952-60)	877	4,288	4.9	89t	35
5. Williams, Delvin (1974-77)	669	2,966	4.4	80t	20
6. Jackson, Wilbur (1974-79)	745	2,955	3.9	80	10
7. Tyler, Wendell (1983- —)	422	2,118	5.0	40	11
8. Washington, Vic (1971-73)	483	1,813	3.8	42	14
9. Hofer, Paul (1976-81)	416	1,746	4.2	47	16
10. Schreiber, Larry (1971-75)	502	1,734	3.5	23	10
14. Craig, Roger (1983- —)	331	1,374	4.2	71	15
15. Cooper Earl (1980- —)	296	1,240	4.2	56	6

Passing
(Completions)

Player	Att.	Comp.	Pct.	Yds.	TD	Int.
1. Brodie, John (1957-73)	4,491	2,469	.550	31,548	214	224
2. Montana, Joe (1979- —)	2,077	1,324	.637	15,609	106	54
3. Tittle, Y.A. (1951-60)	2,194	1,226	.559	16,016	108	134
4. DeBerg, Steve (1977-80)	1,201	670	.558	7,220	37	60
5. Spurrier, Steve (1967-75)	840	441	.525	5,250	33	48
6. Albert, Frank (1950-52)	601	316	.526	3,847	27	43
7. Plunkett, Jim (1976-77)	491	254	.517	3,285	22	30
8. Snead, Norman (1974-75)	237	138	.582	1,705	11	11
9. Mira, George (1964-68)	240	112	.467	1,711	17	14
9. Owen, Tom (1974-75)	235	112	.477	1,645	11	17
17. Cavanaugh, Matt (1983- —)	61	33	.541	449	4	0
22. Solomon, Fred (1978- —)	13	7	.538	122	0	1

Receiving
(Catches)

Player	No.	Yds.	Avg.	Long	TD
1. Wilson, Billy (1951-60)	407	5,902	14.5	77t	49
2. Washington, Gene (1969-77)	371	6,664	17.9	79t	59
3. Clark, Dwight (1979- —)	367	4,961	13.5	80t	31
4. Solomon, Freddie (1978- —)	285	4,614	16.2	93t	42
5. Casey, Bernie (1961-66)	277	4,008	14.5	68t	27
6. Willard, Ken (1965-73)	273	2,156	7.8	62	16
7. Soltau, Gordy (1950-58)	249	3,487	14.0	54t	25
8. Cooper, Earl (1980- —)	209	1,863	8.9	73t	12
9. Parks, Dave (1964-67)	208	3,334	16.0	83t	27
10. Stickles, Monty (1960-67)	207	2,993	14.5	54	14
22. Craig, Roger (1983- —)	119	1,102	9.3	64t	7

Receiving
(Yards)

Player	No.	Yds.	Avg.	Long	TD
1. Washington, Gene (1969-77)	371	6,664	17.9	79t	59
2. Wilson, Billy (1951-60)	407	5,902	14.5	77t	49
3. Clark, Dwight (1979- —)	367	4,961	13.5	80t	31
4. Solomon, Freddie (1978- —)	285	4,614	16.2	93t	42
5. Casey, Bernie (1961-66)	277	4,008	14.5	68t	27
6. Soltau, Gordy (1950-58)	249	3,487	14.0	54t	25
7. Parks, Dave (1964-67)	208	3,334	16.0	83t	27
8. Stickles, Monty (1960-67)	207	2,993	14.5	54	14
9. Owens, R.C. (1957-61)	176	2,926	16.6	75t	20
10. McElhenny, Hugh (1952-60)	195	2,666	13.7	77	15
15. Cooper, Earl (1980- —)	209	1,863	8.9	73t	12
24. Craig, Roger (1983- —)	119	1,102	9.3	64t	7

Scoring
(Total Ponts)

Player	TD	PAT	FG	TOTAL
1. Davis, Tommy (1959-69)	—	348	130	738

2. Wersching, Ray (1977- —)	—	272	139	689
3. Soltau, Gordy (1950-58)	25	284	70	644
4. Gossett, Bruce (1970-74)	—	163	99	460
5. Willard, Ken (1965-73)	61	—	—	366
6. Washington, Gene (1969-77)	59	—	—	354
7. Perry, Joe (1950-60, 1963)	57	6	1	351
8. McElhenny, Hugh (1952-60)	51	—	—	306
9. Wilson, Billy (1951-60)	49	—	—	294
10. Solomon, Freddie (1978- —)	47	0	0	282
12. Clark, Dwight (1979- —)	31	0	0	186

Field Goals
(Made)

Player	Att.	Made.	Pct.	Long
1. Davis, Tommy (1959-69)	276	130	.471	53
2. Wersching, Ray (1977- —)	188	139	.739	53
3. Gossett, Bruce (1970-74)	153	99	.641	54
4. Soltau, Gordy (1950-58)	138	70	.507	43
5. Mike-Mayer, Steve (1975-76)	56	30	.536	54
6. Gavric, Momcilo (1969)	11	3	.273	32
7. Bahr, Matt (1981)	6	2	.333	47
7. Patera, Dennis (1968)	8	2	.250	21
9. Wittum, Tom (1977)	2	1	.500	28
9. Perry, Joe (1950-60, 1963)	6	1	.167	14

Interceptions
(Number)

Player	No.	Yds.	Avg.	Long	TD
1. Johnson, Jim (1961-76)	47	615	13.1	63	2
2. Alexander, Kermit (1963-69)	36	499	13.7	66t	1
3. Hicks, Dwight (1979- —)	26	518	19.9	72	3
4. Wagner, Lowell (1950-53, 1955)	25	331	13.2	40	0
5. Berry, Rex (1951-56)	22	404	18.4	44t	3
6. Baker, Dave (1959-61)	21	294	14.0	40	0
7. Moegle, Dick (1955-59)	20	232	11.6	40	1
8. Taylor, Bruce (1970-77)	18	201	11.2	70	0
9. Lott, Ronnie (1981- —)	17	260	15.3	83t	4
10. Woodson, Abe (1958-64)	15	159	10.6	61	0
14. Wright, Eric (1981- —)	13	221	17.0	60t	2
19. Williamson, Carlton (1981- —)	10	137	13.7	28	0
26. Turner, Keena (1980- —)	7	66	9.4	21	0

Interceptions
(Yards)

Player	No.	Yds.	Avg.	Long	TD
1. Johnson, Jim (1961-76)	47	615	13.1	63	2
2. Hicks, Dwight (1979- —)	26	518	19.9	72	3
3. Alexander, Kermit (1963-69)	36	499	13.7	66t	1
4. Berry, Rex (1951-56)	22	404	18.4	44t	3
5. Wagner, Lowell (1950-53, 1955)	25	331	13.2	40	0
6. Baker, Dave (1959-61)	21	294	14.0	40	0
7. Lott, Ronnie (1981- —)	17	260	15.3	83t	4
8. Moegle, Dick (1955-59)	20	232	11.6	40	1
9. Wright, Eric (1981- —)	13	221	17.0	60t	2
10. Randolph, Alvin (1966-70, 1974)	10	208	20.8	94t	1

Punting
(Yards)

Player	No.	Yds.	Avg.	Long	Blk.
1. Davis, Tommy (1959-69)	511	22,841	44.7	82	2

	No.	Yds.	Avg.	Long	TD
2. Wittum, Tom (1973-77)	380	15,494	40.8	68	9
3. Spurrier, Steve (1967-75)	230	8,818	38.3	61	1
4. Miller, Jim (1980-82)	214	8,686	40.6	80	1
5. Albert, Frank (1950-52)	139	5,828	41.9	70	0
6. McCann, Jim (1971-72)	113	4,439	39.3	63	1
7. Connell, Mike (1978)	96	3,583	37.3	59	0
8. Jessup, Bill (1951-52, 54-58)	75	3,076	41.0	63	0
9. Orosz, Tom (1983-84)	70	2,747	39.2	61	1
10. Melville, Dan (1979)	71	2,626	36.9	53	0
12. Runager, Max (1984- —)	56	2,341	41.8	59	1

Punt Returns
(Yards)

Player	No.	Yds.	Avg.	Long	TD
1. Taylor, Bruce (1970-77)	142	1,323	9.3	76	0
2. McLemore, Dana (1982- —)	83	1,008	12.1	93t	3
3. McGill, Ralph (1972-76)	105	964	9.2	54	1
4. Woodson, Abe (1958-64)	105	949	9.0	85t	2
5. Solomon, Freddie (1978- —)	106	804	7.6	57t	2
6. Alexander, Kermit (1963-69)	120	782	6.5	70t	2
7. Arenas, Joe (1951-57)	124	774	6.2	67t	1
8. McElhenny, Hugh (1952-60)	99	648	6.5	94t	1
9. Leonard, Tony (1976-78)	65	473	7.3	60t	1
10. Hicks, Dwight (1979- —)	54	403	7.5	39	0

Punt Returns
(Number)

Player	No.	Yds.	Avg.	Long	TD
1. Taylor, Bruce (1970-77)	142	1,323	9.3	76	0
2. Arenas, Joe (1951-57)	124	774	6.2	67t	1
3. Alexander, Kermit (1963-69)	120	782	6.5	70t	2
4. Solomon, Freddie (1978- —)	106	804	7.6	57t	2
5. McGill, Ralph (1972-76)	105	964	9.2	54	1
5. Woodson, Abe (1958-64)	105	949	9.0	85t	2
7. McElhenny, Hugh (1952-60)	99	648	6.5	94t	1
8. McLemore, Dana (1981- —)	83	1,008	12.1	93t	3
9. Leonard, Tony (1976-78)	65	473	7.3	60t	1
10. Hicks, Dwight (1979- —)	54	403	7.5	39	0

Kickoff Returns
(Yards)

Player	No.	Yds.	Avg.	Long	TD
1. Woodson, Abe (1958-64)	166	4,873	29.4	105t	5
2. Arenas, Joe (1951-57)	139	3,798	27.3	96	1
3. Alexander, Kermit (1963-69)	137	3,271	23.9	56	0
4. Washington, Vic (1971-73)	84	2,178	25.9	98t	1
5. Owens, James (1979-80)	72	1,728	24.0	101t	2
6. Cunningham, Doug (1967-73)	68	1,613	23.7	94	0
7. McElhenny, Hugh (1952-60)	65	1,494	22.9	55	0
8. Hofer, Paul (1976-81)	68	1,474	21.7	48	0
9. Lyles, Lenny (1959-60)	42	1,091	25.9	97t	1
10. Moore, Manfred (1974-75)	44	1,048	23.8	52	0
11. McLemore, Dana (1981- —)	49	1,009	20.6	50	0
16. Monroe, Carl (1983- —)	27	561	20.8	44	0
22. Ring, Bill (1981- —)	21	457	21.8	41	0

Club Leaders By Years
Rushing

Year	Player	Att.	Yds.	Avg.	Long	TD	NFL/NFC Rank
1946	Standlee, Norm	134	683	5.1	—	2	—

1947	Strzykalski, John	143	906	6.3	50	5	—
1948	Strzykalski, John	141	915	6.5	—	4	—
1949	Perry, Joe	115	783	6.8	59	8	—
1950	Perry, Joe	124	647	5.2	78t	5	5
1951	Perry, Joe	136	677	5.0	58t	3	5
1952	Perry, Joe	158	725	4.6	78t	8	3
1953	Perry, Joe	192	1,018	5.3	51t	10	1
1954	Perry, Joe	173	1,049	6.1	58	8	1
1955	Perry, Joe	156	701	4.5	42	2	5
1956	McElhenny, Hugh	185	916	5.0	86t	8	3
1957	McElhenny, Hugh	102	478	4.7	61	1	15
1958	Perry, Joe	125	758	6.1	73t	4	3
1959	Smith, J.D.	207	1,036	5.0	73t	10	2
1960	Smith, J.D.	174	780	4.5	41	5	5
1961	Smith, J.D.	167	823	4.9	33	8	5
1962	Smith, J.D.	258	907	3.5	28	6	6
1963	Smith, J.D.	162	560	3.5	52t	5	13
1964	Kopay, Dave	75	271	3.6	64	0	32
1965	Willard, Ken	189	778	4.1	32	5	4
1966	Willard, Ken	191	763	4.0	67t	5	5
1967	Willard, Ken	169	510	3.0	20	5	17
1968	Willard, Ken	227	967	4.3	69t	7	2
1969	Willard, Ken	171	557	3.2	18	7	13
1970	Willard, Ken	236	789	3.3	20	7	9/6
1971	Willard, Ken	216	855	4.0	49	4	15/9
1972	Washington, Vic	141	468	3.3	33	3	42/20
1973	Washington, Vic	151	534	3.5	25	8	32/15
1974	Jackson, Wilbur	174	705	4.1	64	0	17/8
1975	Williams, Delvin	117	631	5.4	52	3	21/13
1976	Williams, Delvin	248	1,203	4.9	80t	7	3/2
1977	Williams, Delvin	268	931	3.5	40	7	10/5
1978	Simpson, O.J.	161	593	3.7	34	1	39/19
1979	Hofer, Paul	123	615	5.0	47	2	33/17
1980	Cooper, Earl	171	720	4.2	47	5	23/12
1981	Patton, Rickey	152	543	3.6	28	4	35/16
1982	Moore, Jeff	85	281	3.3	19	4	37/16
1983	Tyler, Wendell	176	856	4.9	39	4	19/10
1984	Tyler, Wendell	246	1,262	5.1	40	7	5/5

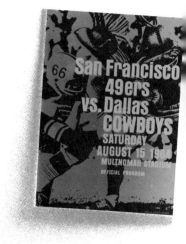

Passing

Year	Player	Att.	Comp	Pct.	Yds.	TD	Int.	Rating	NFL/NFC Rank
1946	Alhert, Frank	197	104	52.9	1,404	14	14	—	—
1947	Albert, Frank	242	128	52.9	1,692	18	15	—	—
1948	Albert, Frank	264	154	58.3	1,990	29	10	—	—
1949	Albert, Frank	260	129	49.6	1,862	27	16	—	—
1950	Albert, Frank	306	155	50.7	1,767	14	23	52.6	8
1951	Albert, Frank	166	90	50.7	1,116	5	10	60.2	8
1952	Tittle, Y.A.	208	106	51.0	1,407	11	12	66.4	5
1953	Tittle, Y.A.	259	149	57.5	2,121	20	16	84.0	3
1954	Tittle, Y.A.	295	170	57.6	2,205	9	9	78.4	7
1955	Tittle, Y.A.	287	147	51.2	2,185	17	28	56.5	4
1956	Tittle, Y.A.	218	124	56.9	1,641	7	12	68.5	7
1957	Tittle, Y.A.	279	176	63.1	2,157	13	15	79.6	1
1958	Tittle, Y.A.	208	120	57.7	1,467	9	15	59.1	3
1959	Tittle, Y.A.	199	102	51.3	1,331	10	15	58.2	4
1960	Brodie, John	207	103	49.8	1,111	6	9	57.8	5
1961	Brodie, John	283	155	54.8	2,588	14	12	84.5	4
1962	Brodie, John	304	175	57.6	2,272	18	16	78.1	6
1963	McHan, Lamar	195	83	42.3	1,243	8	11	54.3	15
1964	Brodie, John	392	193	49.2	2,498	14	16	64.3	12
1965	Brodie, John	391	242	61.9	3,112	30	16	95.2	3
1966	Brodie, John	427	232	54.3	2,810	16	22	65.5	8
1967	Brodie, John	349	168	48.1	2,013	11	16	57.5	11
1968	Brodie, John	404	234	57.9	3,020	22	21	77.9	3
1969	Brodie, John	347	194	55.9	2,405	16	15	74.9	7
1970	Brodie, John	378	223	59.0	2,941	24	10	93.9	1/1
1971	Brodie, John	387	208	53.7	2,642	18	24	64.7	12/6
1972	Spurrier, Steve	269	147	54.6	1,983	18	16	76.2	8/5
1973	Spurrier, Steve	157	83	52.9	882	4	7	59.2	21/13
1974	Owen, Tom	184	88	47.8	1,327	10	15	54.8	25/11
1975	Snead, Norm	189	108	57.1	1,337	9	10	77.2	11/5

1976	Piunkett, Jim	243	126	51.9	1,592	13	16	62.8	17/8
1977	Plunkett, Jim	248	128	51.6	1,693	9	14	62.1	17/8
1978	DeBerg, Steve	302	137	45.4	1,570	8	22	39.8	28/17
1979	DeBerg, Steve	578	347	60.0	3,652	17	21	70.3	13/5
1980	Montana, Joe	273	176	64.5	1,795	15	9	87.8	5/4
1981	Montana, Joe	488	311	63.7	3,565	19	12	88.2	4/1
1982	Montana, Joe	346	213	61.6	2,613	17	11	87.9	5/3
1983	Montana, Joe	515	332	64.5	3,910	26	12	94.6	5/3
1984	Montana, Joe	432	279	64.6	3,630	28	10	103.0	2/1

Receiving

Year	Player	No.	Yds.	Avg.	Long	TD	NFL/NFC Rank +
1946	Beals, Alyn	40	586	14.7	—	10	—
1947	Beals, Alyn	47	655	13.9	54	10	—
1948	Beals, Alyn	46	591	12.8	—	14	—
1949	Beals, Alyn	44	678	15.4	—	12	—
1950	Loyd, Alex	32	402	12.6	38	0	18
1951	Soltau, Gordy	59	826	14.0	48t	7	2
1952	Soltau, Gordy	55	774	14.1	49t	7	4
1953	Wilson, Billy	51	840	16.5	61t	10	6
1954	Wilson, Billy	60	830	13.8	43	5	2
1955	Wilson, Billy	53	831	15.7	72t	7	2
1956	Wilson, Billy	60	889	14.8	77t	5	1
1957	Wilson, Billy	52	757	14.6	40	6	1
1958	Conner, Clyde	49	512	10.4	26	5	5
1959	Wilson, Billy	44	540	12.3	57t	4	6
1960	Conner, Clyde	38	531	14.0	65t	2	1
1961	Owens, B.C.	55	1,032	18.8	54	5	7
1962	Casey, Bernie	53	819	15.5	48t	6	11
1963	Casey, Bernie	47	762	16.2	68t	7	14
1964	Casey, Bernie	58	808	13.9	63t	4	6
1965	Parks, Dave	80	1,344	16.8	53t	12	1
1966	Parks, Dave	66	974	14.8	65t	5	3
1967	Witcher, Dick	46	705	15.3	63t	3	17
1968	McNeil, Clifton	71	994	14.0	65t	7	1
1969	Washington, Gene	51	711	13.9	52	3	10
	Cunningham, Doug, RB	51	484	9.5	58	0	11
1970	Washington, Gene	53	1,100	20.8	79t	12	4/3
1971	Kwalick, Ted	52	664	12.8	42t	5	4/2
1972	Washington, Gene	46	918	20.0	62t	12	13/7
1973	Kwalick, Ted	47	729	15.5	48	5	10/6
1974	Schreiber, Larry, RB	30	217	7.2	16	1	60/36
1975	Washington, Gene	44	735	16.7	68t	9	31/10
1976	Washington, Gene	33	457	13.8	55t	6	52/25
	Jackson, Wilbur, RB	33	324	9.8	32	1	53/27
1977	Washington, Gene	32	638	19.9	47t	5	52/22
1978	Solomon, Freddie	31	458	14.8	58	2	83/42
1979	Hofer, Paul, BB	58	662	11.4	44	2	17/7
1980	Cooper, Earl, RB	83	567	6.8	66t	4	2/1
1981	Clark, Dwight	85	1,105	13.0	78t	4	2/1
1982	Clark, Dwight	60	913	15.2	51	5	1/1
1983	Clark, Dwight	70	840	12.0	46t	8	11/5
1984	Craig, Roger	71	675	9.5	64t	3	11/6

+ Ranked by number of receptions, not yards

Punting

Year	Player	No.	Avg.	Long	Had Blocked	NFL/NFC Rank
1946	Albert, Frank	54	41.0	73	—	—
1947	Albert, Frank	40	44.0	69	1	—
1948	Albert, Frank	35	44.8	82	—	—
1949	Albert, Frank	31	48.2	72	—	—
1950	Lillywhite, Verl	26	39.1	64	1	11
1951	Albert, Frank	34	44.3	66	0	2
1952	Albert, Frank	68	42.6	70	0	5
1953	Powers, Jim	42	40.6	55	1	8
1954	Brown, Hardy	10	38.4	58	0	11

Year	Player					
1955	Luna, Bob	63	40.6	63	3	8
1956	Jessup, Bill	14	40.2	63	0	16
1957	Barnes, Larry	19	47.1	86	0	13
1958	Atkins, Bill	25	39.3	51	0	11
1959	Davis, Tommy	59	45.7	71	0	3
1960	Baker, Dave	3	47.7	55	0	19
1961	Davis, Tommy	50	45.4	67	0	3
1962	Davis, Tommy	48	45.6	82	0	1
1963	Davis, Tommy	73	45.4	64	2	4
1964	Davis, Tommy	79	45.6	68	0	4
1965	Davis, Tommy	54	45.8	65	0	2
1966	Davis, Tommy	63	41.4	60	0	6
1967	Spurrier, Steve	73	37.6	61	1	12
1968	Spurrier, Steve	68	39.0	54	0	12
1969	Davis, Tommy	23	41.5	55	0	17
1970	Spurrier, Steve	75	38.4	58	0	24/11
1971	McCann, Jim	49	38.7	54	1	25/12
1972	McCann, Jim	64	39.7	63	1	21/10
1973	Wittum, Tom	79	43.7	62	0	4/1
1974	Wittum, Tom	68	41.2	67	1	4/2
1975	Wittum, Tom	67	41.9	64	3	3/2
1976	Wittum, Tom	89	40.8	68	2	6/3
1977	Wittum, Tom	77	36.4	54	3	26/13
1978	Connell, Mike	96	37.3	59	1	21/10
1979	Melville, Dan	71	37.0	53	1	25/14
1980	Miller, Jim	77	40.9	65	0	10/5
1981	Miller, Jim	93	41.5	65	0	15/6
1982	Miller, Jim	44	38.1	80	1★	25/13
1983	Orosz, Tom	65	39.3	61	1★	25/11
1984	Runager, Max	56	41.8	59	1	17/7

★ Recorded to the team

Scoring

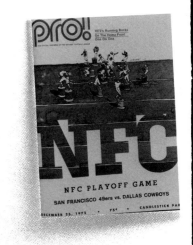

Year	Player	TD	PAT	FG	Points	NFL/NFC Rank
1946	Beals, Alyn	10	1	—	61	—
1947	Beals, Alyn	10	—	—	60	—
1948	Beals, Alyn	14	—	—	84	—
1949	Beals, Alyn	12	1	—	73	—
1950	Soltau, Gordy	1	26	4	44	22
1951	Soltau, Gordy	7	30	6	90	5
1952	Soltau, Gordy	7	34	6	94	1
1953	Soltau, Gordy	6	48	10	114	1
1954	Soltau, Gordy	2	31	11	76	4
1955	Soltau, Gordy	1	27	3	42	24
	Wilson, Billy	7	0	0	42	25
1956	Soltau, Gordy	1	26	13	71	6
1957	Soltau, Gordy	0	33	9	60	9
1958	Soltau, Gordy	0	29	8	53	20
1959	Davis, Tommy	0	31	12	67	9
1960	Davis, Tommy	0	21	19	78	5
1961	Davis, Tommy	0	44	12	80	8
1962	Davis, Tommy	0	36	10	66	16
1963	Davis, Tommy	0	24	10	54	21
1964	Davis, Tommy	0	30	8	54	24
1965	Davis, Tommy	0	52	17	103	4
1966	Davis, Tommy	0	38	16	86	12
1967	Davis, Tommy	0	33	14	75	10
1968	Davis, Tommy	0	26	9	53	19
1969	Willard, Ken	10	0	0	60	21
1970	Gossett, Bruce	0	39	21	102	6/4
1971	Gossett, Bruce	0	32	23	101	5/3
1972	Gossett, Bruce	0	41	18	95	13/7
1973	Gossett, Bruce	0	26	26	104	7/4
1974	Gossett, Bruce	0	25	11	58	25/8
1975	Mike-Mayer, Steve	0	27	14	69	22/9
1976	Mike-Mayer, Steve	0	26	16	74	25/9
1977	Williams, Delvin	9	0	0	54	14/10
1978	Wersching, Ray	0	24	15	69	22/9
1979	Wersching, Ray	0	32	20	92	12/5
1980	Wersching, Ray	0	33	15	78	18/10
1981	Wersching, Ray	0	30	17	81	22/13

1982	Wersching, Ray	0	23	12	59	9/4
1983	Wersching, Ray	0	51	25	126	3/3
1984	Wersching, Ray	0	56	25	131	1/1

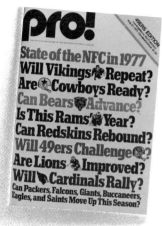

Kickoff Returns

Year	Player	No.	Yds.	Avg.	Long	TD	NFL/NFC Rank
1946	Eshmont, Len	10	264	26.4	—	—	—
1947	Eshmont, Len	9	177	19.7	—	—	—
1948	Hall, Forrest	13	369	28.4	—	—	—
1949	Perry, Joe	14	337	24.1	—	—	—
1950	Cathcart, Sam	14	329	23.9	62	0	20
1951	Arenas, Joe	21	542	25.8	49	0	8
1952	McElhenny, Hugh	18	396	22.0	40	0	16
1953	Arenas, Joe	15	551	34.4	82	0	1
1954	Arenas, Joe	16	362	22.6	41	0	11
1955	Arenas, Joe	24	594	24.8	42	0	7
1956	Arenas, Joe	27	801	29.7	96t	1	2
1957	Arenas, Joe	24	657	27.4	64	0	2
1958	Smith, J.D.	15	356	23.7	39	0	8
1959	Lyles, Lenny	25	565	22.6	46	0	10
1960	Lyles, Lenny	17	526	30.9	97t	1	2
1961	Woodson, Abe	27	782	29.0	98t	1	3
1962	Woodson, Abe	37	1,157	31.3	79	0	1
1963	Woodson, Abe	29	935	32.2	103t	3	1
1964	Woodson, Abe	32	880	27.5	70	0	4
1965	Alexander, Kermit	32	741	23.2	46	0	20
1966	Alexander, Kermit	37	984	26.6	56	0	7
1967	Cunningham, Doug	31	826	26.6	94	0	5
1968	Alexander, Kermit	20	360	18.0	35	0	24
1969	Smith, Noland	14	310	22.1	60	0	16
1970	Tucker, Bill	25	577	23.1	43	0	13/9
1971	Washington, Vic	33	858	26.0	74	0	12/8
1972	Washington, Vic	27	771	28.6	98t	1	4/3
1973	Washington, Vic	24	549	22.9	38	0	26/10
1974	Holmes, Mike	25	612	24.5	57	0	15/6
1975	Moore, Manfred	26	650	25.0	52	0	10/5
1976	Leonard, Anthony	26	553	21.3	39	0	29/13
1977	Hofer, Paul	36	863	23.9	48	0	12/7
1978	Williams, Dave	34	745	21.9	89t	1	23/8
1979	Owens, James	41	1,002	24.4	85t	1	5/3
1980	Owens, James	31	726	23.4	101t	1	4/3
1981	Lawrence, Amos	17	437	25.7	92t	1	3/2
1982	McLemore, Dana	16	353	22.1	45	0	1B/9
1983	McLemore, Dana	30	576	19.2	39	0	30/14
1984	Monroe, Carl	27	561	20.8	44	0	19/9

Field Goals

Year	Player	Att.	Made	Pct.	Long	NFL/NFC Rank
1946	Vetrano, Joe	7	4	.571	—	—
1947	Vetrano, Joe	8	4	.500	—	—
1948	Vetrano, Joe	8	5	.625	—	—
1949	Vetrano, Joe	4	3	.750	—	—
1950	Soltau, Gordy	7	4	.571	26	9
1951	Soltau, Gordy	18	6	.333	42	10
1952	Soltau, Gordy	12	6	.500	31	6
1953	Soltau, Gordy	15	10	.667	39	4
1954	Soltau, Gordy	18	11	.611	37	4
1955	Soltau, Gordy	12	3	.250	28	10
1956	Soltau, Gordy	20	13	.650	40	2
1957	Soltau, Gordy	15	9	.600	37	7
1958	Soltau, Gordy	21	8	.381	39	8
1959	Davis, Tommy	26	12	.462	43	2
1960	Davis, Tommy	32	19	.594	40	1
1961	Davis, Tommy	22	12	.545	46	9
1962	Davis, Tommy	23	10	.435	42	10
1963	Davis, Tommy	31	10	.325	46	10
1964	Davis, Tommy	25	8	.320	53★	14
1965	Davis, Tommy	27	17	.630	53★	4

1966	Davis, Tommy	31	16	.516	46	12
1967	Davis, Tommy	33	14	.424	50	13
1968	Davis, Tommy	16	9	.563	38	10
1969	Davis, Tommy	10	3	.300	48	24/15
	Gavric, Momcilo	11	3	.273	32	26/17
1970	Gossett, Bruce	31	21	.677	48	6/3
1971	Gossett, Bruce	36	23	.639	48	10/5
1972	Gossett, Bruce	29	18	.621	50	15/5
1973	Gossett, Bruce	33	26	.788	54	1/1
1974	Gossett, Bruce	24	11	.458	46	26/14
1975	Mike—Mayer, Steve	28	14	.500	54	24/13
1976	Mike—Mayer, Steve	28	16	.571	45	15/9
1977	Wersching, Ray	17	10	.588	50	17/5
1978	Wersching, Ray	23	15	.652	45	11/5
1979	Wersching, Ray	24	20	.833	45	3/1
1980	Wersching, Ray	19	15	.789	47	2/1
1981	Wersching, Ray	23	17	.739	45	5/4
1982	Wersching, Ray	17	12	.706	45	17/9
1983	Wersching, Ray	30	25	.833	52	5/3
1984	Wersching, Ray	35	25	.714	53	2/2

★ Longest Field Goal in NFL that year

Forty Niners' Big Days

Rushing

194—Delvin Williams at St. Louis . . . . October 31, 1976 (34 Carries)
190—Wilbur Jackson vs New Orleans . . . . . . November 27, 1977 (16 Carries)
180—Delvin Williams vs Washington . . . . . . November 7, 1976 (23 Carries)
174—Joe Perry vs Detroit . . . . November 2, 1958 (13 Carries)
170—Hugh McElhenny at Dallas Texans . . . . October 5, 1952 (7 Carries)
168—J.D. Smith vs Minnesota . . . . November 26, 1961 (28 Carries)
162—Ken Willard at Atlanta . . . . December 15, 1968 (25 Carries)
159—Hugh McElhenny at Green Bay . . . . . . November 23, 1958 (22 Carries)
156—Wilbur Jackson vs Minnesota . . . . . . November 29, 1976 (30 Carries)
153—Delvin Williams vs Minnesota . . . . . . November 29, 1976 (20 Carries)
153—Joe Perry at Green Bay . . . . November 22, 1953 (16 Carries)

Passing

408—Joe Montana at St. Louis . . . . November 21, 1982 (26 of 39)
381—Joe Montana vs Washington . . . . September 10, 1984 (24 of 40)
371—Y.A. Tittle vs Baltimore . . . . December 13, 1953 (29 of 44)
366—Joe Montana vs San Diego . . . . December 11, 1982 (31 of 46)
365—Joe Montana vs Los Angeles Rams . . . . October 28, 1984 (21 of 31)
358—Joe Montana at Los Angeles Rams . . . . October 23, 1983 (25 of 39)
356—John Brodie at Los Angeles Rams . . . . November 9, 1969 (25 of 42)
353—Joe Montana at Houston . . . . October 21, 1984 (25 of 35)
348—Steve DeBerg vs Chicago . . . . October 28, 1979 (26 of 41)
347—Joe Montana at Washington + ... January 8, 1984 (27 of 48)
345—Steve DeBerg vs Atlanta . . . . September 28, 1980 (32 of 51)
345—Steve DeBerg at Atlanta . . . . December 16, 1979 (29 of 54)
341—Joe Montana at St. Louis . . . . September 18, 1983 (20 of 32)
341—Y.A. Tittle at New York Giants . . . . . November 9, 1952 (16 of 29)
336—Joe Montana at Denver . . . . September 19, 1982 (26 of 37)
334—Joe Montana vs New Orleans . . . . . . November 28, 1982 (27 of 42)
328—John Brodie vs Green Bay . . . . December 10, 1961 (19 of 29)
327—John Brodie at Chicago Bears . . . . . . November 13, 1966 (28 of 54)
324—George Mira at Atlanta . . . . December 10, 1967 (20 of 34)
322—John Brodie vs Chicago Bears . . . . . . November 19, 1961 (11 of 19)
321—Steve DeBerg at Houston . . . . September 17, 1978 (20 of 32)
320—Steve Spurrier vs Minnesota . . . . . . October 14, 1973 (31 of 48)

Receiving

231—Dave Parks at Baltimore . . . . October 3, 1965 (9 Catches)
225—Bernie Casey at Chicago Bears . . . . . November 13, 1966 (12 Catches)
196—Gordy Soltau at New York Giants . . . . November 9, 1952 (10 Catches)
192—Billy Wilson vs Chicago Bears . . . . . October 23, 1955 (8 Catches)
186—Dick Witcher at Atlanta . . . . December 10, 1967 (11 Catches)
181—Jim Johnson vs Detroit . . . . November 11, 1962 (11 Catches)
169—Bernie Casey at Philadelphia . . . . . . September 20, 1964 (6 Catches)
165—Hugh McElhenny vs Baltimore . . . . . . December 8, 1957 (8 Catches)
164—Gene Washington at Green Bay . . . . . November 5, 1972 (6 Catches)
160—Gene Washington vs New England . . . . October 31, 1971 (5 Catches)

+ Postseason

Forty Niners' Longest Plays

Top-Ten Long Runs from Scrimmage
89t —Hugh McElhenny at Dallas Texans, October 5, 1952
86t —Hugh McElhenny at Green Bay, November 18, 1956
82t —Hugh McElhenny vs Dallas Texans, October 26, 1952
80 —Wilbur Jackson vs New Orleans, November 27, 1977
80t —Delvin Williams vs Washington, November 7, 1976
80t —J.D. Smith vs Green Bay, December 7, 1958
78t —Joe Perry vs Dallas Texans, October 26, 1952
78t —Joe Perry vs Green Bay, December 10, 1950
75t —Jimmy Thomas vs Chicago Bears, December 6, 1969
73t —J.D. Smith vs Detroit, November 1, 1959
73t —Joe Perry vs Detroit, November 2, 1958

Top-Ten Long Forward Passes
93t —Steve DeBerg to Freddie Solomon vs Atlanta, September 28, 1980
85t —Jim Plunkett to Delvin Williams vs Washington, November 7, 1976
83t —John Brodie to Dave Parks at Los Angeles Rams, October 18, 1964
81t —Steve Spurrier to Ted Kwalick vs New Orleans, October 22, 1972
80t —Joe Montana to Dwight Clark at Houston, October 21, 1984
80t —John Brodie to Clifton McNeil at Green Bay, September 28, 1969
80t —John Brodie to Dave Parks vs Minnesota, October 25, 1964
80t —John Brodie to Jim Johnson at Chicago Bears, October 14, 1962
79t —John Brodie to Gene Washington at Chicago Bears, November 8, 1970
79t —George Mira to Dave Parks at Minnesota, November 8, 1964

Top-Ten Long Punts
86 —Larry Barnes vs Chicago Cardinals, September 29, 1957
82 —Tommy Davis vs Minnesota, September 30, 1962
81 —Tommy Davis at St. Louis Cardinals, November 25, 1962
80 —Jim Miller at Denver Broncos, September 19, 1982
79 —Tommy Davis at Chicago Bears, October 14, 1962
76 —Larry Barnes vs Baltimore, December 8, 1957
75 —Verl Lillywhite vs Cleveland, September 30, 151
74 —Tommy Davis vs Chicago Bears, October 30, 1960
72 —Jon Kilgore vs Chicago Bears, December 6, 1969
71 —Tommy Davis vs Chicago Bears, October 25, 1959

Top-Ten Long Punt Returns
94t —Hugh McElhenny at Chicago Bears, October 19, 1952
93t —Dana McLemore vs Los Angeles Rams, January 2, 1983
88t —Manfred Moore vs Atlanta, November 24, 1974
88t —Abe Woodson at Green Bay, October 21, 1962
80t —Abe Woodson vs Detroit, November 5, 1961
79t —Dana McLemore at New York Giants, October 8, 1964
76 —Bruce Taylor at Chicago Bears, November 8, 1970
70t —Kermit Alexander vs Green Bay, November 15, 1964
67t —Joe Arenas vs Baltimore, December 16, 1956
60t —Anthony Leonard vs New Orleans, October 17, 1975
60 —Dave Williams at Minnesota, December 4, 1977

Top-Ten Long Kickoff Returns
105t —Abe Woodson at Los Angeles Rams, November 8, 1959
103t —Abe Woodson vs Minnesota, September 15, 1983
101t —James Owens at Detroit, November 2, 1980
99t —Abe Woodson at New York Giants, November 17, 1953
98t —Vic Washington at Atlanta, October 29, 1972
98t —Abe Woodson at Detroit, October 1, 1951
97t —Vic Washington vs Dallas, December 23, 1972 +
97t —Lenny Lyles vs Baltimore, December 18, 1950
96 —Joe Arenas vs Baltimore, December 16, 1955
95t —Abe Woodson vs Minnesota, September 15, 1983

Top-Ten Long Interception Returns
94t —Alvin Randolph vs Chicago Bears, December 11, 1966
83t —Ronnie Lott at Kansas City, December 26, 1982
72 —Dwight Hicks at Washington, October 4, 1981
70 —Bruce Taylor vs Green Bay, November 1, 1970
69 —Ed Beard at Chicago Bears, November 10, 1968

66t —Kermit Alexander at Pittsburgh, November 24, 1968
65 —Jim Cason at Pittsburgh, October 14, 1951
63 —Jim Johnson vs Green Bay, December 10, 1961
62t —Dwight Hicks at New Orleans, October 16, 1983
61 —Abe Woodson vs Los Angeles Rams, December 1, 1963

Top-Ten Long Fumble Returns
80t —Dwight Hicks at Washington, October 4, 1981
75t —Clark Miller at Detroit, November 14, 1965
73t —Skip Vanderbundt at Dallas, November 23, 1972
71 —Gerard Williams vs New Orleans, September 23, 1979
66t —Windlan Hall vs Philadelphia, December 2, 1973
63t —Tommy Hart at St. Louis, October 24, 1971
40t —Matt Hazeltine at Detroit, October 18, 1959
39 —Bruce Taylor at Kansas City, October 5, 1975
37t —Abe Woodson at Chicago Bears, October 14, 1962
34t —Gary Johnson at Atlanta, December 2, 1984

Top-Ten Long Field Goals
54 —Steve Mike-Mayer at Los Angeles Rams, November 9, 1975
54 —Bruce Gossett vs New Orleans, October 21, 1973
#53 —Tommy Davis at Los Angeles Rams, October 17, 1965
#53 —Tommy Davis at Los Angeles Rams, October 17, 1965
53 —Ray Wersching at Detroit, September 2, 1984
52 —Ray Wersching at New Orleans, October 16, 1983
52 —Bruce Gossett at Houston, November 15, 1970
51 —Steve Mike-Mayer vs Chicago Bears, November, 16, 1975
50 —Ray Wersching at New York Giants, October 16, 1977
50 —Bruce Gossett at Green Bay, November 5, 1972
50 —Tommy Davis vs New Orleans, October 22, 1967
50 —Tommy Davis vs Los Angeles Rams, November 21, 1965

Long Returns of Field Goal Attempt
92t —Bruce Taylor at New Orleans, December 13, 1970
38 —Kermit Alexander vs Philadelphia, November 20, 1966
30 —Kermit Alexander at Philadelphia, September 20, 1964

+ postseason
#Two kicked in same game

Bruno Banducci

PHOTO CREDITS

AP/Wide World Photos: pp. iv, 31, 35, 38–39, 40, 45, 49 (all), 54, 57, 60, 65, 67, 76, 80, 86, 87 (top), 88, 133, 152, 154

San Francisco 49er Photo File: Cover (Frank Rippon); pp. x, xii (Frank Rippon), 33 (Frank Rippon), 39, 53 (Frank Rippon), 55, 62, 63, 68, 69, 71 (Frank Rippon), 72, 73, 75 (Frank Rippon), 77, 79, 81, 84, 91 (bottom) (Frank Rippon), 95 (top) (Dennis Desprois), 97, 111, 122 (Dennis Desprois), 130, 131, 149

Pro Football Hall of Fame: pp. 28, 41

Stanford University Archives: p. 5

UPI/Bettmann Archives: pp. ii–iii, vi–vii, viii–ix, 2, 4, 7 (top), 8, 9, 11, 12-13, 14, 17, 18, 23, 25, 30, 32, 36, 43, 44, 47, 48 (both), 50 (both), 51, 87 (bottom), 89

Michael Zagaris: pp. 91 (top), 92 (all), 93 (both), 94, 95 (bottom), 96, 99, 100-101, 102 (both), 103 (all), 104 (all), 104-105, 106, 107, 109 (both), 110, 114 (both), 115, 117 (both), 118-119, 124 (both), 125, 127 (all), 128-129, 134, 135 (all), 136, 137, 139, 140 (both), 141, 142-143, 144, 145, 147, 148 151, 184

INDEX

INDEX